CHINA'S AUTOMOBILE INDUSTRY

"From   ly to
draw le   he future
of the   sophisticated   ularly
industr

                    Berkeley

"At a t   n undergoing   tful
picture   d auto-
mobile   retical
and hi   ned
accou   ch vari-
ables   g strategies, o   hinese
politic   extremely
valuab   ues
surrou

                    Berkeley

Studies on Contemporary China

Studies on Contemporary China

CHINA'S AUTOMOBILE INDUSTRY

POLICIES, PROBLEMS, AND PROSPECTS

ERIC HARWIT

An East Gate Book

M.E. Sharpe
Armonk, New York
London, England

An East Gate Book

Copyright © 1995 by M. E. Sharpe, Inc.

Library of Congress Cataloging-in-Publication Data

Harwit, Eric, 1962–
China's automobile industry : policies, problems, and
prospects / Eric Harwit.
p.   cm.
"An East gate book."
Includes bibliographical references and index.
ISBN 1-56324-441-1. — ISBN 1-56324-442-X (pbk.)
1. Automobile industry and trade—China.
2. China—Economic conditions—1976–   I. Title
HD9710.C529H37 1994   94-27011
338.4′76292′0951—dc20
CIP

Printed in the United States of America

MV (c)   10   9   8   7   6   5   4   3   2   1
MV (p)   10   9   8   7   6   5   4   3   2   1

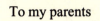
To my parents

Contents

Figures and Tables

Figures

Tables

Acknowledgments

I extend thanks to Lowell Dittmer, who patiently read each of the following chapters as they were completed, and who offered valuable encouragement over my years as a graduate student at Berkeley. Thomas Gold gave detailed criticism of my writing, and I am grateful for his concern and attention over the writing process. Robert Scalapino kindly gave advice since my first days in California, and I thank him for all his support. Kenneth Lieberthal also gave me very useful suggestions and encouragement.

My interviews depended on many Chinese and foreign sources related to the automotive industry in China. Though most preferred to remain anonymous, I am obviously very grateful for their help. Special thanks to Christiane Finckenstein of Volkswagen, for her advice during my fieldwork year in Beijing; to Don St. Pierre of Beijing Jeep, for his early help and encouragement of my work; and to Zhang Liangming, of Guangzhou Peugeot. In Beijing, Tian Chenyang provided valuable research assistance, and I had similar helpful aid from Alan Adcock in Hawaii. I am grateful to Barbara Boettcher for drafting the two maps in this volume.

The United States Education Department's Fulbright Doctoral Dissertation Research Abroad (DDRA) fellowship made possible the fieldwork I conducted for this project from October 1989 to January 1991. I express gratitude for the fund's generous aid.

Finally, I thank my parents for their support during my student days in Berkeley. Their concern helped me persevere over my years of thesis writing, and made the process easier and more enjoyable.

CHINA'S AUTOMOBILE INDUSTRY

1

Bureaucratic Politics and the Chinese Automobile Industry

With the dawning of the reform era in China in the late 1970s, political leaders and industrial planners focused their strategy for redressing decades of isolation by pursuing a paramount goal of "modernization" in nearly all areas of industrial development. One prominent measure of the nation's economic status, however, projected a clear image of backwardness: China's urban streets and country roads were largely populated by inefficient, unattractive, and often unreliable passenger cars, automobiles designed in the early 1960s or even decades earlier. A subsequent flood of vehicle imports in the early post–Mao Zedong years enhanced the country's transport capabilities, but proved a major drain on hard currency reserves.

Reform of the domestic automotive sector, then, became an important part of the nation's drive toward industrial modernization. At a minimum, the Chinese hoped to develop a successful program of car and truck import substitution; with persistence and some luck, they might even emulate their more prosperous neighbors, Japan and South Korea, in fostering a remunerative export-oriented industry. To achieve such goals, however, the Chinese realized they would have to depend on help from more technologically advanced nations. Given a tradition of self-reliance, in both domestic and international interaction, the task of successfully coordinating the absorption and utilization of the complex and expensive foreign technology would be

---

Portions of this and following chapters are adapted with permission from Eric Harwit, "Foreign Passenger Car Ventures and Chinese Decision-Making," *The Australian Journal of Chinese Affairs*, 28 (July 1992): 141–66.

formidable for both national and local political leaders.

This volume uses the experiences of foreign passenger car companies in China to assess the forces acting on the industrial bureaucracies over the past decade, and the outcome for the newly established foreign ventures. In particular, it asks: What institutions and political leaders have helped shape the policy process, and what are their motivations? How has power devolved with decentralized reforms of the 1980s and 1990s? What role have local governments played in industrial development? How have the goals of the foreign companies themselves helped shape the investment landscape, and were any investment strategies particularly effective? Has there been any tangible bureaucratic learning in successive interaction with these foreign investors? Finally, what does the future hold for the development of the nascent automotive industry?

In order to address these points, this study employs a structure based on analyses of bureaucratic politics, governmental bargaining, and political misperception. These tools shed light on what will most likely be a key industrial sector of the Chinese economy in the coming decades. The results, presented from an expanded viewpoint in the concluding chapter, also help paint a broad picture of Chinese foreign economic policy making.

The analytical structure here stands in contrast with many prior approaches, which assume dominance of the Chinese decision-making process by the very top of the political leadership. Below, I briefly discuss past China studies research, before introducing this study's own framework.

Why Study the Bureaucracy?

Few past researchers have devoted their attention to in-depth case studies of specific issue areas and their associated bureaucracies; even fewer have employed theoretical models in such endeavors. Instead, scholars often look primarily to the top leadership in Beijing for clues to the direction of China's development. Why, then, is it important to study the lower-level Chinese administrative institutions?

Several authors have pointed out that increasing decentralization of the foreign trade apparatus has in fact made the lower levels of the bureaucracy more important. Harry Harding presented evidence showing the expanding power of such institutions as the Ministry of Foreign

Economic Relations and Trade (MOFERT).[1] Barry Naughton pointed out a significant rise of decentralization in the decision-making apparatus for assigning capital construction investment throughout China.[2] Still others, discussed below, directed attention to the developing bureaucratic entities responsible for foreign economic policy making. Few of these authors, however, attempted a detailed analysis of the increasingly important institutions, or used case studies to bolster their arguments.

Why have scholars avoided looking closely at the Chinese bureaucracy? First, the Chinese system has, until recently, been quite difficult to penetrate. Chinese citizens were to avoid divulging "state secrets" to foreigners; even general communication with such outsiders was discouraged. Much of the relevant information, then, was found in statements of the top leaders, published in newspapers or journals or broadcast over the radio. Foreign researchers in the 1960s and 1970s found that exiles and migrants from southern China to Hong Kong were also good sources, but the scarcity of central government bureaucrats among their numbers made many types of focused, in-depth interview research nearly impossible.

Although China remains a relatively secretive society, the amount of personal contact allowed with foreigners has vastly increased. The requirement for efficient functioning of economic transactions forces the Chinese to be more open in publicizing their bureaucratic procedures. In other words, even in the face of the June 1989 crackdown on dissent, it is now easier to gain access to the lower levels of power than in the years preceding the economic opening to the outside world.

Previous work has also tended to focus on top leaders because, in the past, the top leadership retained a tight grip on power. Ezra Vogel described a "politicized bureaucracy" in the late 1960s, one in which political rule (often split along loyalties to rival leaders Mao Zedong and Liu Shaoqi) was disruptive to bureaucratic organization. "When a new policy comes down," Vogel noted, "not only must everyone study the new policy, but all those most closely identified with the old policy must criticize themselves for their errors."[3] A. Doak Barnett asserted that "in a fundamental sense [in the 1960s], it was the policy decisions made by personnel at the top of the system rather than the data or ideas from lower levels which determined the general shape of the plans ultimately adopted."[4] Furthermore, leadership from above was reinforced by Chinese Communist Party (CCP) infiltration of all political and administrative sectors, giving the party "effective monopoly of policy-making on major issues."[5] Barnett did note, however, the deepening schism between technically competent bureaucrats (called "experts") and ideologically loyal administrators (those who were "red"), and saw some nascent "passive resistance" based in lower-level administrative competition.[6]

As this volume's historical chapter (chapter 2) and the following case studies try to show, the demands of a complex international economy, introduced to China in the late 1970s, gave the less politicized bureaucratic institutions and their experts gradually more exalted positions, with the result that top leaders became more limited in their choice of action; the influence of politics from above had waned. To focus solely on the highest leaders in the China of the 1990s, then, was to miss much of the important process that went on at more removed levels of power.

Of course, one could not completely ignore the actions at the top level of decision making, particularly among those who made political and ideological decisions. One part of this study, chapter 3, also focuses on some of the highest political and bureaucratic leaders. That chapter, however, together with sections of the volume's later case studies, will try to take into account the procedural and other constraints imposed on even the top political figures. These parts of the text will also look for evidence of "misperception" among the decision makers. Were leaders, for example, constrained by distortion in the information available to them? Were they further detrimentally affected by past experiences? In asking these questions, the study begins to reveal some of the analytical approach lacking in previous, mostly atheoretical, work, some of which is outlined in the following sections.

Why Study the Automotive Industry?

The case of the automotive industry, used in the empirical chapters of this volume, is valuable for several reasons. First, this sector typically accounts for a large share of the industrial production in countries that do manufacture vehicles. In the United States in early 1993, for example, motor vehicles alone accounted for some $20 billion in sales; this was about 9 percent of total U.S. manufacturing output.[7] In Japan, 1990 automobile production made up 13 percent of total production in the manufacturing sector.[8] Furthermore, several nations have made automotive export the backbone of their foreign economic policy: Japan's $69.5 billion in sales of automobiles abroad accounted for some 22 percent of the total value of the country's exports in 1990[9]; these exports, furthermore, constituted nearly 75 percent of Japan's $40 billion trade surplus with the United States.[10] In South Korea, exports of passenger cars brought in $2.5 billion in 1992, though this sum was only about 3 percent of total exports. Still, the vehicle industry was one of the fastest growing sectors of South Korea's export-led economy, with foreign sales rising by nearly 20 percent from 1991 to 1992.[11]

In a study of China, the automotive industry is useful because it has encompassed both domestic and foreign economic and decision processes, as the following chapters chronicle. It is therefore possible to investigate problems not only of industrialization in general, but also of technology transfers. Furthermore, major investments were made in the 1980s by companies from several nations, including the United States, Germany, France, and, to a lesser extent, Japan; this phenomenon therefore allows some cross-national comparison.

Finally, the automotive industry in China is one generally open to foreign scrutiny. Industries with more obvious defense-related applications, or ones at the often secretive cutting edge of technological advance, may be less viable subjects for analytical study.

This sector, then, serves as a useful focus for application of the research approach outlined below. The study differs, however, in some respects from previous empirical work.

Empirical Studies of Chinese Foreign Economic Policy-Making Institutions

Some Sinologists have ventured overview analyses of bureaucratic sectors without choosing case-study formats. Most of this research tends to be descriptive and lacks a theoretical framework. One finds work ranging from political economy analyses to the popular "how to do business in China" type of book.

Michael Yahuda, for example, discussed the early stages of China's post-Mao foreign economic relations in a context of international security competition, and analyzed the role of domestic economic reform in foreign policy making.[12] James H.T. Tsao provided a wealth of statistics and empirical analyses of Chinese foreign trade dating back to

1950, but, again, did little more than describe technical problems and make economic predictions.[13] Nicholas Lardy combined some of Yahuda's ideas with the description of Tsao. He outlined the role of China in the world economy, and suggested implications for American strategy.[14]

A. Doak Barnett, in one of his more recent works, took a somewhat different approach. He looked specifically at foreign policy making by examining various organizations within the Chinese government. He examined the roles of top-level leaders, the Communist Party Politburo, the Party Secretariat, the national state council, the Foreign Ministry, and other actors. This study, however, was mainly descriptive; it lacked analysis linking the various policy-making bodies. Furthermore, Barnett's discussion of the foreign economic policy-making institutions was limited, with only a small portion of his attention devoted to such organizations.[15]

One of the best early analyses of the reforming Chinese foreign trade bureaucracy was Rosalie Tung's 1982 study.[16] Tung traced some of the significant changes enacted between 1978 and 1982, and related them to the relevant bureaucratic organizations. She had relatively detailed descriptions of such entities as the Ministry of Foreign Trade (now MOFERT), the China International Trust and Investment Corporation (CITIC), the Bank of China, and others. Like Barnett, however, she did not discuss the interaction of these various parts of the bureaucracy.

A few researchers have introduced foreign economic case studies to the scene. Ryosei Kokubun looked at China's policy vacillations over the import of Japanese factory equipment during the late 1970s and early 1980s, but his work was largely empirical.[17] Earlier work by Michel Oksenberg investigated the bureaucratic institutions associated with agriculture; this study, however, focused primarily on domestic economic developments.[18] Finally, Margaret Pearson's recent work (discussed below) took a broad view of various foreign-invested industries, using analytical tools from both economics and political science.

Students of business also analyzed Chinese foreign economic relations, often trying to discern the optimum approach for foreigners to take in interacting with the relevant Chinese bureaucrats. Lin Jianhai, for example, studied American motivations for creating joint ventures with China.[19] He investigated the forces that drew American investors to China, and analyzed these factors using statistical methods and theories of joint venture dynamics.

Lin's conclusions included lists of the positive and negative factors Americans faced in choosing to invest in China. He also made some comparison of Chinese and American attitudes toward the joint ventures. He omitted, though, focus on misperceived and misunderstood actions related to divergence in the long-term goals of the two sides.

Victor A.T. Koh analyzed cultural expectations in conducting business in China.[20] He investigated Chinese feelings toward various nationalities, and used these results to predict the future success of some eighteen different nations and regions in trade relations with China. Although this work was useful for examining the Chinese attitudes toward the outside world, no comparison was made of foreign perceptions of and approaches to the Chinese side.

Business journals present a further source of empirical data. Publications such as *The China Business Review* and business school magazines feature articles tailored to potential future investors. Availability of space and the general scope of these journals, however, tend to prohibit a fully developed theoretical analysis of Chinese industrial development.

Finally, there are many "how to" books that offer advice for the businessperson about to be sent to China. Philip Wik, among others, offered an early study of this type.[21] His book includes some history of China, lists of technical requirements for operating in the Socialist country, and a discussion of social life in China. His more valuable chapters, however, offer advice on overcoming cultural differences, and on "navigating the bureaucracy" (he suggests "Preparation. Persistence. Patience"). Randall Stross, whose volume covers the period from the beginning of China's economic reforms up to the early 1990s, presented a more detailed and anecdotally rich example of this school of research.[22] In general, this type of work is useful for understanding the attitudes some foreigners bring along when they first interact with Chinese bureaucrats.

Few of the above-mentioned writers move much beyond empirical description in their analysis of the foreign economic institutions. Because of this shortcoming, they lack the ability to pinpoint some of the most pertinent forces shaping bureaucratic outcomes, and to formulate predictions for future policies. The following section introduces theoretical tools that may help ameliorate this situation.

Decision-Making Frameworks and Their Application
in Chinese Political Studies

One of the most widely read and discussed works on political decision making was done in the early 1970s by Graham Allison.[23] Allison proposed three models for analyzing a nation's political decision making: a rational actor model, an organizational processes model, and a bureaucratic politics model.

The rational actor model ("Model I") focuses on top leadership, assumes that decision makers are rational thinkers, and hypothesizes that leaders could put through courses of action with little resistance. Lower levels of the government were essentially "black-boxed" and ignored. Allison, however, rejected this model because of its failure to take into account the lower levels of political machinery; and this volume has asserted above that China had moved away from resemblance to this model by the late 1970s.

Allison's "Model II" paints a picture of a governmental conglomeration of organizations. Each part of the bureaucracy could produce only limited types of outcomes; change in these results was curtailed by rigid "standard operating procedures" (SOPs). Thus, a top leader might say "do not do A, do B," with the result that, even though those listening *wanted* to do "B," they were only capable of doing "A" (without a period of retraining, anyway).

"Model III" in Allison's scheme proposes that the heads of bureaucratic organizations have their own interests to defend when it comes time to make a decision. During discussion and bargaining sessions, bureaucratic representatives bias their opinions in favor of their own organization ("where you stand depends on where you sit" became a catch-phrase associated with this analysis). The resulting decision was a medley of various organizational preferences.[24]

Extrapolating somewhat from Allison's work, we may postulate that the opinion of a Chinese bureaucratic organization's leader (a ministry or bureau chief, for example) reflects that of his or her organization as a whole. This study, then, focuses on such leaders (particularly in chapter 3) to gain insight on their respective institutions' outlooks.

Researchers of political behavior later in the 1970s sought to apply psychological factors to the decision-making process. John Steinbruner, for example, suggested bureaucracies are not capable of processing all the massive amounts of incoming data to which they are exposed.[25] The resulting overload leads to the same type of behavior Allison predicted: standard operating procedures become automatic responses when stimulated by appropriate incoming information and requests for solutions. Steinbruner went one step further than Allison, however, in suggesting that standard operating procedures could be recombined, under novel circumstances, into a process called "instrumental learning."[26]

Robert Jervis, another analyst of policy making, was a leader in formulating the problems of perception encountered by national leaders.[27] He proposed, for example, that decision makers react to incoming stimuli by turning to memories of similar past occurrences. Decisions are distorted for several reasons: new events are often slightly different from the reference drawn from the past; the past example may be incorrectly chosen; or *one* past example is selected, rather than a combination of several experiences.

Politicians also may suffer from cognitive dissonance, according to Jervis: once a decision is reached, the official experiences a surge of confidence in the correctness of his or her action. Decision makers then close their minds, even in the face of new incoming information. As for possible solutions to the perception problem, Jervis suggested that a "devil's advocate" may be able to point out cases of flagrant misperception of a current problem.

Kenneth Lieberthal and Michel Oksenberg were among the first to apply this kind of policy-making theory to China in a coherent and comprehensive fashion.[28] They somewhat indirectly adopted the work of Allison, again finding the top–down "rational actor" model unsatisfying,[29] and sought to apply decision-making and problem-solving theories to a study of the Chinese energy sector.[30] They looked at the petroleum, hydroelectric, and other related fields in their 1988 volume.

These two authors did a very thorough job in finding detailed information on the institutions they sought to study. They concluded that authority in Chinese decision making was in fact "fragmented" across various bureaucratic levels.[31] Policy making was diffuse, and often depended on bargaining among top central leaders, ministerial officials, and/or influential local politicians.[32] Furthermore, they found that foreign investors also helped shape the development of those projects that were oriented to foreign trade.[33] Finally, they discovered a significant degree of progressive learning and flexibility among policy makers in the petroleum industry; there was, however, less such adaptation in other energy-related areas.[34]

Margaret Pearson's 1990 study[35] also included many elements of Chinese–foreign political interaction, such as foreign investor influence on policy matters, as well as internal Chinese political tension and the resulting bargaining process. Pearson traced the development of Chinese rules and regulations for foreign investment, and found that a combination of Chinese political pragmatism and Western readiness to invest moved the reform process in a steadily more liberal direction. Pearson, however, chose to touch on the whole spectrum of Sino-foreign cooperation, and her study thereby lost some of the analytical power that might be obtained in focusing on one issue area.

These earlier studies also failed to employ Jervis's ideas of misperception. Considering the great differences in culture and past practices of the Chinese and foreign automotive representatives, it would be surprising if misunderstandings did not cloud the stimuli foreigners exerted on the Chinese policy makers. To further utilize Jervis's work, one should also consider the influence of misperception between higher and lower levels of the Chinese political system. Finally, the motivational elements of "wishful thinking" may also distort the policy process at many levels of the Chinese bureaucracy.

My own approach seeks to build on the theoretical framework of Lieberthal and Oksenberg and the analysis of Pearson, while adding new empirical data in a different industrial sector, that of the automobile industry. In doing so, this volume takes into account several variables that shaped both the political and the economic development of the Chinese automotive sector. Four case studies look at the "stimuli" of domestic and foreign economic forces, and discuss their effect on the Chinese central government. The empirical chapters also examine the bargaining that took place between central and local politicians, and the misperception that affected the policy process. Finally, the studies note the differing policy outcomes for the four automotive ventures, and try to make projections of their future progress based on past experiences. Before delving into the details of the following chapters, however, let me give brief explanations of my terminology.

"Domestic economic forces" are defined here as economic factors fostered within China that shape the objective needs of the country as a whole, rather than meeting the narrow desires of some specific constituency. For the automotive sector, domestic economic forces include, for example, the legitimate requirement of work units and individuals for the use of passenger cars; this represents the macroeconomic demand side of the industry. The subsequent need to satisfy such demand pushes the issue of automotive development onto the political agenda. Other domestic conditions, such as recession, that may make foreign automotive investment attractive are also elements here. Finally, domestic economic forces also include the latent wish among many policy makers and ordinary citizens that China might somehow emulate Japan, South Korea, and others in exporting automobiles, thus potentially elevating China's economic status to that of a nation rising quickly out of its early developmental stages. This factor is linked to the process of fostering a sense of pride and improved self-image throughout the whole of the country.

The "foreign forces" in this study are limited to foreign auto companies and their representatives that directly or indirectly persuade the Chinese to put automotive development on the national agenda. European and American companies have proposed and developed cooperative projects with China; in contrast, Japanese manufacturers have tempted the local market with imports, forcing the Chinese to implement import substitution measures to avoid foreign exchange deficits. In the more intimate cooperation with the non-Japanese companies, moreover, elements of misperception have affected the decision-making process within the Chinese government, as the case study chapters reveal.

The actual decision-making process analyzed here highlights the bargaining that must take place within the government before a decision is made. For the central government in Beijing, this study includes the interaction between various pertinent ministries and bureaus and their chiefs, and the top national leaders who traditionally receive much analytical attention. The study also focuses on the conflicts between local and national political bodies in the development of the automotive sector. These bargaining elements are made manifest in the case study chapters.

My decision-making analysis extends to a discussion of misperception among the most important national and local decision makers. Chronicles of these leaders' backgrounds help indicate latent qualities that may shape policy decisions in significant ways.

Finally, as Allison suggests, implementation of policy decisions may be slowed by bureaucratic standard operating procedures. The case studies will try to show how the Chinese automotive bureaucracy was able to cope with the new problems and prospects that arose in the cooperative ventures with foreign manufacturers.

This volume, then, begins in chapter 2 with an overview of China's automotive history. The chapter's goal is to trace the objectives of China's "domestic economic forces," and to explain the emergence of and need for "foreign forces" in the post-Mao reform era. (The goals of the "foreign forces" appear more explicitly in the later case study chapters.)

Chapter 3 outlines the structure and function of the pertinent sections of the Chinese government that form the substratum for the stimuli of these elements. It also introduces brief personal histories of the key officials involved in the auto industry's development, tracing the careers of current Vice Premiers Zhu Rongji and Zou Jiahua, and former automotive czar Chen Zutao. Each of these men influenced the development of the cases under study to varying degrees. As noted above, furthermore, we take their opinions, expressed in the empirical chapters, as generally representative of consensus reached among members of the organizations they led.

The following chapters focus on four case studies. Chapter 4 introduces the first automotive joint venture in China, Beijing Jeep. This case is rather unique among those analyzed, as it presents a crisis situation and the resultant bargaining between the Chinese government and American investors.

Chapters 5 and 6 analyze the joint venture companies of Shanghai Volkswagen and Guangzhou Peugeot. These ventures are noteworthy for their distance from Beijing, and for the subsequent need for coordination and cooperation between the national and local political bodies.

Chapter 7 is devoted to the wholly foreign owned enterprise, Panda Motors, a South Korean/American-invested automotive project in southern China. This venture, which received great scrutiny from foreign media sources, presents a wealth of information for study of local and national political conflict and cooperation, as well as bargaining within the central government, and between the central government and foreign investors.

Finally, chapter 8 gives an overview of the automotive industry and its bureaucratic development over the past decade, and tries to probe for political progress. It then projects the analysis onto a wider view of the foreign-economic policy process, and adds an analysis of prospects for the future of foreign investment in China.

2

China's Automotive History and Policy Development, 1949–1993

From the early days of the People's Republic, the Chinese realized the enormous strategic and economic necessity of a well-developed vehicle industry. This chapter traces the development of what was defined as the "domestic economic forces" faced by foreign firms in the late 1970s and 1980s. It further examines, from a historical perspective, the early government guidance necessary for constructing an automotive industry in a centrally planned system, one that varied considerably with the oscillation of political and economic trends. The chapter outlines these sometimes dramatic policy swings over the decades after the 1949 Communist victory, and thereby provides the necessary historical base for later applications of the analytical framework introduced in chapter 1.

Pre-1949 Conditions

The first automobiles arrived in China in 1901, and ran mainly on the streets of industrialized Shanghai.[1] By the mid-1920s, though, there were only about 7,000 cars and 600 trucks on the streets of major cities;[2] virtually all of these were imported vehicles, and many were owned by foreign residents. American model cars dominated sales in China during these early decades.[3]

Analysts cited several factors that retarded the growth of the automotive sector. First, China had relatively few miles of paved road. In 1923, the country had about 2,000 miles of "highway" (mostly rough trails).[4] By 1937, there were about 25,000 miles of surfaced highway.[5]

(For comparison, the United States had nearly 1.3 million miles of paved road in 1935.)[6] One observer noted that "[n]o matter how wealthy a resident of any [Chinese] district may be or how great his desire to own a motor vehicle, he will not purchase if there is no place in which the car can be used."[7]

Other limits to expansion of automotive sales during the first part of the century included the low standard of living of the majority of China's citizens; for peasant farmers and even industrial workers, the notion of purchasing an automobile was only a distant dream. Low salaries also inhibited the growth of the industry by making the employment of rickshaw pullers or horse cart drivers more economical than the purchase and maintenance of a new automobile. (Often, the purveyors of human transport would even try to block transport companies from using motorized trucks, as such modern conveyance endangered the future of their livelihood.)[8] Finally, political conditions also inhibited the willingness to purchase a private vehicle: during the civil war years of the 1920s, vehicles were subject to confiscation by the armies of feuding warlords.[9] Still, by 1936, China hosted nearly 25,000 passenger cars, some 12,000 of which were in Shanghai.[10]

Domestic manufacture was quite limited in the years leading up to World War II. Vehicle repair stations, of course, were required to service imported cars and trucks. During the 1920s, several larger cities (including Beijing, Shanghai, and Tianjin) established shops making the bodies for imported motors and chassis; these wooden bodies were typically constructed and painted by hand.[11] During the 1930s and war years of the 1940s, a handful of small-scale bus and cargo truck chassis production plants appeared;[12] there was, however, no significant production of complete vehicles in any part of the country until economic recovery began in the postwar Communist era.

Early Production and Policies: 1949–1965

In the face of the prior reliance on imported vehicles, the construction of an indigenous vehicle manufacturing capability came to be a priority for the newly established Communist Chinese government. Why, however, did these leaders feel a pressing need to develop this industrial sector?

First, to help revive the nation's economy, efficient transport of rural produce, now preferably in mechanized trucks, would be vital to spur agricultural development. Furthermore, with the beginning of the Cold War and security threats to China from several fronts, an automotive industry was needed to enhance military mobility. These factors overrode lingering reluctance to replace the still significant numbers of human conveyors with motor transport.

Only one year after the founding of the People's Republic, therefore, the Chinese moved quickly to create their own large-scale vehicle industry. In 1950, they approached the USSR for help in planning an auto factory, and the Ministry of Heavy Industry commissioned a "preparatory office" to guide the motor industry's development.[13] Soviet experts arrived in Beijing to offer advice.

By 1951, the Chinese had chosen Changchun in northeast China as the site of their First Automotive Works (FAW). In the aftermath of Japanese occupation since the early 1930s, the area possessed a high concentration of railway lines and other industrial development conducive to vehicle manufacture.

To develop their nascent freight transport capabilities, the Chinese decided to exclusively manufacture trucks at their new government-owned and managed plant (virtually all private enterprise in China had been nationalized by the mid-1950s). The first product would be a four-ton Soviet model "ZIS 150" (later renamed the "*Jiefang*," or "Liberation" model), and the target was to produce 30,000 vehicles per year.[14] Such initial decisions were approved by the early Finance and Economic Commission of the Government Administration Council (*Zhengwuyuan caijing weiyuanhui*).

In 1953, the government acknowledged the importance of the auto industry by formally establishing the "Automotive Industry Administration Bureau" under the First Ministry of Machine Building. Construction of FAW began, with China's leader, Mao Zedong, contributing an inscription for the factory's founding. The FAW officially opened in 1956, and was soon followed by automotive ventures in industrialized Nanjing, Shanghai, and other cities. These factories also focused on trucks and utility vehicles.

By the mid-1950s, the Chinese recognized the need for a small number of passenger cars, at a minimum, to service top-ranking leaders. In 1958, the FAW produced its first *Hongqi* (Red Flag) model limousine, a luxury vehicle modeled on Daimler Benz's model 220 sedan. That same year, the Shanghai Automobile Assembly Plant began manufacture of its Phoenix model passenger car. Actual produc-

Figure 2.1. **Annual Passenger Car Production, 1957-65**

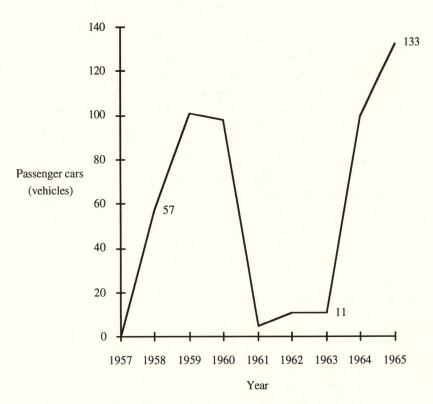

Source: Zhongguo qiche gongye nianjian (China Automotive Industry Yearbook), 1991, p. 124.

tion, however, was negligible; in 1960, the whole nation produced only ninety-eight of its own cars; in 1961, following the shortcomings of the "Great Leap Forward" (noted below), it produced only five (see figure 2.1). To compensate for the small number of domestically produced vehicles, China imported an average of some 1,000 passenger cars per year from 1954 to 1965 (see figure 2.2), mostly from Eastern Europe (Polish cars seemed most prevalent in the 1960s).[15] The pre-1949 cars imported from the West gradually became extinct, as they suffered from a lack of compatible spare parts.[16]

Chinese automotive production policy fluctuated over the course of

Figure 2.2. **Annual Passenger Car Imports, 1954-65**

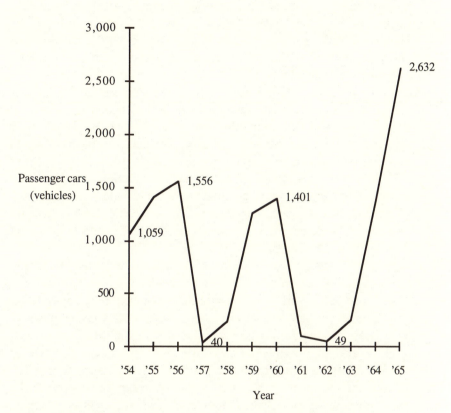

Source: *Zhongguo qiche gongye nianjian* (China Automotive Industry Yearbook), 1991, p. 536.

the Communist nation's first decade. The early 1950s were marked by emphasis on worker innovation at the manufacturing level. With the arrival of Soviet experts in the mid-1950s, however, the Chinese stressed adoption of foreign methods and experiences. The FAW's use of the Soviet model truck plans exemplifies such technology absorption: the "Liberation" model trucks had 81 percent Russian parts in 1956 (by 1965, though, they were 100 percent Chinese-made).[17] During the mid-1950s, worker input was in fact discouraged, as it was thought to interfere with successful utilization of Soviet technique.[18]

The "Great Leap Forward" years (1958–60) again reversed the

attitude toward automotive innovation. The Chinese shifted on a national scale toward reliance on their own working styles, and campaigned against dominance of foreign technologies and equipment. Such a shift was characteristic of Great Leap policies; one historian has noted that "Mao's program, simply put, envisioned the development and application of modern science and technology without professional scientists and technocrats."[19]

In the aftermath of the failed "Leap," the Chinese returned to emphasis on raising technical standards, with less stress on the sometimes ill-informed ideas of production-level workers.[20] The flight of Soviet technicians with the Sino-Soviet split, however, weakened China's ability to adopt foreign technology, although in 1965 China did hold talks with France's Berliet company on construction of a truck factory.[21] The focus on domestic bureaucracy-led technical advance, however, ended in 1964, as reliance on the masses again came to the fore, parallel to the beginning of the Cultural Revolution and the renewed dominance of Maoist policies.

The policy swings guiding automotive development roughly parallel the political clashes among China's top leadership over the country's first fifteen years. Early postrevolution development relied on practical measures to rebuild the war-torn nation, and on Soviet technical advice; Mao Zedong's influence was somewhat eclipsed in these years. With the revival of Mao's policies during the Great Leap era, however, the automotive industry emulated policies of self-reliance. The failure of the Great Leap was reflected in the automotive industry's swing back to technological reliance in the early 1960s. This brief pragmatic and technocratic period, however, like the one experienced by the whole nation in the early 1950s, ended with Mao's reasserting power and his launching of the Cultural Revolution in the mid-1960s.

The Auto Industry under Revolutionary Policies: 1966–1976

As relations with the Soviet Union deteriorated in the 1960s, Chinese leaders became worried about the susceptibility to foreign attack of the country's largest vehicle plant in Changchun. In 1965, the newly formed China National Automotive Industrial Corporation (CNAIC) approved the creation of a Second Automotive Works (SAW), and the next year the Chinese decided to build the new truck factory in the relatively isolated mountainous region of Shiyan in Hubei Province.[22]

The SAW factory was to put into practice the ideals of self-reliance, and would depend on the technology and experiences of other domestic Chinese manufacturers. Although ground-breaking in Shiyan began in 1967, the factory was not fully operational until 1975, though some actual production began as early as 1970.[23] Delays were probably the result of turmoil related to the Cultural Revolution, which also lowered total production of cars, trucks, and other vehicles in the whole nation from 55,861 in 1966 to 25,100 in 1968.[24]

Passenger car production received scant attention during the early years of radical Maoist leadership. Such vehicles were still primarily intended for high-level officials, as private car ownership and operation were essentially prohibited[25]; cars accounted for only about 1 percent of Chinese production, with truck and other vehicles heavily dominating manufacture. (For comparison, passenger cars have accounted for 60 to 90 percent of developed nation automotive production over the three decades since the 1960s.)[26]

In 1966, the FAW introduced a more spacious model of its *Hongqi* luxury vehicle, and the First Ministry of Machine Building approved a plan to enlarge the Shanghai factory's "Shanghai Brand" cars in 1972.[27] Still, passenger car production dropped from 302 in 1966 to 196 in 1970[28] (see figure 2.3), and car imports virtually vanished (figure 2.4).

Although overall production growth was slow, the revolutionary years emphasized the spirit of geographical self-sufficiency, mentioned above, and led to a spiraling growth in the number of automotive manufacturers spread around the nation. In 1964, China had 417 factories producing trucks, cars, motorcycles, and fundamental automotive parts; by 1976, the number had more than quadrupled to 1,950.[29] The number of automotive manufacturers experienced a similar jump (see figure 2.5), and nearly every province (including remote Qinghai) came to boast an automotive plant. Of some fifty factories capable of serial production of trucks or other vehicles, however, only four were reported able to manufacture more than 10,000 units per year. Some plants produced only a few thousand or a few hundred vehicles annually,[30] resulting in significant, though generally ignored, diseconomies of scale in many geographical areas. (For a rough comparison, U.S. auto manufacturers in the 1960s targeted equipment for production of some sixty cars per *hour* per assembly line, for an annual plant capacity of 200,000 to 400,000 units; at the time, this was considered an economy of scale).[31]

Figure 2.3. **Annual Passenger Car Production, 1965-72**

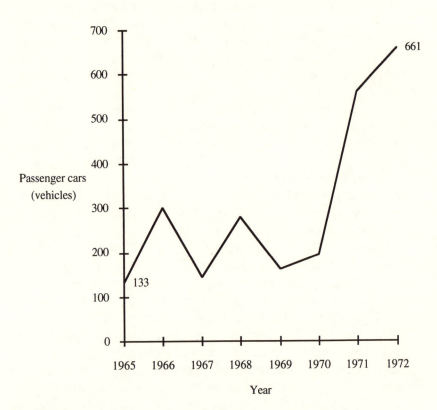

Source: *Zhongguo qiche gongye nianjian* (China Automotive Industry Yearbook), 1991, p. 124.

Automotive policy development in the late 1960s was primarily inspired by Maoist principles. The inherent experiences of the masses, rather than foreign expertise, were termed the best sources for improving production capability. The industry's general aims in the revolutionary times included the development of domestic grass-roots production bases in each province to avoid dependence on foreign technology and production systems, while designing Chinese model vehicles better suited to local conditions.[32] To achieve these goals, the government precluded any meaningful foreign investment in the automotive sector, and tightly controlled exchanges of technicians. The

Figure 2.4. **Annual Passenger Car Imports, 1965-72**

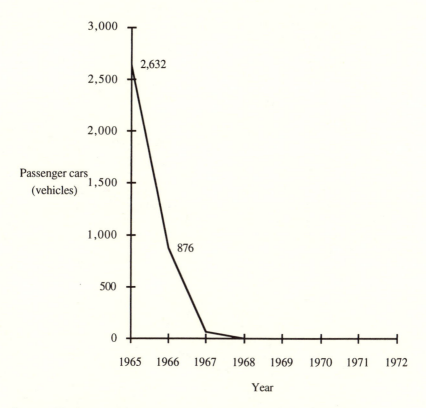

Source: *Zhongguo qiche gongye nianjian* (China Automotive Industry
Yearbook), 1991, p. 536.

Notes: Data are unavailable for the years 1969 and 1970. In both 1971 and 1972,
China imported ten cars.

Chinese eschewed importing completed vehicles, and even rejected the
idea of licensing technology to update local products.[33] One observer
noted in the early 1970s that "industrial backwardness is viewed as an
advantageous force to be harnessed, rather than as an inhibiting factor
in the development process."[34]

  Although China suffered no lack of "industrial backwardness," it
gradually came to realize, as domestic vehicle production volume and

24

Figure 2.5. Growth in Number of Vehicle Manufacturing Factories, 1956-92

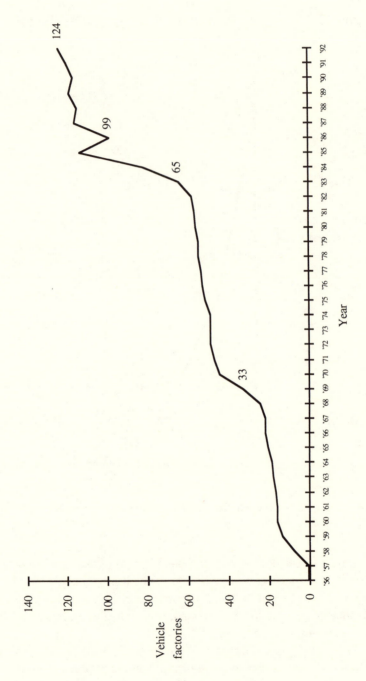

Source: Zhongguo qiche gongye nianjian (China Automotive Industry Yearbook), 1994, p. 94.

quality fell, the value of importing some vehicles developed using foreign, mainly capitalist, technology. Such automotive contact with foreign firms, however, developed slowly. Following the Sino-Soviet split of the early 1960s, total car and truck imports fell from 24,865 in 1958 to a postrevolutionary low of 1,123 in 1961.[35] In 1971, China imported some 10,157 trucks, mostly from Italy, Romania, Japan, and France. Still, the percentage of domestically produced trucks in service rose from some 50 percent in 1970 to about 65 percent in 1975; most of the rest of the vehicles on the road were Soviet and Eastern European imports, and a fraction were from Japan and Western Europe.[36] China also exported a small number of trucks to Tanzania, Albania, and North Vietnam as part of the country's foreign aid program.[37]

Japanese automotive commerce with China was inhibited during the 1960s and 1970s by Chinese restrictions on companies that had ties to Taiwan and South Korea. In 1971, however, Japan's largest manufacturer, Toyota, promised to limit its contacts with those countries, and it subsequently was allowed to participate in China's trade fair in the spring of that year.[38] The Chinese reportedly had a predilection for Toyota, as that company's trucks, captured in the wake of the Japanese surrender after World War II, were a prime resource for the Communist forces fighting the Nationalists in northern China.

Toyota began to explore technological cooperation with the Chinese, ranging from exchanges of technicians to joint production of new vehicle models and importation of a complete integrated automotive plant. An early proposal called for a factory to make up to 150,000 cars and 30,000 trucks per year.[39] Other Japanese firms followed Toyota's lead in the early 1970s, and exchanges of technical experts between the two countries grew quickly during the mid-1970s.[40] Japan supplied some 45 percent of China's truck imports in 1974, and sold nearly $300 million worth of vehicles and parts to China from 1970 to 1975, accounting for about 30 percent of China's import market.[41]

European nations played a smaller part in China's developing auto industry. Their affiliation with the Chinese was limited to exports, mainly of trucks, with France contributing about 17 percent of China's imports. Italy, West Germany, and Sweden provided a limited number of vehicles, and, in 1975, Fiat's president visited Beijing for talks on technical cooperation.[42] The Chinese refused to buy American products, however, until normalization progress came in the mid-1970s.

The period of renewed interest in foreign technology in the early

1970s again paralleled a realignment of China's top leadership as some of the country's pragmatic officials, purged in the opening years of the Cultural Revolution, were rehabilitated. In 1973, Deng Xiaoping, one of the main advocates of reform and opening China to foreign trade and technology import, resumed his political place as vice premier; future premier Zhao Ziyang became party secretary of Guangdong province; and, in 1975, the liberal Wan Li became minister of railroads. At lower levels, automotive experts like future top leader Chen Zutao (discussed in more detail in chapter 3) returned from exile in the countryside to manage the major vehicle factories. The general trend among nearly all leaders, furthermore, was toward greater, though qualified, contact with the West, as exemplified by Chairman Mao's 1972 meeting with U.S. President Richard Nixon.

By the early 1970s, then, the Chinese had reinstated many technical experts to positions of authority, and again saw a need to rely on foreign cooperation to advance their automotive industry. Although the Cultural Revolution only officially ended with Mao's death in 1976, Chinese adoption of Maoist policies in the automotive sector had become somewhat diluted with the introduction of limited cooperation with foreign manufacturers. The period after Mao has shown an accelerated degree of interaction with foreign automotive firms, as the case study chapters will show.

Post-Mao Political Attitudes and Developments in the Auto Sector

In the wake of the political emphasis placed on industrial development following the death of Mao in 1976, and a resultant desire to tap the opinions of rehabilitated automotive experts, a discussion of the proper direction for general automotive policy gradually emerged in the Chinese press in the late 1970s and early 1980s. Automotive planners felt it necessary, first, to stem the mushroom-like proliferation of vehicle factories (see figure 2.5), a legacy of the self-reliant Mao years. These factories, mentioned above, were "small, but complete" (xiao er quan), in the earlier spirit of Maoist policies, but the new Chinese leaders now stressed the need for specialization and coordination among factories.[43] The Chinese eventually succeeded, by the late 1980s, in limiting the total number of the industry's factories (figure 2.5); in 1994 (when there were still some 116 manufacturers), the government said inefficient producers would be allowed to "wither in the face of competition."[44]

In addition to rationalizing the number of vehicle plants, the automotive agenda in the early pragmatic years also listed modernization of factory equipment as a high priority.[45] Furthermore, as vehicles on the road aged, they were to be replaced more quickly with newer automobiles.[46]

The early 1980s were days when the automotive sector in general was beginning to grow at a rapid clip, even compared with other Chinese industries. The total production value of vehicle and parts production doubled in Chinese currency terms from renminbi (the unit of Chinese money; hereafter abbreviated "RMB") 8.84 billion (about U.S. $5.9 billion) in 1980 to RMB 16.45 billion ($7.1 billion) in 1984, and doubled again to RMB 37.3 billion ($10 billion) in 1988 (figured in 1980 constant prices).[47] Over the same period, automotive production value grew from 1.76 percent of China's gross national industrial production to 2.39 percent in 1984, and to 2.53 percent in 1988.[48] Highway transport took an increasing percentage of the country's passenger travel, rising from 72 percent of total traffic in 1983 to 79 percent in 1986; the share of freight transport on the road, however, remained relatively constant.[49]

The Chinese moves to rationalize and modernize factories producing mostly trucks, however, had little initial impact on the still nascent passenger car industry. Production of cars hovered around 2,600 vehicles per year, a slight increase over the 1,819 produced in 1975[50] (see figure 2.6). This small number of cars emanated principally from only two manufacturers, located in the above-mentioned Shanghai vehicle factory, and at Changchun's FAW works. (Truck production, however, rose from 77,606 in 1975 to 119,501 in 1979.)[51]

While the domestic industry languished, the opening to the outside world and the resulting tourist trade created a huge demand for cars to serve as taxis. Guangzhou city, for example, began building its taxi fleet with an initial order for 270 vehicles from Hong Kong in September 1979, and other cities soon followed Guangzhou's example. Furthermore, work units granted permission to retain foreign exchange from export earnings were quick to purchase Japanese cars, buses, minibuses, and vans for their own use.[52]

In contrast to the rather rudimentary modernization priorities of foreign automotive policies in the early and mid-1970s, then, the policy

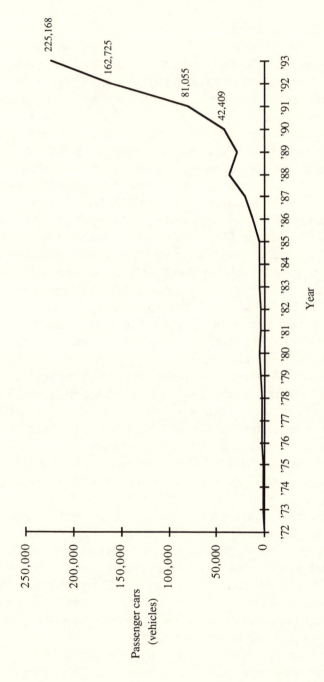

Figure 2.6. **Annual Passenger Car Production, 1972-93**

Sources: For 1972-92, *Zhongguo qiche gongye nianjian* (China Automotive Industry Yearbook), 1994, p. 103. For 1993, *China Auto 4*, no. 1 (January-February 1994): 17.

problems of the new decade were suddenly rooted in the need to impose some limits on the number of foreign passenger cars and other vehicles imported into China. Car imports alone leapt from 52 vehicles in 1977 to 667 in 1979, and to 19,570 in 1980[53] (see figure 2.7). The government responded with tighter import restrictions, and total car and truck imports temporarily fell, to 8,831 in 1982.[54]

Despite the short reprieve, however, relaxed restrictions in the mid-1980s brought a renewed shock to Chinese auto planners, as imports of cars and trucks again skyrocketed (see figures 2.7 and 2.8). The sharp rise from 1984 to 1986 was partly the result of favorable regulations that brought the infamous Hainan Island vehicle binge of 1984. The island was exempted from a 260 percent import duty imposed on the rest of the country, a benefit meant to spur development. Unfortunately, Hainan officials took advantage of the lenient rule to import tens of thousands of cars and other vehicles, mostly from Japan, and resold the automobiles at premiums of three to five times the purchase cost to other mainland provinces.[55] The island's import flood ended in November 1984, as the Bank of China suspended issuance of letters of credit for cars sold to Hainan, but not before 89,000 vehicles had entered China via the island.[56]

The quashing of the Hainan scandal did not, however, signal the end to China's automotive import binge. After a taste of Japanese and other Western vehicle quality, Chinese farmers continued to clamor for the reliable trucks, and taxi companies still thirsted for Toyota Crowns and Nissan Bluebirds. In 1985, China spent a record $3 billion to import some 350,000 vehicles, including 105,775 passenger cars.[57] A November 4, 1985, edict, however, significantly curtailed imports by requiring the approval of both the revitalized CNAIC and the State Planning Commission's[58] Office for Import Investigation before the purchaser could receive an import license.[59]

By the mid-1980s, the Chinese finally began to turn their attention to solving their import troubles by shifting production from heavy trucks, which was sufficient to meet demand, to lighter trucks and domestically produced passenger cars. The percentage of cars in total vehicle production subsequently rose rapidly (see figure 2.9). As the case study chapters of this work indicate, the Chinese had quickly realized that cooperation with foreign manufacturers in the form of joint ventures would be the key to a rapid increase in this type of vehicle production. These later chapters will focus in detail on specif-

Figure 2.7. **Annual Passenger Car Imports, 1972-93**

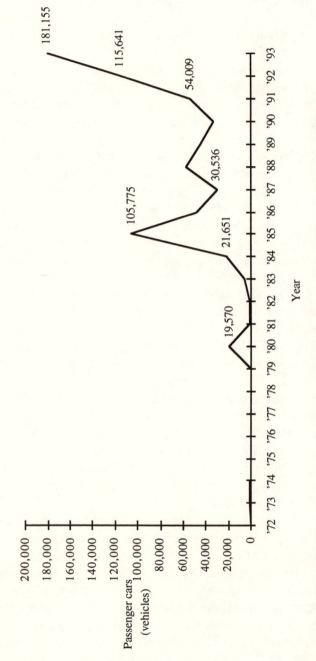

Sources: For 1972-91, *Zhongguo qiche gongye nianjian* (China Automotive Industry Yearbook), 1994, p. 425. For 1992, 1994 correspondence with China Automotive Technology and Research Center, Tianjin, China. For 1993, *China Auto 4*, no. 1 (January-February 1994): 12.

Notes: Data are unavailable for the years 1975 and 1976. In 1977, China imported 52; in 1978, three.

Figure 2.8. **Annual Total Vehicle Imports, 1980-92**

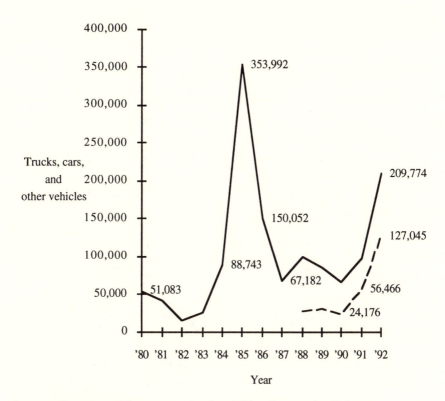

Source: Zhongguo qiche gongye nianjian (China Automotive Industry Yearbook), 1994, p. 425.

Note: The dotted line indicates disassembled vehicle parts kits (CKDs) for the years 1988-92.

ics of the foreign ventures that did appear in China, and the various political conflicts that ensued with the births of the new companies. Some of the general concerns of the automotive bureaucracy over the approach to foreign investors, however, are included below in this chapter.

The high import numbers inspired, for example, some radical suggestions to remedy the automotive dilemma. The new leader of the

Figure 2.9. **Passenger Car Production as a Percentage of Total Vehicle Production, 1980-93**

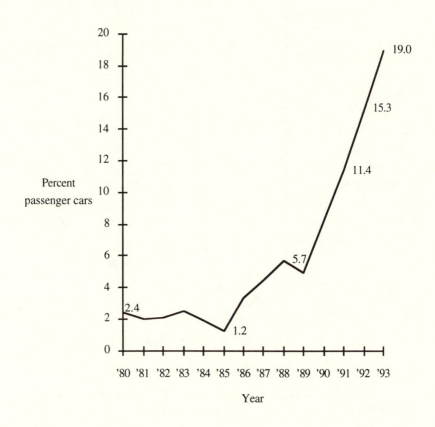

Sources: For 1980-92, statistics derived from *Zhongguo qiche gongye nianjian* (China Automotive Industry Yearbook), 1994, p. 103. For 1993, statistic derived from *China Auto 4*, no. 1 (January-February 1994): 17.

Note: Total vehicle production includes truck, car, bus, off-road vehicle, chassis, and other utility vehicle manufacture.

CNAIC, Chen Zutao,[60] proposed in 1985 that a new large-scale, specialized vehicle plant should be built in China every five years.[61] Chen also called for an increase in the number of automotive joint ventures and foreign loans to the industry,[62] and an increase in automotive exports, which had advanced at an uneven pace[63] (see figure 2.10). Other voices made somewhat irrational or contradictory suggestions. One called for limiting new vehicle technology to that of Japan only, in order to capitalize on the apparently boundless export potential of Japanese car models, and for completely excluding further import of European and American technology.[64] Others sought to reduce or suspend the use of scarce foreign currency reserves to import the disassembled vehicle kits[65] (commonly known as "completely knocked down," or "CKD" sets, discussed in more detail in later chapters) that were processed at Chinese factories.

Although viewpoints opposing increased automotive production are virtually invisible in the public press of the early 1980s, some automotive planners may have been aware of arguments that would have slowed or even reversed investment in the vehicle sector. For example, did the experience of other nations provide negative examples for those contemplating expansion of China's automotive production? Japan and South Korea seemed to be shining models to emulate; other nations, however, had less successful results.

Automotive Models for China?

Several studies of comparative automotive development look to South America for cases of vehicle industries in less developed nations struggling to come to life. Argentina, for example, after many years of investment in the industrial sector, found itself in the 1960s unable to generate the high volume production necessary for economies of scale. The country also failed to coordinate parts standardization among automotive suppliers.[66]

Probably the best comparative case for China, however, can be found in the large, developing nation of India. That country began cooperating with foreign investors in the interwar years, as a British colony, when its manufacturers assembled imported vehicle kits. By the 1980s, essentially all component parts were made in India, under license from various European manufacturers.[67]

India suffered from several problems the Chinese would also be sure to face. The domestic market lacked the financial means to support high-volume production, meaning factories had few economies of scale. Furthermore, low quality standards inhibited exports (though

Figure 2.10. **Annual Total Passenger Car Exports, 1982-92**

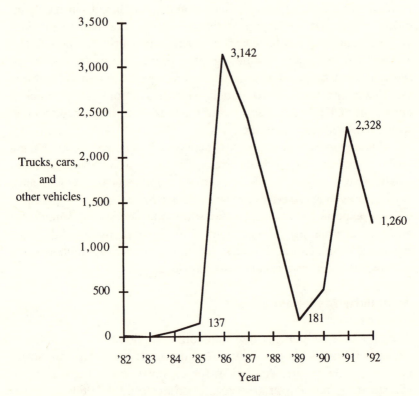

Sources: *Almanac of China's Foreign Economic Relations and Trade*. For 1982-83, p. 1065 in 1984 ed. For 1984, p. 925 in 1985 ed. For 1985, p. 1075 in 1986 ed. For 1986, p. 481 in 1987 ed. For 1987, p. 534 in 1988 ed. For 1988, p. 447 in 1989 ed. For 1989, p. 433 in 1990 ed. For 1990, p. 488 in 1991 ed. For 1991, p. 537 in 1992 ed. For 1992, p. 577 in 1993 ed.

Note: Figures do not include jeep exports.

some developing nations did take Indian products).[68] Finally, government import restrictions protected the inherent inefficiencies of production; locally manufactured cars were both poorly built and expensive.[69] The Indian government's reluctance to allow foreign investment beyond licensing agreements, and its view of the industry as less than vital to the national economy, may also have retarded the growth of the automotive sector.[70] Production of passenger cars, then, rose from 24,790 in 1965 to only 30,538 in 1980; the latter figure is actually lower than the production figure of 38,827 in 1972.[71] In the early 1980s, then, the Indian example should have given Chinese officials both an instructional model and some cause for concern.

The Chinese, however, may have been mesmerized by the successes of their other Asian neighbors, Japan and South Korea. By the mid-1970s, the Japanese automotive industry had already begun reaping significant profits by exporting vehicles to the United States. The Korean case, however, was probably more salient to China: though still a developing nation, South Korea had managed to begin with a kit assembly operation in 1967, and, using imported technology and management skill, to develop its own model vehicle (Hyundai's "Pony") by the mid-1970s. A 1979 projection forecast production of up to one million vehicles by the end of the 1980s; 1979 production of 113,000 cars was already nearly four times that of giant India.[72] The South Korean government, however, played a significant role in managing the country's vehicle industry; it encouraged, for example, restriction of passenger car manufacture to one assembler (Hyundai).[73] The Koreans, though, remained dependent on technology imports to maintain export competitiveness.

Chinese Policy in the Late 1980s and Early 1990s

Despite the mixed success of developing countries' automotive industries in the 1970s, by the mid-1980s the drive to foster a domestic passenger car industry in China had become nearly unstoppable. The latter years of the 1980s saw several published articles calling for accelerated small-car production. Many Chinese writers noted such vehicles would not only stem imports, but might also develop into an export industry;[74] these authors undoubtedly hoped their country could emulate the examples of the rapidly developing automotive export industry in Japan and South Korea. In what was perhaps a display of national pride, other automotive researchers argued that bicycles and subways could never truly substitute for passenger cars in moving people within urban areas, and, furthermore, that no other truly modern country in the world lacked a developed passenger car mode of transport.[75] (In 1994, a move in Guangzhou to eliminate two-thirds of the bicycles on city streets represented a somewhat ominous echo of this earlier sentiment.)[76]

Some more scientifically oriented researchers analyzed the need for steel, fuel, and roads to support an automotive industry, and found that China's raw materials and infrastructure, though then inadequate, could develop with proper technical aid.[77] Others undoubtedly noted the multiplier effects possible from the creation of productive parts supplier industries. Factories producing steel, electronics, and glass needed for automobiles would increase their output to meet the car manufacturers' requirements. One American study calculated, for example, that such so-called "backward-linkage" industries contributed (in the United States' industry) nearly 60 percent of the value of the vehicle produced.[78] A Chinese analyst summarized all of the above arguments by stating, "Without passenger car production, there can be no modernization of the automotive industry."[79] China would continue to devote attention to building such vehicles; and, as figures 2.6 and 2.9 and the case studies in this volume show, the result was a rapidly growing passenger car industry.

A consensus among central leaders in the late 1980s, then, recognized the need to acquire advanced technology and to rationalize and concentrate far-flung production facilities, many of which, though not passenger car producers, were vital parts suppliers to the new foreign cooperative plants. The Chinese also saw value in reforming factory management procedures. To develop a long-term strategy, China formed a study group with Japanese specialists in early 1986,[80] and the policy bureau of the central State Science and Technology Commission carried out a major study of the passenger car industry in 1987.

Once the initial decisions to develop the vehicle industry were made, however, the central leaders took a diminishing role in managing the sector's growth; this was part of the movement in the 1980s to devolve economic management away from the national government. The case study chapters chronicle these developments in more detail.

By the late 1980s, however, the central government did make a rather feeble effort to reassert greater control over the industry's direction. Top political leaders in 1988 considered the so-called "Big Three, Little Three" (*San Da, San Xiao*) scheme proposed at their annual autumn Beidaihe leadership conference. According to this plan, China's main vehicle manufacturers would be the First Auto Works in Changchun, the Second Auto Works in Hubei, and the Shanghai vehicle factory, which by then had formed the joint venture with Volkswagen discussed in chapter 5. The three minor players would be the joint venture companies of Beijing Jeep (see chapter 4), Guangzhou Peugeot (see chapter 6), and the Tianjin Automotive Corporation, which had a licensing agreement with Japan's Daihatsu Motor Company.[81] The plan also called for increasing passenger car output to 40 percent of vehicle production by the year 2000.[82] To further stimulate domestic production, in late 1989 the Chinese again tightly restricted vehicle imports from Western countries, limiting incoming vehicles mainly to Soviet and Eastern European models.

With the enunciation of the *San Da, San Xiao* plan, some Chinese analysts further stipulated that the industry should refrain from blindly building any other new passenger car factories.[83] The desire somehow to emulate the United States' concentrated auto industry in the Michigan and Ohio region, or Japan's centralized Nagoya-Tokyo area factories, manifested itself in various Chinese references to several of their main factories as "China's Detroit," or of their localities as "Motor City."[84] By fostering rational parts supply industries and manufacturing efficiency, focused automotive factory sites would promote production.

With diffuse manufacturing facilities already spread around the nation, however, a result of the policies of the 1950s and 1960s, China was reluctant to simply concentrate production in one or two regions. The six major facilities, therefore, stretched from Changchun to Guangzhou, and included nearly every major region in between (see figure 2.11). The proposed Panda automotive venture in Huizhou, Guangdong Province (see chapter 7), threatened to further dilute passenger car production, as did two new planned passenger car facilities, joint ventures between Hubei's SAW and France's Citroën, and Changchun's FAW and Volkswagen, both of which signed contracts in late 1990. In early 1994, however, the government reiterated its determination to refuse authorization of any major new vehicle factories.[85]

Finally, as China entered the 1990s, some automotive analysts again began a reassessment of the industry's rapid development. One official renewed the call for an end to imports of CKD kits in any future automotive ventures, citing high costs and China's difficulty in absorbing advanced technology.[86] (Such a move, however, would have stifled the extant passenger car producers, all of which were joint venture factories importing CKDs.) In mid-1989, a scholar at one of China's

Figure 2.11. **Locations of the Major Passenger Car Producing Factories, 1994**

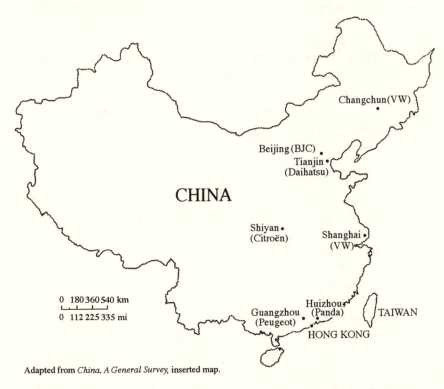

Changchun(VW)

Beijing (BJC)
Tianjin
(Daihatsu)

CHINA

Shiyan
(Citroën)   Shanghai
(VW)

0 180 360 540 km

0 112 225 335 mi

Guangzhou   Huizhou
(Peugeot)   (Panda)   TAIWAN

HONG KONG

Adapted from *China, A General Survey*, inserted map.

most prestigious research institutes wrote a strongly worded criticism of the assumed need for passenger car development in China. He enunciated some of the shortcomings already cited above, and pointed out the serious traffic problems, tremendous requirement of funds to build highways, and general transport inefficiencies accompanying a large-scale auto industry.[87] (By 1988, however, the length of paved roads had increased to nearly 525,000 miles, up from 411,000 in 1980.)[88] Still, such criticism had little effect on the industry's development.

In 1991, the influential *Jingji ribao* (Economic Daily) published a series of articles designed to chart a new path for car production.[89] The newspaper proposed targeting private purchasers for sales of small cars, noting that many cities in China had standards of living high enough to comprise such a market. (By early 1993, in fact, there were some 37,000 private car owners in China.)[90] It further pointed out that the existing purchasers of small cars—namely, government officials—represented a drain on national funds, as well as potentially corrupt abusers of their privilege to buy such vehicles. (As figure 2.7 shows, imports had begun to creep up to previous high levels in the early 1990s.) The inability of the joint ventures to meet world-level quality standards prohibited compensating exports. Therefore, to maintain and increase passenger car production, the government was encouraged to promote sales to the domestic private market. As of this writing, it was not clear whether the newspaper's call would significantly affect policy makers, and prices of $30,000 and up (including taxes) in 1994 for passenger cars further dampened such prospects. Still, as the rest of this book will show, nearly all of the joint venture producers maintained dreams of tapping just such a market. The concluding chapter notes, however, that China's imminent entry into the General Agreement on Tariffs and Trade (GATT) regime presented further complex policy dilemmas.

This study focuses primarily on the experiences of the passenger car joint ventures that have operated in China for several years. Although the Japanese have had extensive contact with the Chinese automotive industry, they have refrained (as of mid-1994) from signing a major joint venture contract and are therefore excluded from close analysis here. A brief discussion, however, of some of the salient points of the Japanese participation in Chinese passenger car development is in order.

The Japanese Investment Role

In spite of the previously noted cooperative efforts offered by Japanese companies in the 1970s, the Japanese initial preference in China was to sell finished vehicles. Thus, the early 1980s saw Japan snatching the lion's share of China's import market, with Toyota alone selling some 40,000 vehicles to China in 1984, mostly in Hainan.[91] Japanese passenger car exports peaked in the mid-1980s, however, and gradually declined for the rest of the decade as the Chinese relied more on joint venture products, barter imports from the USSR and Eastern Europe, and the Japanese vehicles already on the road.[92] By 1991, however, sales had begun to increase again: Nissan sold 20,000 vehicles to

China in 1991, and 60,000 in 1992.[93] (Figure 2.7 indicates this was part of a larger surge of imported vehicles.)

In addition to exports, the Japanese have at times considered some more lasting automotive cooperation with the Chinese. Representatives from Japan explored prospects in the early 1980s for joint ventures in Beijing and Shanghai; these cities, however, later turned to the Americans and West Germans, respectively, to sign contracts. The Japanese thereafter failed to form any large-scale joint venture for car manufacture.[94]

The only significant Japanese passenger car cooperative venture has been between Daihatsu and Tianjin Automotive Industrial Corporation. The venture was a technology licensing agreement, signed in November 1986, for a seven-year term. The Chinese soon began producing the small Charade model car, and by 1992 annual production had reached nearly 30,000 vehicles (see table 8.1), with some 40 percent of the parts made in China.[95] In 1988, the factory was named one of China's "Little Three" manufacturers. The contract also stipulated that Tianjin workers would receive some training in Japan.

Two other car venture agreements to make minicars, signed with Suzuki Motor Company and Fuji Heavy Industries (the manufacturer of Subaru cars), were by the mid-1990s still in the planning stages of production. The small cars to be manufactured had engines with displacement less than 1.0 liters. (For comparison, Shanghai Volkswagen's Santana models had 1.8-liter engines.) Fuji, moreover, had none of its own capital invested in the project.[96]

Chinese automotive officials interviewed for this study almost universally criticized Japan for what they saw as unwillingness in the 1980s to part with the advanced technology needed to establish a large-scale joint project. They noted that the Japanese may have feared future competition from China for export markets, and some events led them to believe the Japanese much preferred to reap the greater profits of assembled vehicle sales to China.[97] One Toyota assembly operation in Guangdong to build Dyna light pickup trucks, for example, stopped after 2,000 vehicles had been manufactured, reportedly because Toyota refused to cooperate beyond simple kit assembly.[98] A Shanghai official who had been rebuffed by Toyota in 1983 commented, "I told Toyota that after several years have passed, you will not see any Toyotas in Shanghai—only VWs."[99]

This pattern of Japanese investment was not restricted to the automobile industry; by early 1993, only 1.6 percent of Japan's overseas investment had gone to China.[100] In addition to some actual fear of future competition, Japanese businesses were also wary of the investment climate in China, and tended to withhold their funds pending stronger legal guarantees of their capital's safety; for automotive manufacturers, the United States and Europe seemed safer investment targets.[101] Technology-transfer agreements, furthermore, were subject to strict Cold War–era security regulations until 1986; even joint venture television factories and other commercial electronics firms, which took the bulk of Japanese investment, were affected by these rules.[102] Problems of Chinese quality control further complicated cooperation.[103] Finally, general cultural animosity, based in historical antagonism, created a further barrier to increased Chinese economic interaction with the wealthiest and most technologically advanced nation in Asia.

By the mid-1990s, some Japanese officials and car manufacturers looked back in frustration at their past failure to invest in China. Kazuo Yawata, of Japan's Ministry of International Trade and Industry's North and East Asia Division, claimed in late 1993 that Western nations' protectionism had forced the Japanese to divert investment funds to build plants in the United States and Europe in the 1980s; little money, then, had been left to invest in China.[104] In the future, Japan would have to focus its attention on automotive investment: "From a long-term perspective, we can't afford not to be here," said Yutaka Kume, chairman of both the Japan Automobile Manufacturers' Association and of Nissan Corporation.[105] Toyota's general manager in China, Etsuo Hattori, however, believed it might be too late for Japan to catch other investors. "We have been using our power in America and Europe. Now China is the biggest market in the world. We have lost our chance."[106]

Conclusion

This chapter has outlined the early pendulum-like policy swings of the 1950s and 1960s, illustrating the contradiction between Maoist policies of grass-roots innovation and self-reliance, and the pragmatic forces preferring rational industrial development and use of foreign technology. Both sides, however, seemed to recognize the importance of a viable vehicle industry: the continuous construction of production facilities, and resultant increases in automotive output over the decades, testify to this assertion.

With Mao's death, those favoring foreign technology and investment, a rationalized production system, and meaningful passenger car manufacture seem to have won the day. The precipitous advent of domestic vehicle demand reinforced the pragmatists' calls for such steps. There followed, then, basic agreement on the ultimate goals for the automotive sector, even given the evidence of uneven progress in the vehicle industries of other developing nations.

As the first chapter has indicated, however, concurrence on goals does not necessarily form the basis for coherent bureaucratic action. This chapter has shown that the post-Mao era fostered public debate and a divergence of opinion on the precise path China should take on the way to a healthy passenger car industry. It has also indicated that, by allowing foreigners a chance to participate in the country's automotive development, the Chinese had introduced a new element to the equation, one less subject to the central leadership's control.

The case study chapters will focus on the foreign interaction with the more free-thinking bureaucratic structures of the 1980s. Before the cases are introduced, however, chapter 3 assesses the substrata on which the foreigners could act, by examining in some detail the most relevant political institutions and actors participating in the automotive industry's reform-era development.

3

Automotive Political Structures
and Individual Leaders

This discussion of the political actors and institutions that helped determine the foreign-invested automotive climate in the 1980s is divided into three sections. First, it looks at the central government structure for regulating the industry, taking a snapshot view of the highest levels (elder leaders, the State Council, and central government commissions) and presenting a more in-depth examination of lower levels (the various machine-building ministries and automotive corporations). This section seeks to gauge central control over the automotive sector, and to pinpoint bureaucratic rivalries in regulation of the industry.

The following section focuses on local automotive governmental bodies. What responsibilities are these levels assigned, and how is policy-making power allocated within the municipal unit? Later case study chapters provide further detail, and examine the interaction of the cities with the Beijing leadership. This chapter gives an overview of the four locations (Beijing, Shanghai, Guangzhou, and Huizhou) of the ventures under study.

The final part of the chapter provides brief biographies of three leaders closely associated with one or more of the ventures under study. In looking at Chen Zutao, Zhu Rongji, and Zou Jiahua, this section asks: How have these men's backgrounds shaped their outlook on automotive policy? Do personal rivalries, institutional loyalties and connections, or private goals color their policy-making efforts? Do what may be thought of as "typical" bureaucratic backgrounds inspire the expected political actions?

The Automotive Industry and Central Government Structure

Elder Leaders

Over the first fifteen years of China's economic reform era, the central government's political leadership was heavily influenced by elderly CCP revolutionary leaders. Though generally lacking formal titles, these officials often functioned as invisible hands to approve broad policy propositions decided at lower bureaucratic levels. The powers and responsibilities of this elite group have been described in other works;[1] this section therefore briefly focuses on three elderly leaders who are closely identified with the automotive sector.[2]

Bo Yibo, born in 1908 and a member of the CCP beginning in 1925, was one of China's top elderly leaders throughout the 1980s and early 1990s. Following stints as finance minister and chairman of the State Construction Commission, Bo was the first director of China's new State Economic Commission (SEC), serving from 1956 to 1966; he thereby established a firm base in implementation of economic and industrial policy. After the Cultural Revolution, Bo served as chairman of the State Machine Building Industry Commission from 1980 to 1982. Though he relinquished many of his posts in the mid-1980s, Bo remained a force in the moderate-conservative policy-making camp. As vice chairman of the CCP's Central Advisory Commission, Bo joined other elderly leaders who advocated restraint in economic transformation, although in 1993 he pledged support for Deng Xiaoping's capitalist-style economic policies. He defended, however, the 1989 decision to use force against Tiananmen Square democracy demonstrators.

Bo took an active interest in the automotive sector, participating in planning and giving several speeches on the progress of the industry. He expressed some caution in the early 1980s on cooperating with foreign firms, putting self-reliance before full collaboration.[3] A later speech, however, acknowledged trends in reform and decentralization of the automotive industrial structure.[4] Perhaps in part to help him keep a check on automotive policy development beyond his retirement, Bo's son Bo Xiyong took a position as vice president of the CNAIC in the late 1980s.[5]

A second senior leader, Gu Mu, also reportedly had considerable interest in the automotive sector.[6] Born in 1914 and a CCP member since 1932, Gu was an SEC vice minister under his close ally, Bo Yibo, from 1955 to 1965. Gu was nominal chairman of the State Construction Commission from 1965 to 1970, though he had in fact been purged in 1967. As director of both the State Import and Export Administration and State Foreign Investment Administration in the first post-Mao years, Gu had the opportunity to shape China's "open" policy in the early 1980s. By the end of the decade, though, Gu's highest official post was that of vice chairman of the Chinese People's Political Consultative Conference.

Gu was generally looked on as a conservative leader, one favoring central control and planning, while demonstrating ambivalence about the West.[7] He helped shape the metallurgy and petroleum industries in the early 1980s, and was subsequently embarrassed by the troubles of the expensive Japanese-imported Baoshan steel plant.[8] According to one foreign source, Gu also maintained a particular interest in automotive development, taking a position as manager of the State Council Automobile Leading Small Group (discussed below) in the late 1980s. He therefore had some significant influence in formulating automotive policy.[9]

Finally, Ma Hong, though not quite in the top echelons of elderly leaders, also took a notable role in shaping the course of automotive development. Born in 1920, Ma joined the CCP in 1937. He served as secretary general of the State Planning Commission from 1952 to 1954 and was leader of the Policy Research Office of the SEC from 1956 to 1965. During the reform era, Ma took a position as vice chairman of the State Machine Building Industry Commission, serving under Bo Yibo. In 1988, he was named vice chairman of the National People's Congress's Financial Economic Committee, though his true power base lay in his leadership of the State Council Economic and Technological Development Research Center, a post he acquired in 1985.

Though Ma's political bent was unclear, sources report he took a great technocratic interest in automotive policy making. He apparently held a post in the State Council's automobile group, working under Gu Mu, and his own research center was a further source of automotive policy making.[10] In a 1987 speech at an automotive strategy conference, Ma demonstrated some detailed knowledge of China's vehicle requirements, calling for an increase in small car production and quality to reduce automotive imports, and advances toward a planned market economy.[11] He praised the reformist leader Zhao Ziyang's policies several times in this address, indicating a more liberal stance toward industrial reform. In the early 1990s, he called for renewed efforts in making China's economy available to foreign investment, saying "[t]he commercial, transport, banking, and foreign trade sectors could open up to the outside step-by-step."[12]

Although the actions of these leaders are difficult to document, their influence was probably manifested in some efforts to moderate rapid moves for cooperation with foreign automotive investors. Their age kept them from playing detailed decision-making roles, but their status, power bases built during tenures at industrial-related institutions, and interest in automotive policy made these leaders part of the anonymous group of top officials whose informal approval was apparently required for major policy initiatives.

The State Council and Commissions

At the top of the central government's bureaucratic structure in the early 1990s lay the State Council, headed by the premier. (As of mid-1994, this was Li Peng, in office since 1988.) The State Council played little day-to-day role in managing the automotive industry, but it did approve large joint venture or wholly foreign-owned enterprise (WFOE) projects, ones in excess of a RMB 200 million ($54 million in 1988) investment;[13] automobile ventures typically surpassed this level. The State Council also certified import quotas for motor vehicles, and for disassembled vehicle kits. This duty was assigned the Machinery and Electronics Import Inspection Office, led in 1990 by former Machine Building Industry minister Zhou Jiannan.

Under the State Council came the State Planning Commission (SPC.) The SPC was responsible for formulating and carrying out the national economic plan. For the foreign-invested auto industry, this power was of vital importance, as it gave the commission virtual control over the numbers and types of vehicles factories could produce. The SPC also had to approve joint ventures, and, in most cases, WFOEs (though, as we will see, Panda Motors was able to bypass the need for an SPC chop). Automobile ventures were greatly dependent on the Planning Commission to ensure approval of a constant, reliable supply of raw materials and energy resources.

The SPC had its own set of experts to help formulate its policies toward auto industry development. Under the top ministers lay the

Second Comprehensive Industrial Branch; this group's deputy director in 1990, Xu Bingjin, was directly accessible to the foreign auto manufacturers. The automobile department under this branch had approximately fifteen staff members.

The State Economic Commission (SEC) existed throughout most of the 1980s; its task was to implement the plans formulated by the SPC. It was concerned in the middle of the decade with technological improvement, management reform, and rational distribution of raw materials and energy.[14]

Several SEC officials had ties to the development of the automobile industry, including Ma Hong, Rao Bin, and Zhu Rongji. In 1988, the SEC was dissolved, with many of its functions going to the SPC and a new Ministry of Materials. In early 1992, however, Zhu Rongji led a movement to reconstitute the SEC; this maneuver is discussed later.

Finally, a State Council Automobile Leading Small Group was created in July 1987, to coordinate national automotive policy. It included representatives of the Planning, Economic, Machinery, and other committees, and the CNAIC.[15] This group, however, apparently ceased to function by 1989, and it is not clear how much influence it actually held during its brief tenure, though foreign business sources indicate it may have held veto power over major automotive projects.[16]

The Ministerial Level

The next level of bureaucracy (coordinated, but not directly governed, by the SPC) brings us to the ministerial ranks. The most important of these for the automotive industry was the machine-building ministry, which receives in-depth examination below. The discussion is followed by analysis of the China National Automotive Industrial Corporation (CNAIC), subordinate to the machine-building ministry.[17] Finally, we note other ministries more peripherally related to the automotive sector.

Machine-Building Ministerial Bodies

After the founding of the People's Republic in 1949, the Ministry of Heavy Industry was the first ministry-level organization supervising machine building; under it came a Bureau of Machinery Industry.[18] In 1952, however, with the cessation of the Korean conflict, the First

Ministry of Machine Building (FMMB), which would exist for the next thirty years, took charge of developing civilian machinery production.[19] With Huang Jing as minister (until 1956), the FMMB had bureaus devoted to automobiles, machine tools, ship building, electrical machinery, and other products.

As the new nation turned its attention toward automotive production, the ministry formed various automotive production bureaus and offices. The FMMB itself, moreover, underwent several transformations over its first decades. In February 1958, for example, the First Ministry absorbed the Ministry of Electrical Equipment and part of the Second Machine-Building Ministry.[20] By 1966, there were eight machine-building ministries; most of the second through eighth ministries, though, were military-related, and provided little competition with the FMMB.

Automotive planning and construction seem to have been tightly controlled at the ministry level until the early 1960s, when experiments in lower-level devolution of authority (namely, to the CNAIC) pulled some of the planning powers away from the First Ministry. In 1960, furthermore, the Ministry of Transport took over the functions of production, supply, and sales of auto parts from the FMMB.[21] In 1963, however, the FMMB was granted control over China's motorcycle production. That same year, the ministry regained its authority over parts production from the Transport Ministry, indicating the FMMB may have won a small interministerial power struggle.

The chaos of the Cultural Revolution ended such decentralizing and realigning trends, as purges at the ministerial level tended to freeze bureaucratic responsibilities. Furthermore, as chapter 2 indicated, planning and development of the automotive industry generally suffered on a broad scale.

As the chaos of the Cultural Revolution subsided, the FMMB took up the reins of automotive planning as best it could. In 1972, for example, it approved a plan for increasing production of Shanghai brand sedans. The following year, it helped chart the expansion of Jinan's auto factory.[22]

In the post-Mao era of industrial reorganization, China's machine-building ministries were revamped on several occasions. Bo Yibo became chairman of a new State Machine Building Industry (MBI) Commission in February 1980; this commission oversaw the various machine-building ministries. In May 1982, the FMMB merged with the Agricultural Machinery Ministry, the State Instrument and Meter Bureau, and the State Electrical Equipment Bureau to form the Ministry of Machine-Building Industry (MMBI).[23] The first minister was Zhou Jiannan; the former FMMB minister, Rao Bin, became board chairman of the CNAIC. The CNAIC itself assumed quasi-ministry-level status, though it officially remained under the MMBI.

The MMBI's authority began to diminish with a 1984 State Council proclamation calling for a separation of China's political and industrial sectors. Rather than existing as simple extensions of the bureaucracy, enterprises gained some rights to decide on personnel, product, and profit-sharing policy. The ministry (and the CNAIC) thereby lost some powers it had previously enjoyed.

In the wake of this process, MBI minister Zhou Jiannan left his job in November 1985, and moved to become an adviser to the party's Financial and Economic Leading Small Group.[24] The position of MBI minister then remained vacant for more than a year, probably as a result of indecision over further plans to reorganize the machine-building sector.[25] Finally, in December 1986, the MMBI merged with the Ordinance Ministry, then led by Zou Jiahua, to form a new Commission of Machine-Building Industry, which Zou took over as chair.

The decision to create the new commission was engineered by Premier Zhao Ziyang. Zhao wanted to put machine building and military production under one roof, thereby transferring civilian management expertise and orientation to the military's industrial sector.[26]

Changes in the machine-building structure were still unfinished. Little more than a year after the commission was inaugurated, it merged with the Electronics Ministry (in April 1988) to become the Ministry of Machine-Building and Electronics Industry (MMEI). Again, Zou Jiahua took the minister's post, which he held until his promotion to the State Planning Commission chairmanship one year later. Zou's long-time deputy and reported ally, He Guangyuan, took over the top spot at the MMEI.

By 1990, the MMEI had regained a fairly strong grip on the CNAIC. The ministry had the power to approve the appointment of the CNAIC leadership, as the corporation's chairman merely held vice-ministerial ranking. Furthermore, the CNAIC approached the State Council and SPC only through its superior ministry. The MMEI's jurisdiction also included control over allocation of raw materials among industries (including that of automobiles) and over investment in these industries. At the first session of the eighth National People's Congress (NPC) in March 1993, however, the ministry was again split, with He Guangyuan heading the Ministry of Machine-Building Industry (MMBI), and Hu Qili (resurrected after being purged from the Communist Party's powerful Politburo Standing Committee following the June 4, 1989 Tiananmen massacre) taking the post of Electronics Ministry minister.

In the early years of China's machine-building ministerial development, then, the automotive industry was subject to some rivalry between ministries, as the challenge from the Transport Ministry in the 1960s shows. The creation of the CNAIC in 1964 represented a power play from below (though, as noted below, it was instigated by Liu Shaoqi and other top leaders from above). The Cultural Revolution delayed the development of the semi-independent automotive entity, and a reconstituted CNAIC saw a steady decline of its authority in the 1980s. Over the same decade, however, the machine-building ministerial entities gathered increasing powers, eventually virtually reabsorbing the CNAIC and thereby reasserting their claim to guiding automotive industrial advances.

The CNAIC

The first embodiment of an automotive-specific government entity appeared in 1950 as a "preparatory office for motor industry" under the Ministry of Heavy Industry. Its earliest guidance came from Soviet experts. In 1953, the office became the Automotive Industry Administration Bureau, also known as the Sixth Bureau under the FMMB.

By 1958, the bureau was responsible for regulation of such items as automobile model-number coding; the superior ministry, however, retained such powers as the choice of actual models that factories would produce. In 1964, however, at the suggestion of China's president Liu Shaoqi, an experimental automotive trust emerged, taking the title of China National Automotive Industrial Corporation (CNAIC). The new entity was to be superior to the main auto-producing factories, including those in Changchun, Beijing, Nanjing, Chongqing, and Wuhan. In all, the CNAIC governed some seventy-five industrial plants.

The CNAIC gained further momentum as the State Economic Commission, apparently with the blessing of the FMMB, ratified the plan for an experimental automotive trust.[27] In 1965, then, the CNAIC took a leadership role in planning the Second Auto Works factory in Hubei.

The CNAIC experiment coincided with (although it did not necessarily inspire) great automotive industrial advances. From 1964 to 1965, automotive total output value rose 69 percent, personal productivity 61 percent, and automotive output 64 percent.[28]

With the purge of technical experts during the Cultural Revolution, the CNAIC was accused of being a "revisionist roader organization," and was eliminated.[29] Its functions were apparently reabsorbed (in name, anyway) by the FMMB. As chapter 2 indicated, however, automotive planning evaporated, leaving each small industrial sector isolated and uncoordinated.

Following Mao's death in 1976, pragmatic reformers moved to revive the earlier goal of coordinated automotive production. In 1980, then, the State Machine Building Industrial Commission promulgated a scheme for reorganizing the automotive industry; two years later, the State Council reestablished the CNAIC in Beijing.

As noted above, the first post-Mao CNAIC director was Rao Bin. Rao, known as the "Father of China's Auto Industry," had been an important figure in the PRC's early years, serving as mayor of the northeastern city Harbin in 1949, secretary of Songjiang Province from 1950 to 1954, and a vice chairman of the State Economic Commission in the early 1960s. He was also one of the founding managers of Changchun's First Auto Works.

Rao, unlike other early machine-building leaders, apparently received no formal education in the Soviet Union. His work in building both the First and Second Auto Works, however, gave him a stature among auto leaders others found difficult to match.

Rao's attitude toward postreform automotive development was generally conservative. In a 1985 speech, for example, he put little emphasis on the role of foreign cooperation in improving product quality and reliability, even though three major joint ventures (described in chapters 4–6) had already been established.[30] A later talk emphasized the need to substitute Chinese-made auto parts for imported parts, though Rao did mention the need for technical cooperation with foreign manufacturers through joint production.[31] One source noted Rao and Zhao Ziyang feuded over decentralization policies, with Rao fearing loss of central control over the industry's development[32] (a fear realized in the late 1980s).

The CNAIC's reincarnation, however, seemingly brought it some significant potential tools to mold the industry. The corporation's charter gave it the responsibility of planning output according to national goals, and modernizing management and production processes.[33] The CNAIC also became the leader of several "associated companies," including the FAW in Changchun, SAW in Hubei, and factories in Beijing, Tianjin, Shanghai, Jinan, Chongqing, and other cities.[34] As indicated in chapter 2, however, these companies were accustomed to self-reliance, and resisted attempts at CNAIC coordination.

At its founding, in fact, the CNAIC had difficulty establishing its authority. The corporation's budget was small, and the central government generally favored large infrastructural projects over machine building. Furthermore, the CNAIC received little profit from vehicle sales; local governments reaped most of the factory incomes.[35] As a partner in the 1985 Shanghai Volkswagen venture, however, the CNAIC sought a steady, and perhaps increasing, supply of foreign exchange.

The CNAIC's planning powers were further challenged in the mid-1980s. Although it could veto projects, the CNAIC depended on local governments and factories to push through the corporation's own plans.[36] The CNAIC also fought battles with the Machine-Building Ministry over the right to control automotive foreign trade.[37] Eventually, much of this power went to the Ministry of Foreign Economic Relations and Trade's (MOFERT's) machinery import–export branch, MACHIMPEX.[38] (The CNAIC, however, maintained its own import–export entity, the China National Automotive Industry Import Export Corporation [CAIEC]. The division of labor with MOFERT became unclear, though MACHIMPEX reportedly was the dominant force.)[39]

As the automotive industry received growing attention in the middle and latter 1980s (see chapter 2), the powers of the CNAIC paradoxically declined. This development was the result of several factors: First, as noted above, the central government instituted a program of decentralization. Those enterprises taking part in joint ventures, in particular, felt a greater degree of independence from Beijing, as they had foreign partners providing a source of hard currency and planning expertise. By 1986, the CNAIC could regulate only the FAW, SAW, factories in Nanjing and Jinan, and auto parts manufacturers.[40]

A further reason for the CNAIC's decline was the fall in leadership quality. As noted, Rao Bin had brought immediate prestige to the CNAIC in its early years of reincarnation. Rao stepped down as board chairman in July 1985,[41] and was replaced by Li Gang, who had been the CNAIC's general manager. Li gave up his general manager's position, however, in September 1985, to CNAIC chief engineer Chen Zutao, who assumed the actual leadership of the CNAIC.

Chen, described in more detail below, lacked Rao's revolutionary credentials and administrative skills. He tried to instill his ideas of large-scale production and Soviet-style central control at the height of the decentralization movement. The tide of reform ran against Chen, and he apparently lacked the power to resist.

In 1987, then, the CNAIC reached the nadir of its influence: it lost its power as a "corporation" (*zonggongsi*) and became simply a much looser "association" (*lianhehui*) of the nation's automotive manufacturers.[42] As an association, the CNAIC became a body that merely gave advice; it lacked the authority to make final policy decisions, such as those related to technology import, quality control, and domestic sales.

The resulting power vacuum led to some chaos among the automotive factories. For example, many small companies scattered around China produced limited numbers of vehicles, in quantities representing diseconomies of scale. All of these companies hoped to survive and to continue to make profits, of course, and therefore many spent scarce hard currency on foreign technology license agreements, contracts the CNAIC could no longer veto. The result was a spate of inefficient factories, purchasing exactly the same technology, with little benefit for the expenditure.

To rectify such problems, the State Council attempted in early 1990 to restore the preeminence of the CNAIC. In February, it was again made a corporation, and, on paper, it had the power to prevent technology duplication, to decide on the types of vehicles to produce, and other functions. In fact, however, it found the current of decentralization too strong to resist, and, as of early 1991, had actually regained few of the powers it enjoyed in the early 1980s.[43]

At this critical juncture, the organization's leadership did little to enhance the CNAIC's position. When Chen Zutao retired in 1988, his successor, Cai Shiqing, was reportedly hand-picked by the SPC chairman and concurrent Machinery and Electronics Industry minister, Zou Jiahua. Cai was characterized as a very passive figure, one with little backbone.[44] Even with central attempts to rein in automotive production, then, the CNAIC leadership seemed incapable of response.

Perhaps the CNAIC's major problem in its early history was the reluctance of the top leadership to pursue the development of the automotive industry. Not until 1964 did an automotive corporation emerge, and it was quickly snuffed out. Following its rebirth in 1982, the organization seemed to have a good chance to assert itself, with a clear mandate and influential leader. The retirement of Rao Bin, national decentralization, and the general absence of an automotive advocate in the top leadership levels, however, dimmed the CNAIC's development prospects. During the first decade of reform politics, then, the CNAIC saw its authority gradually erode, as it surrendered its powers to local-level factories, and, as the case study chapters will show, played a diminishing role in regulating the joint venture companies.

Although strong leadership at the helm of the CNAIC would probably not have greatly affected the course of events, the downward-sloping quality of Rao Bin's successors may have accelerated the corporation's decline. Finally, though it had struggled for many years to establish some independence from the various superior machine-building ministries, the appointment of Zou Jiahua's ally as CNAIC chief indicated the corporation would closely follow ministerial policy (and that of Zou, reportedly a proponent of rail transport) for at least the first years of the 1990s.

Other Ministries

Although the machine-building ministry and the CNAIC took the lead in shaping automotive development and policy, many other ministries naturally had peripheral functions. Two played prominent roles in shaping the joint venture automotive corporations: MOFERT was responsible for considering and approving all joint venture contracts involving the use of foreign capital. After a contract was certified, MOFERT generally did not take part in regulating a joint venture. The ministry did, however, take an interest in insuring that foreign exchange would be balanced by the companies it approved. As later chapters will show, MOFERT felt some responsibility for such a balance.[45] The Ministry of Aeronautics and Aerospace (MAAS) was interested in the passenger car industry mainly as a market for its civilian industrial parts-producing factories. The MAAS became determined to make sales to the auto industry, particularly during the late 1980s, as cuts in military manufacturing hurt the ministry's ability to fill its coffers. MAAS played a significant part in the progress of Panda Motors. In March 1993, however, the ministry was abolished, and was reorganized as the China Aerospace Industry Corporation, a new economic organization under the State Council.

The case studies will provide empirical evidence of the role the above institutions took in developing the foreign-invested automotive sector. First, however, we briefly examine local political industrial bodies.[46]

The Automotive Industry and Local Government Structure

At the top of the municipal structure, the mayor had potentially the most power in directing the course of such a capital-intensive industry as auto manufacturing.[47] Mayoral participation in this sector, however, varied. In the early 1990s, Beijing mayor Chen Xitong (who was also a state councilor at the national level) simply had too much on his political plate to take time to direct the industry's development in his city, but mayors of Shanghai, Guangzhou, and Huizhou (sites of the case studies) took an active interest in automotive development within their jurisdictions. Of course, with their many other duties, they could devote a limited amount of time. They concentrated on major decisions, such as the creation of new ventures, significant restructuring of existing projects, and mediation of serious problems the enterprises encountered.

In addition to the role played by city mayors, each city had delegated one or more vice mayors to put the auto industry into their portfolios. By the late 1980s, Beijing vice mayors Zhang Jianmin and Wu Yi had absorbed municipal authority over their city's automotive development. Guangzhou's vice mayor in charge of the sector, Xie Shihua, was the board chairman of Guangzhou Peugeot from 1985 to 1987, and Shanghai and Huizhou vice mayors also took special interest in their cities' auto industries. These vice mayors seemed to have significant power when the mayor was otherwise occupied. Zhang Jianmin, for example, helped negotiate the settlement of the Beijing Jeep crisis in 1985. Shanghai's vice mayors fell somewhat in the shadow of that city's more active mayor, Zhu Rongji, though at this writing it was not clear whether the city's new mayor, Huang Ju, or Communist Party leader Wu Bangguo, both of whom served under Zhu for several years, would take such a dominant role.[48] Huizhou's vice mayor, Li Hongzhong, held extensive authority over his city's Panda project.

Beijing and Shanghai both had automotive leading small groups in 1990, and Guangzhou had plans to establish one. (Huizhou's industry was not extensive enough to warrant such a body.) The small groups included one or more vice mayors (and, in Shanghai, the mayor was the symbolic head) and representatives from the cities' economic, planning, and international trade committees, and from their automotive industrial corporations. Beijing's group had fifteen people in the fall of 1990, and Shanghai's had about twenty. These small groups tried to chart a general course for the local industry, and to provide a forum for coordination among the disparate government bodies.

Other municipal committees had various planning and management roles, taken in coordination with the municipal automotive industrial corporations. In general, a planning commission formulated long-term development schemes, and an economic commission carried out these plans. Implementation in the automotive sector consisted of regulating energy allocation, seeing that industrial laws were followed, and other functions. The foreign economic relations commission considered joint venture and other foreign investment projects, but, like MOFERT, played a minor role in implementing the approved project.

The importance of the auto industry was evident by the composition of some of these committees. In Shanghai, a vice chairman of the city's economic commission until 1989, Lu Ji'an, was head of the city's automotive corporation in early 1991; Lu's power in the economic commission remained strong, though. In Guangzhou, the board chairman of Guangzhou Peugeot, Xie Gancheng, was concurrently the vice chairman of the machinery and electronics department under the economic committee; he was, by a special mayoral order, the only high-ranking city official allowed from the commercial sector.

In Huizhou, much of the municipal power for regulating the auto industry was vested in a committee-level Economic Construction Leading Group. The group consisted of forty to fifty people in late 1990, and was responsible for macromanagement of municipal programs related to the Panda company and other projects. A vice manager of the group was devoting almost all of his time to the new auto project.

The powers of automotive industrial groups varied in each city. Their main function was to coordinate the suppliers to the main auto manufacturers in their jurisdiction.[49] The Beijing Automotive Industrial Corporation (BAIC) had relatively loose control over the city's factories, partly because of the fairly large number of producers in the capital. In Shanghai, however, the SAIC had powers to regulate the finances of the city's companies; they depended to a great extent on SAIC for loans, and SAIC decided how much money each factory would receive. The Guangzhou Automotive and Agro-Machinery Industrial Corporation (GAAIC) controlled many of Guangzhou's auto parts production and vehicle plants, but it competed with factories under the control of the city's military and transportation committees. Indirectly, GAAIC also competed with parts suppliers in other areas of Guangdong province.

Finally, Guangdong Province had a special Panda Automotive Small Group office, set up directly under the governor's office, to help Panda coordinate itself with the rest of Guangdong Province. In early 1991, this group consisted of eleven people, representing the provincial economic commission, the machinery and electronics bureau, and the automotive office. It is noteworthy that there was no such provincial-level group for the Peugeot venture; the relationship between the Guangzhou venture and Guangdong Province is discussed in chapters 6 and 7.

By the end of the 1980s, Chinese localities had developed extensive regulatory institutions for guiding automotive development. The case studies will examine their interaction with the foreign-invested corporation under their jurisdiction, and their ability to work with the central government to solve problems. The following section briefly returns to the central level to spotlight three leaders who helped shape automotive policy development.[50]

Automotive Industry Decision Makers:
Three Personal Profiles

These biographical sketches focus on three men closely associated with the automotive industry or related government offices. As noted in chapter 1, the personal backgrounds and experiences of individual decision makers can affect the perception of administrative choices and the rationality of the eventual decision. Furthermore, institutional loyalties and obligations, based in past occupational experiences, can also play a major role in shaping policy selection.

Chen Zutao, Zhu Rongji, and Zou Jiahua each played a major role in the development of one or more of the joint venture case studies discussed in chapters 4 through 7; these latter chapters give further detail on their policy-making roles.

Chen Zutao

Chen Zutao was born January 20, 1928, in Hubei Province. He was the son of Chen Changhao (1906–67), a high-ranking military-revolutionary figure during the 1930s.[51] Chen's early years were significantly affected by his father's career. The elder Chen left for study in the Soviet Union in December 1927, one month before his son's birth. One of the Soviet-trained "Twenty-eight Bolsheviks" who clashed with Mao Zedong in the 1930s, Chen Changhao studied at Moscow's Sun Yatsen University for more than two years. His son most likely remained in China during this period.

Chen Changhao returned to his home nation in 1931, and took up a military post as political commissar in the Communist New Fourth Army, serving under future top Communist military leaders Xu Xiangqian and Ye Jianying. Chen Changhao took part in the 1934–35 Long March, though it is unlikely his son was present.[52] Following the elder Chen's alliance with the rebel Communist Zhang Guotao, Chen Changhao, in some disgrace, left for the Soviet Union in August 1939 (officially going for medical treatment), where he remained until he returned to China in 1952.

Chen Zutao reportedly spent part of his childhood in Yan'an, thereby acquiring the moniker "*hongxiaogui*," (young revolutionary).[53] With his father's departure, however, Chen left China and spent his high school years in the USSR.

It is unclear whether Chen Zutao returned to China at or before the Communist victory in 1949, but, in any case, by 1950 he had begun advanced study at Moscow's Bauman Engineering Institute, where he remained until about 1953. He acquired part of his practical training at the Stalin Automobile Factory.[54] During these years abroad, Chen had a chance to interact with China's future premier, Li Peng, then the leader of the Chinese student association in the USSR.

On his return to China, Chen took a post at Changchun's First Auto Works, becoming a vice chief engineer in the early 1960s. He stayed in Changchun until 1967, when he was sent to the countryside at the beginning of the Cultural Revolution. By 1969, however, he had resumed work as a senior official at the Second Auto Works in Hubei. In May 1982, Chen was picked to be chief engineer at the newly reconstituted China National Automotive Industrial Corporation, and in September 1985, he became CNAIC general manager, a post he held for three years.

Chen played a significant role in shaping the development of foreign-funded automotive projects. Chapter 2 already noted his interest in expanding the number of foreign-invested factories and foreign loans, and in increased automotive exports. Later chapters chronicle his actual intervention in the resultant ventures.

During his tenure at the CNAIC, Chen became further known for his deep admiration of General Motors. One source noted Chen favored the company because of its size and management abilities; another source said that, to Chen, GM was like a "beautiful American girl," one that the Chinese automotive industry should court. Other sources report that GM shared some personal interest in Chen, sponsoring one of his sons to study in the United States. For all of the "romance" with General Motors, however, the company failed to establish a joint venture car manufacturing plant in China during Chen's tenure.[55] (In 1992, however, GM established a large-scale truck joint venture in Shenyang. See chapter 8.)

Chen's exit from the CNAIC paralleled the rise to prominence of Zou Jiahua. In 1988, Chen, at age sixty, retired from his CNAIC positions, though it is unclear whether he left willingly. Many sources note a personal enmity between Chen and Zou, who became the head of the SPC virtually simultaneously with Chen's removal.

Although he left the CNAIC, Chen's affiliation with the auto industry was by no means finished. He was, first, given the somewhat symbolic post as a standing commissioner of the State Science and Technology Commission.[56] Soon, however, Chen took an assignment as adviser to Guangdong Province on matters related to Panda Motors. Meanwhile, Chen's son also solidified ties to the automotive industry in the early 1990s, holding a managerial job at the Second Auto Works.

Chen generally fit the description of a conservative, Soviet-educated official, suspicious of ties to the West. He was, however, eager to enhance his own status, and to advance the career of his offspring. As later chapters will show, Chen's personal ties to Li Peng and animosity toward Zou Jiahua played significant roles in shaping at least one of the cases under study. The blemishes on the career of his father, Chen Changhao, however, seem to have had little ill effect on Chen Zutao's rise to prominence in the 1980s, perhaps indicating that such negative stigmas are not necessarily inherited.

Zhu Rongji

Zhu Rongji, a native of Hunan's provincial capital, Changsha, was born in 1929. Zhu's parents were poor, and they died when he was still young. Zhu raised himself, however, and funded his own high school education through scholarships. In 1947, Zhu entered Qinghua University and immediately took an active role in student politics. He became head of the university's student union and joined the Chinese Communist Party in October 1949, as Communist People's Liberation Army (PLA) troops marched into Beijing.

In 1951, Zhu graduated from Qinghua with a degree in electrical motor engineering and was named deputy chief of the Product Planning Section in the planning office of the Industrial Department under the Northeast China People's government. The following year, he assumed the post of deputy division chief of the newly established State Planning Commission.

In spite of his early success, a brief speech critical of some elements of the Communist system caught Zhu in China's antirightist campaign of 1957. He was expelled from the CCP and demoted. During the Cultural Revolution, he was sent to the countryside for five years of labor.

Zhu began his rehabilitation in 1975, when he was made a deputy chief engineer in a company regulated by the Petroleum Ministry. After the third plenum of the eleventh CCP Congress in 1978, Zhu was completely exonerated, with the support of his former superior at the State Economic Commission, Ma Hong, and assigned in 1979 to be a deputy bureau director at the SEC. In 1982, he was named director of the Technical Transformation Bureau under the State Economic Commission, and the following year was promoted to be an SEC vice minister. That year, Zhu edited a book advocating modernization of China's economic managerial practices based on Western theories.[57]

In March of 1984, Zhu led an economic delegation to Hungary, Czechoslovakia, and other East European Socialist states. Later that year, he became vice president of China's Industrial Economics Society. In January of 1986, Zhu led another delegation abroad, this time to

France and West Germany; he evolved into one of China's top officials charged with attracting Western investment.

Zhu's work in helping the Beijing Jeep venture resolve its crisis of early 1986 is discussed in some detail in chapter 4. By early 1987, however, Zhu was headed to Shanghai, where he became deputy party secretary, serving under Jiang Zemin. In November 1987, Zhu was promoted to alternative CCP Central Committee membership.

Zhu became mayor of Shanghai in April 1988 (even though he could not speak the Shanghai dialect).[58] He succeeded Jiang Zemin, who retained his post as the city's party secretary. When Jiang left to become general secretary of the national CCP, Zhu became simultaneously party chief and mayor of Shanghai, imitating Jiang, who briefly held both posts from November 1987 to April 1988.

Zhu soon developed an enthusiastic following in Shanghai among foreign businesspeople, and particularly among Volkswagen investors. He formed a municipal commission empowered to quickly approve foreign investments of up to U.S.$30 million; foreigners, pleased with the opportunity to avoid the need for many signatures, dubbed the commission the "one-chop stop."[59] Zhu also created a committee of foreign businessmen to offer the city special counsel.[60]

During Shanghai's protests in the wake of the June 1989 Tiananmen massacre, Zhu avoided polemics in appealing for calm in his city. He refrained from calling in the military, instead using civil servants to end demonstrations. Zhu also promoted economic modernization as a solution for China's social problems; his program to develop East Shanghai (the Pudong area) using foreign investment was key to his local strategy.

In July 1990, Zhu led a mayors' delegation to the United States; his trip represented one of the first high-level delegations to visit the United States after the 1989 Tiananmen events. By this time, foreign press reports had begun to call him "China's Gorbachev," comparing him to the Soviet Union's reformist leader.[61] Zhu was later promoted to vice premier, along with Zou Jiahua, in April 1991, apparently at the insistence of paramount leader Deng Xiaoping. By the end of 1992, Zhu had been promoted to "executive" vice premier; he was to be acting premier when Li Peng traveled abroad and was then ranked above Zou Jiahua and other vice premiers[62] (who in 1994 were Foreign Minister Qian Qichen and former MOFERT chief Li Lanqing).

In late 1991, Zhu made a further bid for power, as he used his position as chief of the State Council Production Office to promulgate further reforms. In this capacity, Zhu wanted to see, for example, conglomeration of state enterprises, implementation of bankruptcy laws, reduced stockpiles of unsalable goods, and higher quality standards in the passenger airline industry.

The Production Office, introduced in early 1991, assumed many of the powers of Zhu's former State Economic Commission. As noted above, the SEC was partly absorbed into the SPC in April 1988; in late 1991, the Production Office was struggling to regain the powers previously held by the SEC. One report predicted it would soon assume status as a commission-level agency.[63] In March 1993, however, the NPC's annual session instead created an Economic and Trade Commission, led by Wang Zhongyu. At the national Fourteenth Party Congress in October 1992, however, Zhu, who had previously only been an alternate member of the party's Central Committee, was elevated to the small group of leaders on the Politburo's Standing Committee (again, Zou Jiahua remained behind Zhu, as an ordinary member of the Politburo). Finally, in July 1993, Zhu took the reigns of China's banking system, becoming governor of the People's Bank of China and head of the "Leading Group for Reforming the Banking System" under the State Council.

Zhu represented a rare political breed in the top post-Mao echelons of the government, as the only victim of the 1957 antirightist movement to be elevated to the vice premier level. He was also expelled from the Communist Party in 1957; purge victims of the Cultural Revolution (including such top figures as Deng Xiaoping) typically retained their party membership. This made Zhu's later rise to power even more striking. Furthermore, unlike other top leaders of his age, Zhu received no education in Eastern Europe.[64] Finally, Zhu's lack of familial or pre-1949 revolutionary connections makes his rapid ascension in the 1980s and 1990s almost unbelievable.

In general, Zhu's basic orientation was Western-looking. He spoke fluent English, and one of his sons was a university student in Wisconsin.[65] (Many other top leaders, of course, also had children studying in the United States.) Zhu's rather unique background, then, placed him in the forefront of the liberal economic reformers. Chapters 4 and 5 focus more closely on his activities in the middle and late 1980s. In conclusion, however, one should note that Zhu's activism in the early

1990s was generally confined to the economic arena. Perhaps sensing the problems inherent in the type of political reform promoted by former CCP Chief Hu Yaobang, and that applied by Soviet President Mikhail Gorbachev, Zhu's efforts focused on continuing and expanding economic liberalization. (When he did discuss politics, he sometimes clung to conservative party doctrine, as reflected in remarks in 1992 critical of Hong Kong's democratic reform proposals.)[66] His power base, moreover, lay more in the government and in connections to elder leaders than in the party or the military. With the incipient leadership changes of the 1990s, however, Zhu stood as a possible heir to the highest levers of control, ones that could have potentially presented him the ability to significantly reorganize China's political apparatus.

Finally, as the case studies indicate, Zhu favored foreign-funded automotive development in the few chances he had to influence the industry's progress. Earlier discussion noted the industry had few powerful advocates devoted to foreign cooperation among the top leadership in the late 1980s and early 1990s; with his record of supporting Beijing Jeep and Shanghai Volkswagen, and Western ventures in general, Zhu stood to be a useful ally for the rapidly growing foreign-invested automotive ventures.

Zou Jiahua

Zou Jiahua was born in October 1926, in Shanghai, the son of revolutionary journalist and publisher Zou Taofen (1895–1944). He was one of three children born to Zou Taofen's second wife, Shen Cuizhen.[67]

There is little history of Zou's childhood years, though his father spent most of the pre–World War II years in Shanghai, criticizing the KMT government for failing to counter Japanese expansionism. With the outbreak of war, Zou Taofen traveled to various parts of China (including a brief residence in Hong Kong) before settling in Communist-controlled northern Jiangsu in November 1942, where he was welcomed by the CCP's New Fourth Army.[68] Although the elder Zou soon surreptitiously left for medical care in Japanese-controlled Shanghai (where he died in 1944), Zou Jiahua remained in the CCP guerrilla area.

The younger Zou launched his own career in 1944, studying in the finance and economic department at the New Fourth Army's Huadong

Construction University in the Huainan base area. He joined the CCP in 1945 and took a post in the construction section of the industry and commerce office under the Shandong provincial people's government.

Zou spent the rest of the civil war years in Northeast China, taking various party posts in Songjiang Province. In 1948, he attended Russian classes at Harbin's industrial university, and moved on to Moscow (in a group that included future premier Li Peng) to study mechanical engineering at the Bauman Engineering Institute.[69]

On returning from the Soviet Union in 1955, Zou held a variety of factory posts, including the directorship of Shenyang's Number Two Machine Tool Factory, and delegation chief engineer of the Northeast Electric Power Administration. From 1964 to 1966, he was head of the Number One Ministry of Machinery's research institute. With the start of the Cultural Revolution, however, Zou was sent to the countryside to labor.

In 1972, Zou was rehabilitated, taking the job of deputy director of the Machinery research institute's revolutionary committee. The following year, he was named deputy director of the State Council's Defense Industrial Office. In 1974, he took a further military-related post on the PLA Science and Technology Commission for National Defense.

Zou's status rose quickly with the post-Mao rehabilitation of pragmatic leaders, as he was elected an alternate member of the CCP Central Committee in August 1977. From 1982 to 1985, he served as vice minister of the Commission of Science, Technology, and Industry for National Defense. Zou was minister of Ordnance Industry from mid-1985 to December 1986, when that ministry merged with the Ministry of Machine-Building to form the Commission of Machine-Building Industry; Zou became commission chairman. In April 1988, Zou was appointed head of the new Ministry of Machine-Building and Electronics Industry (MMEI); that year he also was named a state councilor.

The latter years of the 1980s saw further leaps for Zou's career. He became a CCP Central Committee member in 1985, and a Politburo member in October 1992. In December 1989, Zou took the chairmanship of the State Planning Commission from a frail Yao Yilin, and in the spring of 1991, he was elevated with Zhu Rongji to a vice premiership (though he was later listed as subordinate to Zhu, who, as noted above, became "executive" vice premier in late 1992). Unlike Zhu, who lost his position of power in Shanghai, Zou was initially allowed to keep his top job at the SPC.

In late 1991, the Chinese leadership felt Zou, like Zhu Rongji, presented a friendly face to foreign nations, and he was sent to Germany in October of that year as China's highest-level envoy to visit since June of 1989. Led by Volkswagen's automotive ventures, Germany's foreign investment in China topped that of all other European nations.

Zou's career presents many close parallels to that of Premier Li Peng. Like Li, two years his junior, Zou was the son of a famous revolutionary, and spent part of his youth in the CCP guerrilla base areas.[70] Both studied engineering in Moscow over the years 1948 to 1955, when they undoubtedly became well acquainted. During the Cultural Revolution, however, Li's close personal ties to Premier Zhou Enlai saved him from persecution; Zou was not so lucky, even though his wife, Ye Chumei, was the daughter of the late marshal Ye Jianying (one of the few top leaders not purged during the turmoil of the late 1960s).

Considering Zou's background, one might assume he would hold political views similar to those of Li or Chen Zutao. In the aftermath of the 1989 Tiananmen massacre, however, Zou apparently said little to support the prevailing hard-line policy.[71] Chapter 7, moreover, shows Zou's clear split with Li and Chen over the approval of Panda Motors, and reveals further insight into his attitude toward cooperation with foreign investors.

In general, Zou supported development of the foreign-funded automotive sector in the 1980s and early 1990s, making publicized visits to Shanghai Volkswagen, Beijing Jeep, and Guangzhou Peugeot. Some sources, however, reported Zou had doubts about the feasibility of Chinese automotive development, favoring instead the railway system for freight and passenger transport.[72]

Zou's elevation in 1991 to the vice premiership simultaneously with Zhu Rongji prompted some comparisons. Zou's generally centrist policies, and his more extensive connections to the military, the CCP, and the powerful SPC, together with his notable family ties (his wife and late father), gave him a much broader power base than that of Zhu. Zou, however, seemed to lack the type of reformist vision found in Zhu's economic policies; were Zhu to succeed in strengthening China's economic system, his resultant prestige might make him a formidable rival even for the well-positioned Zou. By 1994, in fact,

Zou's star had begun to fade. He lost his position (to Zhu Rongji) as head of the government's panel overseeing debt defaults in August 1991,[73] and relinquished his chairmanship of the SPC to Chen Jinhua in March 1993.

Conclusion

This chapter has analyzed the bureaucratic institutions that constitute China's automotive policy-making structure. By understanding the history and hierarchy of the most important offices and leaders, we can now look to the case studies for evidence of the policy-process problems predicted in the introductory chapter's framework. Based on the information presented here, one might expect to see, for example, conflict among top leaders or commissions and the subordinate ministries; competition between the machine-building ministry and its subordinate CNAIC; or disagreement among central policy makers and local automotive structures. Several personality clashes, based on backgrounds described above, may also influence policy formulation and implementation. Finally, personal backgrounds could also indicate the tenor of relations with the foreign automotive investors.

4

Beijing Jeep's Bumpy Road

As the first Sino–foreign automotive joint venture, the Beijing Jeep Corporation (BJC) stood to be a prototype for future cooperative projects. The company would be a test case, one that would reveal the kinds of problems, both political and economic, that would appear for other investors the Chinese hoped to attract.

Beijing Jeep, however, did not always shine as a model for other foreign firms eyeing the Chinese automotive sector. The company was plagued by early problems, some of which threatened to extinguish the nascent venture. After a significant crisis and confrontation in 1986, though, BJC skillfully capitalized on conditions in the Chinese political and investment environment to help assure the venture's continued progress for the next several years.

Jeep Talks

The spark for the Jeep venture came on a day in 1978, when the Chinese-American businessman C.B. Sung was lecturing to officials of the First Ministry of Machine Building.[1] Representatives of the Beijing Automotive Works (BAW) approached Sung about finding a joint venture partner for their rough terrain vehicle factory. Sung contacted the American Motors Corporation (AMC) in Detroit, which manufactured Jeep-model vehicles. He then became an intermediary for the earliest talks between the Americans and the Chinese. After contacting other car manufacturers in Japan, Great Britain, France, and the United States, and comparing bids, BAW chose to focus on AMC as a potential partner.[2]

BAW had its own roots in preliberation China as an assembly plant.

67

In the PRC's first five-year plan, the factory was assigned the task of providing fuel pumps and other parts to Changchun's First Auto Works. In 1958 the company began producing its own vehicles, and, after expansion, in 1966 made its first model 212 rough-terrain automobile,[3] a jeep-like car based on a design supplied by the Soviet Union.

In early 1979, AMC officials arrived in Beijing to begin discussions on forming the new company. The Americans met with a team of Chinese negotiators, including Rao Bin, then a vice minister at the First Ministry of Machine Building, and later the first director of the CNAIC. The two sides agreed at these early meetings that a venture had promise. A memo projected cooperation on improvement of the Jeep already manufactured at BAW, production of a new family of vehicles, and manufacture of parts in China for export.[4]

Subsequent talks made little progress over the following two years, as the Chinese reportedly considered, then rejected, an alternative venture with Japan's Toyota.[5] Furthermore, the Chinese government was slow to approve the AMC feasibility study. One Chinese source noted that "no one [among those studying the report] would take the responsibility of approving the plan until more than a year after the report was submitted"[6] in 1979. Each department apparently feared taking responsibility for any resulting problems with the new joint venture.

At the same time, however, the top levels of the automotive bureaucracy itself were also undergoing rapid post-Mao structural reorganization, and this is also cited as a factor delaying the talks.[7] BAW had "more than ten government sections overseeing its operation and interfering with its work."[8] Over four years of negotiations, the factory "reported to its leaders on the situation of their talks with AMC more than 300 times, averaging one every five days, but heard little in response."[9] Such hesitancy may have been rooted in official wariness of the motivations of the foreign investors: "there were still people involved with the Beijing company who had misgivings about entering into a joint venture with foreigners—a result of the mental shackles imposed by years of 'leftist' ideas."[10]

In 1982, however, following the establishment of the CNAIC, the Chinese formed a group of five department heads to face AMC in the negotiations. This group apparently had "complete negotiating and decision-making authority in the talks."[11] Among the new Chinese team was Chen Zutao, then chief engineer at the CNAIC. Chen was the senior CNAIC official taking part in the discussions. On the AMC side were Tod Clare, vice president of the company's international operations, and Ronald Gilchrist, manager of Far East operations.

Although the discussions quickened, several areas of disagreement confounded the Americans. The Chinese, for example, were slow to comprehend the importance of registering the American company's "Jeep" trademark name in China,[12] a step that would provide penalties for other domestic manufacturers attempting to adopt the brand name. The Chinese were also unfamiliar with standard contract clauses, such as *force majeure*, and AMC officials were forced to explain these to their negotiation partners. A significant turning point in the discussions came when the AMC team decided to abandon a rough contract outline it had brought to the talks, and began to move toward the Chinese contract format.[13] The Chinese, for example, required a seven-year financial feasibility plan for the venture. AMC was accustomed to planning for only three years of a project, with two more years of rough estimations sometimes added. Clare noted he

> felt rather uncomfortable about that [seven-year plan], because that's really getting into the unknown. But they wanted seven years. We did seven years and we did an intelligent job with it. And as you look back, it's rather comforting to see the seven-year story in front of you.[14]

Clare's comfort, however, proved to be short-lived. After nearly four years of negotiations, the Americans and Chinese finally signed a contract on May 5, 1983. The Beijing Jeep Corporation, Ltd., was born.

The Venture's Early Years

Under the terms of the agreement, AMC contributed $16 million to the $51 million venture, for a 31.35 percent share of the corporation; BAW, which contributed the factory site and equipment and $6.6 million in cash, held the balance of the venture. The new company took BAW's assembly facilities at its southern Beijing plant; the northern factory would continue to produce BAW's own products. BJC's contract was to run for a twenty-year term.

The Chinese had several goals in creating the venture. As with most cooperative agreements between China and the West, the Chinese auto manufacturers hoped to acquire valuable technology. AMC agreed to provide not only vital equipment and designs, but also managerial techniques useful to an industry hampered by lax standards that had existed for decades. In the contract, the Chinese put a value of $8 million on AMC's technology, which constituted half of the American side's contribution to the initial capitalization fund (the other half consisted of $8 million in cash).

Foreign exchange earning was also a Chinese goal. Both sides believed exports would be a result of the joint venture, bringing a chance for American repatriation of profits, and Chinese garnering of much needed hard currency.

The Chinese also hoped to develop a new, light cross-country vehicle that could be both used in China and sold abroad. The car previously produced by the Beijing plant was seen as "technically out-of-date and stylistically dull, and therefore not competitive on [the] international market."[15] The contract called for development of a new type of vehicle to correct these shortcomings, one that would appeal to the world market. The Chinese military was hoping this new vehicle could also fill its needs for a soft-top (canvas-roof) transport tool. Until this vehicle was developed, however, the joint venture was to continue producing BAW's model BJ212 for its first five years.[16]

Both sides soon found the new vehicle was not easy to design. Not only did the prototype have several serious structural defects, but the Americans predicted that it would take hundreds of millions of dollars in further investment to create a new model.[17] The Chinese therefore agreed to import AMC's "Cherokee XJ" Jeep in a disassembled kit form known as a "completely knocked down," or "CKD," vehicle. Unfortunately, this decision came without a firm agreement on the source of foreign exchange currency (that is, Western-denominated convertible funds) to pay AMC for the kits. A memorandum stipulated that Chinese customers, mainly state-owned work units, would pay such "hard" currency to BJC for the assembled vehicles, and the venture would build up a fund for "localization"—that is, developing machinery in China to produce the Cherokee parts at the Beijing plant. The memorandum, however, never formally superseded the original contract.[18] This error, as we will see, was a primary factor leading to the later crisis.

AMC, of course, also had hopes for the venture. Access to the Chinese market offered a potentially enormous pool of consumers.

Poor road conditions seemed to make China a good market for the rugged Jeep model, and BAW had a monopoly on domestic Jeep sales, with 90 percent of produce going to civilian work units and 10 percent to the military.[19] Low wages for Chinese workers increased profit potential. Hopes for hard currency gain, however, seemed tied to the ability of the venture to export its product. Under the original contract, AMC was expected to wait approximately five years until the new joint venture vehicle was designed and ready for market; until then, the venture would reinvest soft currency (Chinese renminbi) profits from sales of the domestically produced BJ212 into BJC. Without exports, though, hard currency that could be repatriated would not be available.

With imports of Cherokee kits, the Americans had shifted their focus from designing the completely new vehicle to the localization of the Cherokee parts manufacture. With localized production, and low wages at the factory, the Americans hoped to make a reasonable profit on exports of the Cherokee. BJC officials predicted that more than 80 percent of the vehicle would be produced in China by 1988, and that the venture could be exporting some 25 percent of the Cherokee Jeeps by 1990.[20]

Despite such predictions, the localization process was painfully slow. The problem with finding local parts to substitute in the imported kits lay with the quality levels of Chinese supplier factories. After decades of isolation, these plants were unfamiliar with high foreign standards, and were furthermore financially unable to raise quality until they were given economy-of-scale orders for their product; they balked at the large investments needed to reach American levels when BJC initially required only a few hundred or a few thousand items. (In 1985, for example, China only imported some 450 disassembled Cherokees.)

Until export actually began, then, AMC stood to make money by selling CKD kits to the joint venture at a profit. Such sales provided those eager to tap the "China market" with immediate gratification.

The BJC Crisis

The crisis of 1986 was precipitated by a foreign exchange shortage within the venture. At the time, the Chinese government's supply of hard currency was limited. In 1985, China's balance of trade was hurt by a surge of Japanese motor vehicle imports noted (see chapter 2), and the Chinese were reluctant to allow state-owned enterprises to spend more foreign exchange to finance the kit purchases. Foreign exchange reserves in 1985 were $11.9 billion, off some 29 percent from 1984's reserves of $16.7 billion. The Chinese hoped to pay for the American parts using the nonconvertible Chinese renminbi, but this proposal was not acceptable to the American side. The Chinese renminbi was only useful for purchases within China; to recoup the funds, the Americans would have had to buy goods (such as textiles, toys, or other products) that were potentially saleable in Western markets, and then export them to earn convertible currency.

Don St. Pierre, who took over as BJC's president in September 1985, found the Chinese unwilling to allow the company to continue its practice of charging Chinese customers $10,000 in hard currency to cover the import cost of one kit (the remaining $9,000 of the vehicle's $19,000 price tag, inflated by import duties, could be paid in RMB).[21] Soon, some 1,008 kits were sitting at the docks on the United States' East Coast.

Foreign exchange was also required to import an engine and stamping plant, machinery vital for localization of production of the Jeep model. The Chinese claimed the original contract did not oblige them to pay for this equipment—this was, of course, true, because the original agreement did not envisage the necessity of localization of production of a purely American model. Still, the Americans balked at paying an estimated $70 million over three years for localization costs.[22]

As the lack of hard currency became acute, the American side began to look at debts owed the venture. The State Bureau of Supplies owed the company $2 million, a result of nonpayment in hard currency for 200 Jeeps ordered by Chinese no longer allowed to spend foreign exchange. BJC was also owed some RMB 30 million by Beijing Auto Works for the venture's other product, the BJ212. Without these funds, according to St. Pierre, the venture would have collapsed.[23]

In order to defuse the situation, St. Pierre took several steps that, at the time, he considered standard procedure. Beginning in the last months of 1985, he first spoke with the Beijing municipal government to try to convince those responsible for financial matters to release foreign exchange to the venture to pay for the imported kits and machinery. He started there because he believed it was the first appropriate level of government to contact; furthermore, the municipal government had its own foreign exchange reserves. When this strategy had no immediate effect, however, he wrote to the responsible central government organizations, including the Ministry of Foreign Economic Relations and Trade (MOFERT), the State Planning Commission, and the general manager of the CNAIC, Chen Zutao.

"The Chinese could not understand the problem, and seemed to be groping in the dark," according to St. Pierre, who soon became frustrated with the lethargic reaction of the Chinese side. At the end of November, representatives from AMC's Far East division visited China to try to resolve the currency exchange problems. Upon realizing the situation would not be resolved quickly, the Americans presented a concrete challenge: unless the Chinese were willing to allocate foreign exchange to finance the purchase of the kits and localization equipment, AMC would cut off further investment, stop technology transfer, cancel technical training, and recall its foreign experts from China. The Chinese referred to these conditions as the "Three Stops and One Removal" (*San Ting Yi Che*),[24] and CNAIC Chief Chen was reportedly "furious" about the threat.[25] On December 17, 1985, though, AMC people met the Chinese ambassador in Washington. The discussions with him were encouraging enough that AMC withdrew its threat to recall experts and cancel training programs, but an end to investment was still being considered. And the 1,008 kits still sat in the docks.[26]

On February 18, 1986, St. Pierre wrote a letter to then-Premier Zhao Ziyang, describing the crisis and including a "veiled threat." St. Pierre rhetorically asked the Chinese premier, "What will world opinion be of the investment climate in China if this venture fails?"[27] The implication, of course, was that other foreign companies would react negatively to a collapse of such a major joint venture.

Two weeks later, St. Pierre still had no reply from the Chinese authorities, and decided to try a different tactic: he would put further pressure on the Chinese by publicizing the venture's problems. In mid-March, St. Pierre spoke with a Reuters reporter and a correspondent from *Business Week* magazine in Beijing. The first mention of the venture's problems appeared in *Business Week* in the April 7 edition.[28] The story was later picked up by the *Wall Street Journal*, though this article appeared much later in the crisis, on April 30.[29]

When all of these maneuvers failed to resolve the shortage of foreign exchange, St. Pierre left Beijing in mid-April, returning to Detroit to "wind down" the operation. The April 30 *Wall Street Journal* article announced to the world that production at BJC had stopped, pending relief of the hard currency deficiency. This article described the situation as "a big embarrassment to the Chinese government," and quoted P. Jeffrey Trimmer, general manager of Far East operations at AMC, stating that the plant would be closed for at least two months, and that the closure would be extended "one day for each day that AMC doesn't receive a new letter of credit" to pay for the kits.[30] Trimmer added a positive note to his warning, however, hoping that AMC could ride out the problems and saying that "I can't see us turning our back on China."[31]

Although the Americans perceived little action on the Chinese side in early 1986, one Chinese source from BAW claimed the agencies St. Pierre had contacted were actually working with the joint venture to solve the crisis.[32] Following pressure from BAW, the Beijing municipal planning commission, Beijing's foreign economic relations and trade department, and the State Planning Commission, MOFERT and the CNAIC had at least three joint meetings from January to March 1986. The Chinese were concerned by AMC's challenge, even at the early stages. Still, the lack of results from these sessions indicates that the Chinese partners in the BJC venture had little leverage when they tried to solve the problem without direct American involvement.

One factor mitigated St. Pierre's threat to some degree: the joint venture continued to produce the domestic BJ212 model, as imported parts were unneeded. The venture would not necessarily have collapsed, even if Cherokee production were delayed for a long time. Of course, AMC's abandoning production of the Cherokee would probably still have meant an eventual withdrawal by the American company, with the resulting repercussions for the international investment climate that St. Pierre hinted at in his letter to Premier Zhao.

Crisis Resolution

On April 25, 1986, as St. Pierre began talks with his Detroit colleagues on ending the China operation, a telex arrived from Chinese officials. Apparently, the wheels of the bureaucracy had begun turning in the top levels of the Chinese government. On April 4, Zhao Ziyang had reportedly proclaimed that important joint ventures such as BJC should not be allowed to fail, and he called for high-level aid to solve the problem. He received support for this effort from such officials as then-vice premiers Li Peng, Yao Yilin, and Tian Jiyun, and from Bank of China head Chen Muhua.[33] The telex invited AMC to send a high-level delegation to China to speak with a group led by Zhu Rongji, who at the time served as vice minister of the State Economic Commission. The Americans agreed to meet in China from May 8 through May 13.[34]

The main negotiators on the Chinese side were Zhu, CNAIC Chairman Chen, and Beijing Vice Mayor Zhang Jianmin. BJC's board chairman, and concurrently head of the Beijing Automotive Industrial Corporation, Wu Zhongliang, was notably absent, claiming illness. On the American side were P. Jeffrey Trimmer, Tod Clare, Tim Adams (director of new business development at AMC), and Don St. Pierre. The main topic of discussion was the number of Cherokees to be produced in the years 1986 to 1990. The Chinese favored limited production to save foreign exchange. The Americans wanted to raise Cherokee output, both to realize a profit and to attain the necessary economies of scale for the localization effort.

Early in the meetings, according to St. Pierre, the American side achieved some satisfaction by forcing a "self-criticism" from Zhao Nailin, a Chinese vice president at BJC. Apparently under pressure from Zhu Rongji, Zhao admitted he had been deliberately misrepresenting the venture's projected foreign exchange earnings in such a way that the shortage of hard currency to import kits could not have been foreseen. Zhao's goal in doing this may have been to force AMC to commit more of its own money to relieve the deficit once the crisis came to a head. St. Pierre noted in an interview that Zhao had probably acted on his own, out of ignorance, and admitted that AMC should have monitored the situation more closely.[35]

The meetings were marked by several threats by the Americans to leave,[36] actions meant to intimidate the Chinese further. In the end, however, both sides reached agreement. The main points of the settlement were:

1. Beijing Auto Works paid its RMB 30 million debt, and the State Bureau of Supplies delivered its payment of $2 million. AMC was allowed to convert some $6.9 million worth of its RMB earnings to hard currency, at the official government exchange rate.[37] These steps were the key to ending the immediate cash flow problems, and the joint venture could then pay for the Jeep kits waiting to enter the country.

2. AMC received formal permission to require up to 60 percent of Cherokee Jeep payment from Chinese customers in foreign exchange.

3. BJC and the CNAIC, rather than AMC, would be responsible for raising capital for localization costs. Funds would come from hard currency sales and Bank of China loans. AMC, however, pledged to help speed the localization effort.

4. AMC agreed to limit production of the Cherokees, a recognized drain on China's hard currency reserves, to 12,500 vehicles up to 1990.

5. The new Jeep desired by the military would never be possible, both sides agreed, without a large infusion of capital. The Chinese agreed to delay production of such a vehicle.

Postcrisis Venture

Once the 1986 problems were resolved, officials at BJC set out to put the venture back on track. By August 1986, St. Pierre was optimistic enough to comment that "[a]s of now, there is nothing holding this company back. We can do the business that we are supposed to do. It is now a matter of execution."[38] Why was he so optimistic?

The immediate problems the venture faced were solved in the May agreement. The company had enough money to resume production by mid-August, and it began to look toward increasing the percentage of parts produced locally in China. St. Pierre's attitude, however, may have been more closely linked to his assessment of pertinent political forces than to the successful crisis-resolution agreement. That settlement, brokered by Zhu Rongji, was an important sign of significant government support for BJC, and the political aid remained after the problems were resolved. Zhu, then, continued to play a role in the development of the Jeep venture until he became mayor of Shanghai in 1988. When the Chinese Public Security Bureau was considering buying Japanese vehicles, for example, Zhu convinced the policemen to buy Jeeps instead. However, Zhu was unable to meet St. Pierre's request to further increase the number of import licenses for Cherokee kits.[39]

The association with Zhu was valuable even without his direct intervention. St. Pierre claimed that a mere hint that BJC would appeal to the SEC vice minister would be sufficient to resolve bureaucratic problems. At the time, according to one assessment, Zhu was reportedly "virtually running the Chinese automobile industry."[40] Troubles with slow customs procedures, or with Chinese shipping officials, then, would disappear with such threats. After Zhu's departure for Shanghai, St. Pierre redirected his attention to local Beijing officials, such as vice mayors Wu Yi and Zhang Jianmin.[41]

The support of key politicians was perhaps rooted in a larger Chinese effort to make the company a kind of "model joint venture." In some ways, the Chinese may have come to look on Beijing Jeep as a sort of modern-day "Daqing," the oil-producing city held up as a model industrial area during the 1960s' Cultural Revolution. BJC would be a success story, one to act as source of positive propaganda to attract further foreign investment.[42]

While relying on top leaders for help, St. Pierre also felt his company's position was strong enough that he could become personally involved in relevant Chinese political power games. After BJC's Chinese chairman, Wu Zhongliang, had "disappeared" in 1986 following an apparent heart attack, St. Pierre tried to arrange for a successor that he preferred. He wanted the Beijing Automotive Industrial Corporation (BAIC) vice chairwoman, Wang Mei, to take over for Wu as the company's chairman.[43] Not only did St. Pierre see Wang as more knowledgeable, she was also concurrently leading negotiations with General Motors for a possible venture making trucks in China; St. Pierre hoped to get this business for AMC. The American manager mentioned to Chinese auto officials his positive opinion of Wang,[44] and complained to Vice Mayor Zhang Jianmin of his dissatisfaction with Wu.[45] In March of 1987, however, Wu reappeared as BJC chairman, though he later lost his position as chief of the BAIC. (By 1992, following St. Pierre's departure from the venture, Wang Mei had succeeded Wu, who took a position as vice chairman.)

St. Pierre also campaigned for the promotion of BJC Vice President Chen Xulin to the venture's presidency. Chen had become a close friend of St. Pierre, and the American had been training him to take over the position. In early 1988, Chen did become BJC's president.[46] After St. Pierre left the venture in 1988, however, his successor, Richard Ott, declined to imitate St. Pierre's aggressive stance toward China's politicians.

With solid Chinese support, the venture made substantial progress. It continued to manufacture the BJ212 model vehicle, and could make RMB profit on its sale.[47] In 1986, the venture made some 24,000 vehicles, mostly 212s. Production rose to more than 26,000 in 1987,

Figure 4.1. **Localization of the Beijing Jeep Cherokee, 1985-93**

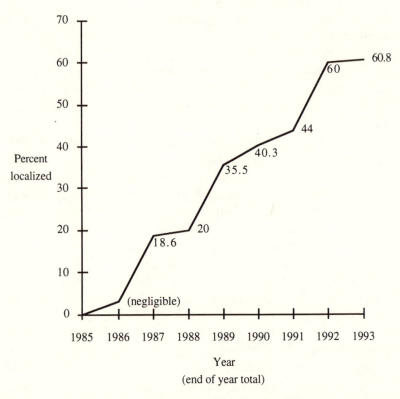

Year

(end of year total)

Sources: For 1986, *New York Times*, April 11, 1986, p. D4. For 1987, *Beijing Jeep Company brochure*, p. 9. For 1988, 1989 interview with Don St. Pierre. For 1989, *China Daily*, February 14, 1990. For 1990, *China Daily*, October 12, 1990. For 1991 and 1992, *China Daily* (North American ed.), February 19, 1993, p. 2. For 1993, *China Auto 4*, no. 1 (January-February 1994): 6.

31,000 in 1988, and almost 40,000 in 1989, including 6630 Cherokees. Although the Americans helped improve the design of the Chinese model, the development of the 212 was far from the old dream of creating a completely new kind of Jeep for China.

BJC also moved ahead in its program to localize production of vehicle parts. Figure 4.1 shows the annual increase of local content in the Cherokee model. (Local content is calculated on the percentage, by cost of parts, of the vehicle manufactured in China.) Once BJC reached 40 percent local content, it was theoretically exempt from the requirement to obtain import licenses for its kit parts.

The Beijing municipal government recognized the importance of the localization drive, and had assigned Vice Mayor Wu Yi to supervise the program.[48] Supplies came from 140 factories across China, with about 40 percent of local parts made in Beijing.[49]

The venture's progress was substantial, and was marked in late 1988 by a visit from Lee Iacocca, whose Chrysler Corporation had purchased AMC in 1987. During his visit, Iacocca proposed raising the American percent holding of the venture from 31.35 to 49 percent. (By early 1994, however, the Americans had only increased their stake to 42 percent.)[50] Iacocca also suggested that Chrysler and the First Auto Works in Changchun cooperate to make a vehicle in Northeast China,[51] but, again, little progress was made in these plans over the following few years. (The FAW venture to make cars went to Volkswagen, though Chrysler concluded a contract to make engines in Changchun.)

In March 1989, the company faced a second crisis, though one much smaller than that of 1986. After customs officials announced a significant increase in duties on Cherokee parts kits, the Americans protested. They employed tactics similar to those used in 1986, threatening to close the Beijing factory and complain to the press. Beijing municipal officials came to the venture's aid, and, after negotiations, the customs people capitulated.[52]

The venture was not significantly affected by the prodemocracy demonstrations in China's capital in 1989. Although most of the American executives left in late May, many had returned within a few months. BJC was, however, hurt by China's economic austerity policy, launched in the autumn of 1988 to continue for some three years. In late 1989, the Chinese government announced plans to spend RMB 350 million (about $94 million) to purchase some 7,440 unsold joint venture automobiles (including those of BJC, Shanghai Volkswagen, and Guangzhou Peugeot); by early 1990, however, it had somewhat reduced the number of vehicles it felt necessary to buy.[53]

By the end of 1990, the company seemed to have recovered from the austerity slowdown. Sales of Cherokees in the first half of 1990 were up by 34 percent over the 1989 period,[54] though the government bailout was probably key to the increase. BJC was named one of China's top ten joint ventures, and was listed as the fifty-third largest company among all enterprises in the country, with sales of $276 million and a profit of $40 million.[55] In 1990, the venture made 7,000 Cherokees; in 1992, production jumped to nearly 21,000, although it slowed (probably temporarily) to 10,400 in 1993.[56] Local content rose to 44 percent in 1991, and 60 percent in 1992.[57] Fixed assets reached RMB 400 million (about $73 million) by the end of 1992.[58]

The company demonstrated further strength by completing work on the site's engine factory in late October 1990. The plant had a capacity of about 100,000 engines, though it would begin producing only about 30,000 in its early years.[59] During 1990, BJC even exported some vehicles (most likely the domestic model, renamed BJ2020); it sent about 350 Jeeps to Thailand, Holland, the USSR, and Latin America for a profit of about $25 million.[60] Finally, in November 1992, a Detroit engineering company signed a $45 million contract to design the long-awaited new Jeep model, though the vehicle was to be restricted to domestic sales.[61]

As the oldest of the auto joint ventures, BJC provides the most data for analysis using the analytical framework suggested in chapter 1. The following sections use that framework to try to highlight the foreign and Chinese political roles in shaping the development of Beijing Jeep.

Stimuli

The shape of each case under study would potentially be greatly influenced by the types of stimuli exerted on the Chinese bureaucracy by both foreign and domestic elements. The following sections characterize the types of factors that shaped the policy process guiding Beijing Jeep's development.

Foreign Forces

The American Motors officials who arrived in China in early 1979 represented an established, relatively large American company, one with technology that would be potentially quite suitable for Chinese manufacturers. These features must have inspired some respect from the Chinese assigned to negotiate with the Americans; the AMC people were no small players.

The Americans proposed a joint venture with the Chinese, and were therefore pledging to become integrated in many ways into the country's economic and political systems. At the time, the Chinese authorities preferred the joint venture form of foreign investment, as the government had more control over such entities than it would over wholly foreign-owned enterprises. Foreign investors also had the advantage of securing a partner knowledgeable of the intricacies of operating a business in China.

As one of the earliest joint ventures, BJC would be an experiment of foreign investment in China. In this sense, the Americans were offering themselves as a guinea pig; but AMC showed willingness to risk its capital only a few years after China's economic reforms had begun. The venture also represented a potential magnet for further foreign investment, and perhaps a test case for large manufacturing projects.

In the latter years of BJC, AMC officials, led by Don St. Pierre, took an active role in trying to shape the Chinese political landscape. For example, St. Pierre's attempts to place Wang Mei in the chairmanship of BJC, and Chen Xulin as president of the company, show an acute, and perhaps atypical, interest by the foreign side in trying to affect pertinent positions within the Chinese bureaucracy. St. Pierre's key role, however, was as a successful agitator moving the bureaucracy to solve the 1986 crisis. He may also have been at least partly responsible for BJC chairman Wu's later dismissal from his position as chief of the BAIC.

In sum, the American side presented Chinese decision makers with a large company, one that offered technology, capital, and a chance to set a good precedent for future foreign investment, while at the same time earning foreign exchange through export. Its representatives in China, led by St. Pierre, showed an active interest in trying to shape the structure of the decision-making hierarchy in the Chinese bureaucracy.

Domestic Economic Forces

By the late 1970s, the Chinese automotive bureaucrats had realized the necessity of modernizing their industry's production capabilities. This step was needed, among other reasons, to stem the tide of imported vehicles, mostly ones from Japan. Any foreign manufacturer, therefore, was potentially a good source of much needed technology and managerial skill.

The first vehicle joint venture would set a precedent for future cooperative projects. Therefore, to ensure that the industry could continue to absorb foreign knowhow, there was some impetus to encourage the success of the earliest Sino-foreign car company.

Of course, there were limits on the Chinese economy's ability to support any one enterprise or industry. By the mid-1980s, it became evident that automotive production would entail spending significant amounts of foreign exchange to finance imports of kit parts, and the nation was pressed to relinquish valuable hard currency for this purpose.

The original vision of some of the automotive planners was an export-driven industry, one that could supply the foreign cash reserves needed for technology importation. The ability of the industry to sell its product overseas was, however, overestimated, as quality and price considerations hampered the effort. The failure of the industry to achieve its goal of exporting vehicles, then, resulted in the need to siphon hard currency from other sectors of the economy.

When the Chinese economic austerity policy was introduced in the late 1980s, as a reaction to high inflation, the prospects for sales of the high-priced and often expendable joint venture vehicles, including both the domestic and Cherokee Jeep models, were temporarily dimmed. Chinese work units were to severely reduce their purchases of such luxury items.

Again, however, the fear of losing technology import was apparently greater than the desire to limit spending on joint venture products. The government-ordered bailout of the ventures, including BJC, was a response induced by the potential loss of future foreign technology and managerial expertise transfer.

Domestic economic forces for the early 1990s would be characterized in part by the need to replace aging imported taxis, at a minimum, and to provide passenger cars for work-unit and, perhaps, private use, at a maximum. The Shanghai Volkswagen and Guangzhou Peugeot ventures seemed best suited for most of these requirements, but one official at Beijing Jeep pointed out that Cherokees could be, and in fact were, used as taxis and for intracity travel.[62] And, of course, Jeeps would still prove useful for rough-terrain travel, a key attribute, considering the often uneven surfaces found on Chinese roads. One source, then, projected that demand for the Cherokees could reach 150,000 by the year 2000.[63]

Government Decision Making

Political Bargaining

The following discussion is divided into studies of both local and central government politics, beginning with an analysis of the national leadership and its policies toward Beijing Jeep.

The Central Government's Role

It is hard to pinpoint the attitude of many top leaders toward the AMC proposal in the early days of reform, and during the venture's existence from 1983 to the present. At the pinnacle of Chinese power, elder leader Deng Xiaoping took pains to stress China's opening to the West, and to encourage foreign investment in his country. He had little, if any, direct influence on the founding of the Jeep venture; and the initial talks in the early 1980s foundered at the same time Deng was touting foreign investment in China. In the venture's later years, Deng failed to meet Lee Iacocca on his 1988 visit to Beijing. During the 1986 crisis, however, former U.S. ambassador to China Leonard Woodcock (who had also previously been head of the United Auto Workers labor union in the United States) offered to approach China's paramount leader to discuss the venture's problems.[64] The Americans declined the offer, fearing that Deng either could not or would not solve the problems.

Premier Zhao Ziyang played a much greater role in shaping the course of the automotive project. Although he did not figure prominently in the early years of the company, Zhao was instrumental in resolving the crisis of 1986. As mentioned above, St. Pierre's letter to Zhao motivated the then-premier to appoint Zhu Rongji as an intermediary in the crisis talks. Zhao was obviously concerned that the venture should survive.

In early 1988, Zhao visited the factory site and stressed the importance of technology transfer.[65] He called for higher quality and lower costs of the domestically produced parts,[66] while noting it was unnecessary to replace every single foreign-made part.[67] Zhao was generally supportive of the venture, mentioning the benefit of import substitution. Such a stance coincided with Zhao's reputation as a staunch supporter of the open door policy, and of cooperation with foreign investors.

Zhao's chief ally in aiding BJC was Zhu Rongji. As noted above, Zhu was instrumental in solving the venture's 1986 crisis, and in helping smooth problems in the postcrisis period. These events showed Zhu's early support for importation of Western technology, and for allowing foreign business to succeed in China. His promotion to Shanghai's mayorship, however, ended his relationship with the Beijing company, as Shanghai Volkswagen then required his allegiance.

As a top official at the SEC, Zhu's support of BJC implies that the commission favored the project, at least to some extent. But neither the SEC nor the State Planning Commission actually approved the key 1984 decision to produce Cherokees instead of a new model vehicle,[68] and no Cherokee manufacture was officially stipulated in China's seventh five-year plan (1985–90) for national production.

As a former leader of the Ministry of Foreign Economic Relations and Trade, and chief of the Bank of China from March of 1985 to 1988, Chen Muhua was potentially quite important to the success of the auto venture. She appeared at several ceremonies marking advances in the company's progress, and publicly agreed with Zhao Ziyang in 1986 that the venture should be saved. MOFERT officials, however, were not key to the resolution of the 1986 problems, and their authority over a venture's import quotas seems to have been at least temporarily usurped by SEC commissioner Zhu.

It is difficult to find sources of opposition to BJC in the top echelons of the Chinese leadership. Li Peng, who replaced Zhao as premier in 1988, may have been skeptical of the company's chances, based on his friendship with BJC detractor Chen Zutao (see chapter 3). Li did, however, publicly support the decision to aid BJC in 1986, and he later met Chrysler president Lee Iacocca on his October 1988 visit to Beijing.

The most prominent critic of the company was found at a lower political level, in the form of CNAIC leader Chen Zutao. Previous discussion described his early enthusiasm for the project, a feeling that turned to disdain for BJC as the company failed to balance its kit imports with vehicle or parts exports, and as the rate of localized production remained low. Zhao Ziyang's 1988 trip to the Jeep factory was, apparently, a response to some of Chen Zutao's public criticism of the joint venture made at a news conference three weeks before Zhao's 1988 visit.[69]

Chen's motivations remain somewhat mysterious. Chapter 3 pointed out his earlier fascination with General Motors, and some Chinese officials believe his hostility toward BJC may have been rooted in frustration that China was not dealing with the largest American company. In 1988, Chen called for ventures to produce axles and motors in China, instead of assembled vehicles.[70] His disenchantment with the joint ventures continued until 1989, when Panda Motors came to China (see chapter 7).

The Chinese military also had reasons to be unhappy with the venture's development. The PLA had hoped for a four-door, soft-top vehicle, and the Cherokee did not fulfill that wish. In fact, the 1986 settlement specifically said such a derivative would *not* be developed.[71] It is difficult, however, to document specific pressure the military may have applied on Chinese officials to forward its desires. Chen Xulin apparently calmed the PLA by noting that the venture was improving the BJ212 model; 10 to 20 percent of that vehicle's output went to the army. Chen later told them a new model might emerge in the mid-1990s.[72] In the meantime, the military *did* buy Cherokees; in 1989, it bought some 2,000 vehicles.[73]

Local Politics

As for any city, a new automotive project represents a potential source of valuable investment and productive capability; multiplier effects could help the whole area's economy. How did Beijing municipality react to the AMC venture? Were the local Beijing officials as supportive of the large enterprise as one might expect a local government to be?

Early representatives to the venture talks seem to have come mainly from the central government. The most prominent figure on the municipal side, however, was Wu Zhongliang, chief of both the BAW and of Beijing's municipal automotive industrial corporation (BAIC). One of the first auto officials to visit AMC's Detroit headquarters in 1979, Wu was a key figure in the venture's history. Once BJC was created, Wu was chosen board chairman.

In the early years of BJC, Wu was a strong proponent of speeding development of the proposed new model. By late 1984, however, Wu had accepted the American argument that such a vehicle would be too costly, and agreed to the kit imports. Wu, along with other municipal officials, was one of the highest-ranking people actually to give permission for the Cherokee project, and the lack of central government approval was a major problem as the 1986 crisis unfolded.

It is not clear how Wu was able to launch the Cherokee project on his own. One source points out that a representative of the national government's CNAIC sits on the eleven-person BJC board, and that the representative agreed to the 1984 plan to import kits; this implied a tacit CNAIC approval to the BJC board.[74] Still, the decision suggested a degree of independence from central government policy makers that was quite impractical, as the municipality lacked sufficient foreign reserves to finance the necessary purchases.

Wu later appeared to regret his action. In 1985, as the national foreign exchange shortfall became evident, Wu blamed higher-level government offices, such as the Customs Bureau, for failing to allow imports of the needed parts.[75] Of course, by then the venture had already invested in the assembly line and other equipment specifically meant for Cherokee production. As the crisis took shape in late 1985, BAW independently tried to rally central government concern, with little apparent result. During the critical talks in early 1986, Wu disappeared, apparently in the hospital with a heart attack. The top Chinese official of both BJC and BAIC, then, was absent at the crisis resolution.

Beijing was instead represented by Vice Mayor Zhang Jianmin.[76] Zhang appeared to be a natural ally of the venture. As a vice mayor with the city's automotive industry in his portfolio, he stood to lose stature if the company failed. During the crisis negotiations, then, the Chinese side could not field a united front, as Zhang seemed much more sympathetic toward BJC than was Chen Zutao, his corepresentative.

Zhang Jianmin also had his differences with Wu Zhongliang. Zhang reportedly disliked Wu, and may have influenced Wu's dismissal as head of the BAIC.[77] The Americans at BJC were also frustrated with both the BAIC and BAW; one source claimed the government bodies were inducing the joint venture to buy local parts at high prices, then accepting kickbacks from the parts manufacturers. In sum, the BAIC seems to have had poor relations with both superior and subordinate levels.

Although the city officials initially played a lesser role than that of the central leaders, BJC turned to the Beijing government in the years after Zhu Rongji and Don St. Pierre had passed from the scene. The 1989 customs clash, for example, was resolved with local officials' aid, rather than central help.

Misperception

The 1983 decision creating a venture meant to produce a new model vehicle was perhaps clouded by wishful thinking on the Chinese side, though the problem was compounded by some duplicity among the American negotiators. This first important decision led directly to many of the problems that would later plague the venture's development.

In approving the plan to develop a new four-door, soft-top vehicle, the Chinese decision makers might have simply been careless, ignoring information that planning and production of such an automobile would be lengthy, and impossibly costly to such a small enterprise as BJC. Given the number of years the Chinese spent negotiating the contract, however, such an assertion seems unlikely.

The Chinese may have been induced to consciously discount the potentially high costs of such a project by the American assurances that such a venture was feasible. As noted above, the "seven-year plan" both sides accepted seemed practical, and must have been fiscally within the realm of possibility. As late as January 1984, AMC's Tod Clare claimed BJC would be making a "totally new and fresh" export-model Jeep within two to four years.[78] The Chinese, in the end, were victims of their almost blind acceptance of American promises, what one analyst suggested might be a case of a "bait and switch" tactic to deceive the Chinese.[79] (Remarks made by the Americans who created the venture, particularly those of Clare, imply that AMC actually believed to some extent that its plan was feasible, and not simply a deception intended to launch the venture more quickly.)

How were the Chinese so easily fooled? Perhaps the reverence of a large foreign company and its modern technology made the Chinese believe anything was possible, and that the Americans would be able to finance the project even if it cost more than the estimates predicted. In the early years of the opening to the West, such confidence in foreign capabilities would be expected; perhaps BJC Vice President Zhao Nailin's flawed foreign exchange calculations were partly inspired by his faith in American "deep pockets." In any event, the early Chinese approval of the venture's plan was irrational, and was probably the result of unfounded expectations based more on unattainable hopes and dreams, and an exaggerated view of the foreign investors, than on responsible fiscal analysis.

Policy Process Conclusions

The central government demonstrated early unity in taking a cautious yet positive attitude toward AMC's proposed joint venture. The talks were slowed by some officials still reluctant to embrace China's opening to the West begun in the late 1970s.

As the country's leadership entered the 1980s, there was general agreement that the auto industry required technological assistance from abroad in order to modernize. This consensus, together with the American promises and resulting misperception of possible achievements, strengthened the generally unanimous public support for the Jeep project in its early days. As troubles arose in the mid-1980s, however, central government unity gave way to serious schisms. Chen Zutao, chief of the CNAIC, converted from being a supporter of the BJC venture to acting as its most vociferous critic. The company's allies in the central government, including Premier Zhao Ziyang and SEC Commissioner Zhu Rongji, proved too powerful for the frustrated Chen, and the Americans obtained their desired concessions following the 1986 crisis.

The pro-AMC outcome was further influenced by the activist BJC president, Don St. Pierre. His tactics pointed out the value of maintaining the Chinese reputation as a safe investment site, further strengthening the hand of those supporting the joint venture. St. Pierre's contacts with central and local leaders served as a useful conduit to resolve future conflicts, such as the 1989 customs duty dispute.

The local government seems to have been left playing a junior role in guiding the development of BJC. Once the venture contract had been signed, the BAIC, and its leader Wu Zhongliang, erroneously assumed it could work independently of the national government to permit importation of Cherokee model kits. Perhaps the mid-1980s atmosphere of decentralization had allowed this misconception.

With the crisis of 1986, the Beijing municipal government forces, led by Vice Mayor Zhang Jianmin, rallied to support the local project. These officials faced embarrassment were the venture to fail. Luckily for them, they had powerful allies in the central government who were also willing to aid the venture.

The Beijing city government did seem to perceive significant problems with local government–joint venture cooperation. Wu's removal as head of the BAIC may have been an attempt by Zhang Jianmin to further smooth the way for BJC development. Although the local government was responsible for much of the day-to-day activities at BJC, such as coordinating parts deliveries and developing local suppliers, the national government took the top billing as policy maker for the venture. This outcome was the result of several factors. First, and most obvious, was the location of the venture in the nation's capital. Because of this, central leaders seemed to develop a natural interest in the project's welfare.

The national government also took a major role in BJC's development as local officials deferred to the central will. Unlike the other ventures investigated here, including Volkswagen in Shanghai and two others in Guangdong province, Beijing Jeep lay directly in the shadow of the national government. Local officials probably felt intimidated by the proximity of central leaders; and the settlement of the 1986 crisis and St. Pierre's later dependence on Zhu Rongji reinforce this proposition.

In sum, local government generally played more of a supporting role in policymaking for the auto project. The key central government players began with generally unified optimism about the Jeep venture. As problems arose, however, so did opposing factions within the government; Beijing Jeep was lucky that its supporters were more influential.

Policy Implementation: Did BJC's Road Get Any Smoother?

The joint venture began with an extended period of contract talks. As noted, there were nearly a dozen government offices overseeing the discussions, and some officials had not yet come to appreciate the potential benefits of foreign investment. Such layers of slow-moving bureaucrats delayed the establishment of the first automotive venture, in spite of the general support for the project from top political leaders.

Once the venture was established, however, and had begun its operation, the decision-making process seemed to accelerate. The local Chinese officials, for example, were very quick to approve the importation of Cherokee kits: the Americans suggested the idea in September of 1984, and by mid-October of that year, the Chinese had accepted the plan.[80] Of course, the central government played no role in approving the scheme, but the layers of government overseeing the local officials seemed to have evaporated.

Troubles surrounding the 1986 crisis may have intimidated local officials, who in any case lacked the foreign reserves needed to ameliorate the situation. Local government officials then appeared as obstacles to a solution. Frustrated AMC representatives, therefore, led by St. Pierre, skipped over the city government, and even bypassed the CNAIC and ministerial levels, to seek quick relief with Zhao Ziyang's office. Once the top leadership learned of the crisis, it acted quickly to reach a solution.

BJC was fortunate to win the favor of Zhu Rongji. In future clashes with the Chinese bureaucracy, St. Pierre was able to appeal directly to Zhu for help. Once Zhu left for Shanghai, however, the venture relied more on the city government for needed aid.

Overall, the government displayed a rather significant degree of Steinbruner-type "learning" (see chapter 1 for a definition of this term) in responding to problems facing the joint venture. The early years of talks were marked by inaction, the result of unfamiliarity with foreign entrepreneurs and of a general distrust of outside investors. By the mid-1980s, however, the Chinese seemed to have modified their decision-making apparatus; the major local decision to allow Cherokee production was made in record time. The postcrisis years demonstrate the value of AMC contacts with the top leadership; most local-level obstacles could simply be overridden by orders from the top. The latter years of the venture, however, show BJC's increasing reliance on local officials to solve problems, indicating that this level of government was then organized well enough to encourage generally smooth implementation of policy decisions.

Projections for BJC

As noted, the Beijing Jeep venture achieved a significant degree of success in the aftermath of the 1986 crisis. Its strong gains in vehicle production, steady progress in localization efforts, and ability to generate a profit testify to the company's positive achievements.

BJC's gains, however, came in the wake of preferential treatment by the central government, and sacrifices made to keep the company viable during the difficult times in 1986, 1989, and 1990. Will the central authorities continue to provide aid on demand to the Chinese Jeep company?

During the middle and late 1980s, BJC achieved status as a kind of "model" joint venture, and its success became important for attracting other foreign investment to China. By 1994, however, the utility of such a "model" was in question. Myriad successful ventures, combined with strong, if sometimes erratic, GNP growth, made China a tempting investment target; "Daqing"-type models were perhaps no longer needed.

The importance of Beijing Jeep to China, then, was certainly diluted. Were the venture again to experience problems of the same magnitude as those seen in 1986, it is doubtful the government would again react with such vigor to sustain the company. The success of BJC to the time of this writing, however, and solid contacts the Americans had established with Chinese political forces, provided the company a momentum indicating it would survive, and perhaps even thrive, into the foreseeable future.

5

Shanghai Volkswagen: Success through Foresight and Local Cooperation

As China's most cosmopolitan city before the 1949 Communist revolution, Shanghai had several decades of close contact with Western nations. European influence (predominantly British and French) was particularly strong. It seemed fitting, then, that Shanghai would choose a German auto manufacturer to found the city's first foreign vehicle venture.

This chapter analyzes the successful development of Shanghai Volkswagen, one of the largest single foreign-invested projects ever conceived in China. Compared with Beijing Jeep's course, the German venture's progress was steady and smooth, though somewhat slow. How did the Germans avoid the serious troubles that plagued BJC in its early years?

The Shanghai Industrial Setting

Prerevolutionary Shanghai saw significant industrial growth over the thirty years following World War I. The city was known for its trading enterprises: some 40 percent of China's imports and exports passed through Shanghai in the 1920s and 1930s.[1] Annual industrial growth from 1919 to 1939 reached nearly 14 percent, with textile and light machinery production leading the advance.[2] The municipal banking sector competed with well-established foreign concerns in the city's international treaty settlements, though the Chinese financiers and other business people benefited from foreign capital and expertise.[3] By 1935, about half of all foreign investment in China was found in Shanghai, and the city produced a similar percentage of the nation's industrial output.[4] Japanese occupation in 1941, however, forced out British, French, and American concerns.

Throughout its years of early development, Shanghai maintained a strong fascination with automobiles and their manufacture. In 1902, the city registered its first two imported passenger cars, both of which were American Oldsmobiles. The Shanghai Automobile and Tractor Associated Company was founded in 1910, and was soon joined by a car and bus repair factory in nearby Anting, and by the Shanghai Chassis Factory, created in 1912. In 1918 the Shanghai Fire Truck Factory began operation, and was followed one year later by the Shanghai Heavy Truck Repair Factory. A second wave of manufacturers came three decades later, with the formation of the "7424" assembly factory (in 1941), and the Shanghai Diesel Locomotive Factory (1947).[5] Shanghai residents also displayed a fascination with passenger cars. The city's automotive imports dwarfed those of other areas of the nation, with some 11,900 cars plying the municipal streets by 1936.[6]

Following the Communist takeover in 1949, Shanghai's heavy industrial sector developed quickly. The textile industry had held the lion's share of Shanghai's 1949 output, constituting 62.4 percent; light industry accounted for 24 percent, and heavy industry only 13.6 percent.[7] Over the first ten years of the People's Republic, however, heavy industry (nationalized in the 1950s) grew by some 42 percent annually, leaving it with 52 percent of the city's industrial output in 1959. Textiles had fallen to account for only 27 percent of production by that year.[8]

The Great Leap Forward brought a further rise in Shanghai industrial growth. A nationwide campaign to produce iron and steel helped feed the machinery-manufacturing sector; the city's industrial output soared 50 percent in 1958 and 43 percent in 1959.[9] This period saw the establishment of more automotive factories, including the Shanghai Automotive Electric Motor Factory, the Shanghai Automotive Transmission Shaft Factory, and, most important, the city's first passenger car factory, the Shanghai Automotive Assembly Plant (later known as the Shanghai Car Plant, or SCP), all founded in 1958.

In the wake of uncoordinated Great Leap efforts, Shanghai (and the rest of China) faced severe economic retrenchment in the early 1960s.

In fact, from 1959 to 1973, heavy industrial growth slowed to an average of 6.25 percent per year.[10] Construction of major new automotive factories virtually stopped, though cooperation among the various manufacturers allowed the SCP (Volkswagen's future partner) to produce its first "Phoenix Brand" car in 1958. The hand-crafted production at the factory remained extremely limited, with output barely reaching one hundred vehicles each year (see figure 2.1). In 1964, SCP modified the Phoenix, and thereafter sold its vehicles under the "Shanghai Brand" model name.

Shanghai heavy industrial development continued in the late 1960s and early 1970s, with concerted efforts to modernize steel production. By the mid-1970s, the city's steel output trailed only that of the northeast steel town of Anshan; in 1970, furthermore, Shanghai received one of only two modern oxygen furnaces imported into China.[11]

Given Shanghai's commitment to and investment in heavy industry, it is not surprising foreign automotive companies would look to the city as a prime joint venture site. The following section outlines the city's early attempts to initiate such cooperation.[12]

Joint Venture Exploration

In May 1978, several months before Deng Xiaoping consolidated his power at the key reformist third plenum of the CCP eleventh party congress, First Machine Building Vice Minister Yang Keng led an official delegation to West Germany. Although Volkswagen (hereafter VW) was not on Yang's stated itinerary, the Chinese group requested a meeting with VW officials, and asked whether the Germans would be interested in a cooperative automotive project. The Chinese said they desired technical knowledge, modernization of equipment, and, eventually, the ability to export cars. They envisioned a factory capable of producing up to 200,000 vehicles per year. According to Chinese sources, the overtures were inspired by the State Planning Commission, then led by Yu Qiuli.

VW officials responded positively to this initial contact, and preliminary discussion soon followed. The Germans pointed out in these early contacts, however, that existing Chinese production systems were quite outdated, and that the Chinese goals were far too ambitious. The Chinese, perhaps somewhat disillusioned, withdrew from the talks for several months, and the Germans believed they had lost interest.

In March 1979, however, VW was surprised by an invitation to send a delegation to China. Rao Bin, then FMMB vice minister, greeted them, and renewed his country's cooperation proposal. The Germans again questioned China's ability to produce an export-quality vehicle; the Chinese pointed to Shanghai, however, saying that they were in fact already manufacturing cars. The Germans then decided to convince the Chinese of potential production limitations by staging a manufacturing experiment in that industrial city.[13]

In late 1982, then, the Germans began trial production of their Santana model vehicle at the SCP. VW shipped completely knocked down kits (CKDs) to Shanghai, and the Chinese workers assembled them. In conducting this operation, the Germans had several goals. First, they wanted to test the logistics of shipping car kits to China, noting problems with customs regulations, parts storage, and so on. Second, they wanted to see how the Chinese reacted to the required quality stipulations associated with the new technology. Finally, VW wanted to establish its presence in the country, and to make an early statement that it was seriously considering investing in a Shanghai automotive joint venture.

Shanghai municipal officials, who by then dominated the Chinese negotiating team,[14] felt the trial provided useful training for its assembly-line workers. Furthermore, they could see whether the Santana model was appropriate for domestic road conditions.[15] In 1983, then, the experiment produced some 430 vehicles; the following year, the factory assembled about 450, all of which were bought by the Chinese. Furthermore, eight Chinese workers went to Germany for advanced training, and VW sent technicians to Shanghai to give instruction.

As the negotiations and trial operation proceeded, Shanghai automotive manufacturers publicly proclaimed their own Shanghai Brand sedan production system was in fact ill-equipped for future Chinese market requirements. One study in 1982 asserted the SCP lacked the efficiency to meet the demand of emergent taxi companies and of government officials and other work units, and called for improved technology and a better product.[16] In 1983, the factory came in for further criticism, with one writer noting the SCP's efficiency fell far below that of American or Japanese production levels, and that the vehicle model had hardly changed in two decades. (Like Changchun's luxury Red Flag automobile, the Shanghai sedan was originally modeled after the 1950s Mercedes 220 series.) Furthermore, the car's price was too high, at RMB 20,000 ($10,300), and its top speed too low (130 km/hour).[17]

The above-mentioned 1983 report not only stressed the need for an improved passenger car, but also proposed a major export plan.[18] In order to reach such a goal, however, cooperation with foreign investors was essential.[19]

Shanghai officials did not limit their contact to German automotive representatives. General Motors, Ford, and various European companies also expressed interest in a Shanghai project. As noted in chapter 2, Japanese companies investigated the city's prospects in the early 1980s. The German trial operation, however, demonstrated VW's sincerity, and kept the company in the lead for selection as a partner.

While the discussions in Shanghai continued, AMC's talks in Beijing over the Jeep project were nearing a conclusion. As noted in chapter 4, the Americans had promised to help the Chinese develop a completely new vehicle model. Would not the Germans do the same in Shanghai, asked VW's negotiating partners? If not a new model, then the Germans should at least make some concessions in light of the proven American flexibility.

The Germans, however, were unfazed by the Chinese request. They ruled out any possibility of developing a new model, anticipating BJC's problems, and insisted CKD imports were the only method of producing quality vehicles in Shanghai. The Chinese, apparently impressed by the German frankness and practicality, accepted their position on the issue.

VW officials were struck by early Chinese naivete on other negotiating points. One German representative remarked that in the early stages of the talks, Shanghai automotive officials had difficulty comprehending financial calculations, and often required careful instruction from the foreign side to understand details of the German proposals. VW representatives, though, intent on crafting a clear and precise contract, acted patiently to explain the unclear points.

Finally, the two sides moved toward agreement. VW's partners in the venture were proposed by the central government, though the Germans approved of the choices. VW was to hold 50 percent of the new company, named Shanghai Volkswagen (SVW). The Shanghai Automotive Industrial Corporation (SAIC), which had tight control over the Shanghai Car Plant, took 25 percent of the venture. The rest of SVW was owned by the Bank of China's Shanghai Trust and Consultancy

Corporation, with 15 percent, and the CNAIC, which held 10 percent.

The new company was capitalized at RMB 120 million (about $40 million), with the SCP factory, in Shanghai's suburb, Anting, contributing equipment and about half of its factory space. VW promised advanced technology, but put up most of its RMB 60 million in cash. The contract was to run for twenty-five years. It was signed with much ceremony in October 1984, during a visit by West German Chancellor Helmut Kohl. Premier Zhao Ziyang also attended the signing, showing top-level Chinese concern for the huge foreign-invested project.

SVW's Plan, and Early Problems

The contract VW negotiated with the Chinese was notable for attention to detail, and for its ability to predict future difficulties. (One VW representative said West German experiences with Socialist East Germany may have contributed to an understanding of command economies and their shortcomings, though the automotive company itself had few investments in the preunification nation.) Several clauses in the SVW contract differentiated the venture's agreement from that of the BJC project. As noted above, for example, the Germans insisted on assembly of imported CKD kits.

Other parts of the contract, however, also demonstrated VW's foresight. Anticipating the problem of paying for imported kits with Chinese renminbi remittances, the contract allowed SVW to convert RMB into German marks at the prevailing, official exchange rate until the venture had produced 89,000 cars. Such a clause would help protect the company against the kind of debacle BJC faced when it was unable to pay for Cherokee imports.

The contract took into account the need to localize the Santana model. According to the agreement, however, responsibility for providing quality parts made in China rested squarely with the Chinese; VW had no obligation to hasten the process.

To help balance the foreign exchange flowing out of China to pay for kit imports, the contract called for the venture to export engines produced in Shanghai back to West Germany for use by the foreign partner, VW. It is unclear whether the agreement called for VW to buy a specific number of engines over the life of the contract, but the price VW would pay for each engine was predetermined. As we will see, this clause also played to the German advantage in a later dispute.

In early 1985, then, SVW moved in earnest to transform production at the Shanghai factory. The first session of the venture's board of directors decided to invest RMB 250 million (about $85 million) to renovate the SCP's assembly line and body-finishing section.[20] The Santana price was set at RMB 40,000 ($13,800), comparable at the time to the cost of a Japanese import vehicle before tax.[21] By the end of the year, production had reached thirty cars per day. The SAIC, which had some 140 subordinate companies in its group, encouraged its parts factories to improve quality to meet VW standards. Several of these suppliers licensed foreign technology to raise standards; one factory collaborating with a West German corporation was able to contribute tires to SVW, and, reportedly, exported some of its product to Western nations.[22]

Although the venture had some early success, its first years saw many problems characteristic of foreign-invested Chinese projects. In modifying the SCP facilities, for example, Chinese construction crews were slow: they traditionally measured their achievements in terms of new footage completed, and shunned renovation work. Local banks were inefficient, and failed to budget funds to lend SVW.[23]

Perhaps most disappointing was the mixed support among local political leadership. Municipal construction authorities were late in implementing needed infrastructural improvements. City planners were lax in encouraging localization parts projects, and in raising funds to aid the development of the main factory. One report complained Chinese officials had acquired some of the first cars off the assembly line, then sold them domestically for foreign exchange and failed to reimburse SVW.[24]

In interviews, Chinese officials defended themselves against some of these charges. They noted, for example, that reconstruction and redesign of outdated equipment is always time-consuming. Furthermore, they asserted the city government did try to solve some of the early problems: Vice Mayor Li Zhaoji, for example, called local banks together to press for greater cooperation with SVW.[25] Others made detailed suggestions for remedying the problems, calling, among other proposals, for a leading municipal group to coordinate automotive development (a suggestion later implemented), relaxation of employment rules to attract all sorts of skilled workers, and acquisition of technology from other manufacturing plants around China to conserve investment funds.[26]

Despite these troubles, SVW production showed steady growth in the company's first years. In 1985, the factory turned out 3,356 Santanas. This number more than doubled in 1986, to 8,031, and climbed to 10,470 in 1987.[27] Engine production also grew strongly, rising from 352 complete engines in 1987 to 13,085 in 1988.[28] The Shanghai factory had a short experiment making 100 of VW's Passat Variant models in 1986, and assembled nearly 1,000 Audi 100 cars in 1986 and 1987. (In 1988, manufacturing efforts for the Audi moved to a different VW venture in Changchun, in northeast China.)

Workers at the Shanghai plant were pleased by some special joint venture benefits. Salaries were high, ranging from RMB 140 (including bonuses) to RMB 300 per month; such compensation greatly exceeded most Chinese factory wages in 1986. SVW's allotment of seven days of paid vacation was also attractive to Chinese employees, who had no previous experience with such a perquisite.[29]

In 1988, problems again surfaced for the German venture. The BJC crisis of 1986 had raised central government concerns about CKD imports. These kits were a drain on foreign exchange reserves, and the only method of stanching the outflow of hard currency lay in localizing parts production in China. With the truce over AMC's dispute in place, the central leaders turned their attention to the VW venture in Shanghai.

The Local Content Dilemma

As figure 5.1 shows, localization of Santana parts in the company's early years proceeded fairly steadily, and was in fact on a par with BJC's progress (see figure 4.1) and with that of Guangzhou Peugeot (figure 6.1). Still, CNAIC chief Chen Zutao led a campaign to force more rapid progress in the use of Chinese parts. In 1988, Chen said SVW should move quickly to localize up to 80 percent of the Santana; he implied that the volume of raw materials supplies to SVW might be linked to the localization rate.[30]

In many ways, Chen's demand was naive and generally destructive. First, his timetable was overly ambitious when one considers localization projects in other parts of the world. Honda, for example, began assembling cars in the United States in 1982, starting with 25 percent American parts already suitable for the Japanese-designed vehicle. Ten years later, in 1992, Honda was near its goal of using 75 percent local

Figure 5.1. **Localization of the Shanghai Volkswagen Santana, 1985-93**

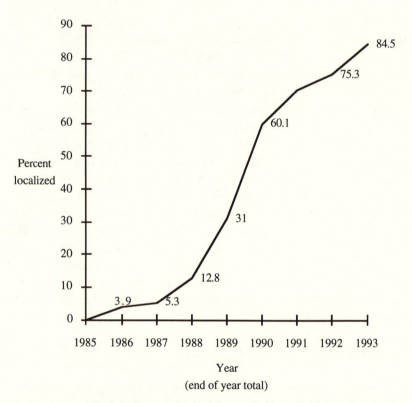

Year
(end of year total)

Sources: For 1985-92: 1992 correspondence with Volkswagen, Germany. For 1992-93: 1994 correspondence with Volkswagen, Germany.

American parts.[31] To expect the Chinese supplier industry to match or exceed this pace seems incredible. The Chinese in fact reached the 80 percent goal after only seven years; the resultant vehicle, however, most likely suffered from parts that were inappropriate or substandard for the Santana model.

The problem for SVW finding local parts for its vehicles was the same problem BJC had faced three years earlier: local quality was too low. The SCP's traditional suppliers of such components as carburetors, cylinders, and chassis were unfamiliar with high foreign standards,

Figure 5.2. **Chinese and German Preferences for Kit Imports and Local Content**

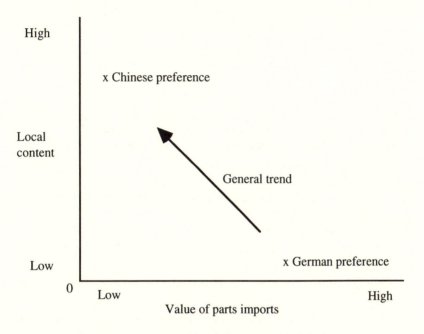

Note: As local content rose, the value of parts needed by the Chinese would generally decrease; at 100 percent localization, the value of imports is, of course, zero.

and refused to invest funds to raise quality until they were given large, economy-of-scale orders for their product. In its early years, however, SVW required only a few hundred or a few thousand items. In a vicious circle, though, the central government was loath to allow a larger number of CKD imports until the joint venture reached higher local content rates.

For the Germans, of course, profits were generally greater when local content was low, as this gave VW the chance to export more parts to China (see figure 5.2). VW also worried about the effect poor-quality products would have on the company's reputation. To overcome this obviously foreign-inspired inertia, and the vicious circle of parts supplies, the Chinese imposed localization taxes on each Santana sold domestically. In late 1988, then, SVW sold its product to SAIC for RMB 70,000 ($18,800). The SAIC then resold the sedans to authorized distributors for an exorbitant RMB 140,000 ($37,600) per car; the RMB 70,000 windfall went to the Shanghai government, which used most of it to subsidize local parts suppliers.[32] The Germans would naturally have preferred a lower price for the vehicles, to spur more demand; but there was little they could do to prevent this process.

The Chinese did grant some incentive for the Germans to increase local content. After 40 percent of parts were localized, the imported parts were no longer considered "CKD" kits and were then taxed at a lower rate. Similar tax reductions were made once the 60 and 80 percent localization barriers were crossed.[33]

In the localization squabble, VW had some further consolation: their contract specifically charged the Chinese with responsibility for providing parts of acceptable quality (which were tested at a special German laboratory transported to Shanghai for this purpose). Furthermore, throughout the Chinese barrage of criticism over localization levels, the Germans refrained from making their problems public. Unlike the Americans at BJC, VW officials patiently allowed the Chinese to find a solution to the problem.

The German patience paid off in the long run. The company reached its goal of 80 percent local content in 1993. This followed the ability of some 200 manufacturing partners to meet the requirements for Santana production.[34] It was unclear, however, whether the supplied parts met the world standards necessary for export capability.

Shanghai's New Leadership

As the controversy over local content abated, the Germans were pleased by the arrival in Shanghai of Zhu Rongji as the city's new mayor. Zhu seemed to make the revitalization of Shanghai industrial development his own private mission. Chapter 3 described some of Zhu's steps to aid foreign investors in Shanghai; he also made moves to help SVW in particular.

Even before he was officially named Shanghai mayor, for example, Zhu (then still an SEC vice minister) came to the city in June 1987 to investigate the auto venture's localization troubles. According to some

Shanghai officials, his experience in helping solve Beijing Jeep's crisis made him realize the complexity of successful vehicle industrial development.[35] In the wake of Zhu's visit, the city moved to create its automotive leading small group; it also raised the SAIC from a deputy bureau to bureau-level status.

On assuming his duties as mayor in April 1988, Zhu encouraged the founding of a Shanghai taxi company that would exclusively use cars from the SVW plant. The joint venture would sell its vehicles to the company, with a price discount as an incentive. The taxi company was officially created in 1989; by the following year, the lion's share of sedan taxis in Shanghai were Santana models, and Japanese imported vehicles became more scarce on the city's streets.

Zhu developed into a strong Shanghai chauvinist in the last years of the 1980s, working hard to promote investment and development in his city. One municipal official noted the major role SVW could play in Shanghai's economic progress: with production of 18,500 cars in 1990, the joint venture already accounted for 2 percent of the city's output value; at the factory's full capacity of 300,000 vehicles, it would potentially contribute up to 17 percent of municipal output.

Once the German venture had acted to overcome its localization troubles, then, it encountered less criticism from central and local officials. Unfortunately, the company was further affected by China's economic austerity measures introduced in late 1988. Like BJC and Guangzhou Peugeot, SVW faced a stockpiling of its output, as the central government restricted domestic vehicle sales. Production of some 15,700 vehicles in 1989 fell far short of the contractual projection of 20,000 cars for that year. Furthermore, the factory operated at only 50 percent of capacity in the last part of 1989, and actually halted production in October because of an oversupply of 3,000 vehicles.[36] Eventually, however, the central government's "emergency purchasing plan" (noted in chapter 4) allocated some RMB 1 billion ($268 million) to buy the inventories of the various ventures. One SAIC official expressed satisfaction with Beijing's move, commenting that "the central government is certainly relaxing its grip on Sino-foreign automotive ventures and making it easier for state institutions and enterprises to buy vehicles."[37] As China's economy rebounded in the early 1990s, SVW's development accelerated. The company looked forward to further advances in the new decade.

Strength into the 1990s

Like the other major automotive projects in China, SVW had a high public profile as a foreign-investment example. The Chinese hoped to reap positive propaganda from such projects to encourage further investment in other industries. SVW's generally good progress, then, inspired the government to name it number two of China's top ten joint ventures for 1988 (for comparison, BJC was number three that year, and Guangzhou Peugeot was number five).[38] SVW continued a strong showing on the list in 1989, as number five. In 1990, the company fell to the tenth spot, but recovered to take the number one position in 1991, and was fourth in 1992. (BJC fell from third in 1989 to ninth in 1990, and was off the list in 1991; Peugeot's company failed to make the list after 1988.)[39]

Production at the Shanghai factory rose quickly. Although 1989 output was limited to 15,688 vehicles (virtually identical to 1988's figure) by the economic austerity policy, production grew in 1990 to 18,500 and leapt to 35,000 in 1991; 1992 saw some 65,000 Santanas roll off the assembly line, to reach full capacity at the existing plant. Following a merger with neighboring Chinese production facilities (discussed below), the company reached the 100,000-vehicle mark in 1993.[40] Accumulated investment in the venture reached RMB 825 million ($220 million) at the end of 1989, and RMB 1.7 billion (about $300 million) at the end of 1992.[41] For 1991, SVW projected $154 million in profits, a fourfold increase over its 1990 figure;[42] profits for 1992, however, were reported to be $87 million.[43] Finally, local content in 1992 approached 80 percent (see figure 5.1). This success was rewarded by SVW's becoming the first joint venture in China allowed to import parts without a license.[44]

The venture, however, was not completely free of problems. In 1990, for example, VW and the Chinese disagreed over the price the Germans should pay SVW for engines exported to the home factory in Europe. The Chinese wanted a high price, to earn more foreign exchange; VW officials countered that a price was already stipulated in the venture's contract. It is unclear exactly how the issue was settled, but SVW did ship some 400 engines to Germany in 1990.

Further difficulties loomed as SVW moved to take over the remaining factory space of its partner, the Shanghai Car Plant. The decision to end the SCP's existence came in 1988 after consultation among

SVW's shareholders. The Shanghai municipal government, however, took some two years to plan and approve the merger. In June 1991, the SAIC announced the demise of the SCP, and the retirement of its old product, the Shanghai Brand sedan.

SVW's seven years of experience in China probably gave it the ability to integrate the new production area without too much difficulty, though the task of converting old machinery and retraining workers seemed daunting.[45] By the end of 1993, however, VW's overseas training program had seen more than 1,000 senior Chinese engineers receive training in Germany.[46] Labor rates, moreover, remained low: "For all practical purposes . . . the cost of labor in China is nothing," said SVW's supply manager, Peter Topp, in late 1993.[47]

Delivery of new cars to customers continued to present a challenge for the German venture into the 1990s. Poor road and rail systems meant cars would have to be driven to customers, or purchasers would have to come to Shanghai and drive them away themselves. (In one case, a VW car arrived at its delivery point with 2,000 miles already on the odometer.)[48]

Finally, the joint venture's most challenging potential problem arose in late 1991, as the company reached its production limit of 89,000 cars, after which it could no longer freely exchange Chinese RMB for hard currency. Although this factor was quite critical in the early and mid-1980s when the venture's contract was written (as the BJC crisis demonstrated), by 1992 it was not quite so troublesome. China had created currency exchange markets, designed particularly for foreign investors; these markets allowed foreign concerns to change renminbi to hard currency, though at a premium (of some 10 to 20 percent or more). As China moved toward full currency convertibility in the early 1990s, however, the issue seemed to be becoming moot.

Stimuli

Foreign Forces

Perhaps most striking in the German approach to the Shanghai automotive project was VW's attention to precise planning. The SVW contract seemed almost clairvoyant in its ability to anticipate troubles. Because of the detailed scheme presented in the charter, the venture avoided problems over CKD imports, foreign currency balancing, rushed localization, and pricing of exported engines.

The negotiation of the contract was characterized by frankness on the foreign side. Unlike the Americans in Beijing, VW representatives refrained from promising difficult deeds in order to secure agreement quickly. Thus, SVW could immediately embark on CKD assembly and avoid arguments over design of a China-specific vehicle. Such early German sincerity probably nurtured Chinese support for solving later problems.

In addition to the helpful contract clauses, the 1984 agreement also displayed some insightful German understanding in accepting joint venture partners. With the SAIC, the Bank of China, and the CNAIC, SVW had a beneficial blend of both local and national shareholders (their respective contributions to the company are highlighted in later sections).

Finally, the Germans were careful in their selection of Shanghai as a factory site. The city had a long history of automotive manufacture, and was the major passenger car producer in China as the nation opened its doors to foreign investors. Below is more detail on the domestic economic factors characterizing the SVW venture; it is noted here, however, that VW did analyze and choose Shanghai over at least one other site, the Second Auto Works in Hubei.[49]

Domestic Economic Forces

As the SVW venture was conceived and developed in a time period nearly identical to that of Beijing Jeep, many structural similarities exist in their economic environments. Both ventures were founded on the basis of contributing foreign technology to China. The two major factors differentiating the projects in this category, however, were the vehicle type produced and the developmental stage of the chosen factory site.

Chapter 2 pointed out that the Chinese were desperate in the early and mid-1980s to stem floods of imported Japanese vehicles by developing their own modern automotive industry. Many of the imported vehicles were passenger cars, used as taxis and for transport of high- and middle-level political leaders.

With BJC producing sturdy Jeeps capable of riding difficult terrain, then, the two ventures were apparently designed to respond to different markets. BJC's product would be adequate primarily for rough-road transport and goods delivery. Shanghai's Santanas would mainly fill the demand niche of intracity passenger conveyance. Although BJC officials interviewed insisted their Cherokee model was quite suitable to take taxi duties, its high chassis and rough appearance made it an undesirable choice for such service. The market forces for BJC, then, behaved differently from those SVW encountered.

The German venture's market outlook was bright. Until Peugeot's factory in Guangzhou began producing sedans in large numbers, SVW would have an enormous potential nationwide demand; at a minimum, it would substitute for Japanese vehicles. In the future, furthermore, a rapidly developing Shanghai economy and its population of more than 10 million would in itself be a valuable captive market for SVW automobiles.

Besides Shanghai's advantage as a potential market, its heavy industrial infrastructure made major contributions to facilitating SVW's development. A large number of parts factories, together with the extant Shanghai Car Plant, and the city's steel and other heavy industries, cried out for the final ingredients necessary for rapid development: modern technology and management skills. Shanghai's local conditions, then, not only attracted the Germans to the city; they also helped ease later problems. When the Chinese complained that the rate of localization was too low, for example, SVW could turn to relatively advanced municipal suppliers to help ameliorate the troubles. Shanghai city leaders, furthermore, had experience in guiding heavy industrial development, and were another source of aid to the new company.

Again, Shanghai had advantages in this aspect over BJC and the other case study ventures, Guangzhou Peugeot and Panda. We have already noted some of the difficulties BJC had with finding quality suppliers; the other two companies initially found even more rudimentary local industrial conditions for their projects in southern China (chapters 6 and 7).

Government Decision Making

Political Bargaining

Beijing's Role

Like the BJC venture, VW's project required the approval of most of China's top political and planning organizations. The Shanghai auto plan therefore had to pass by the CNAIC, MOFERT, the Ministry of Finance, the Bank of China, and the State Planning and Economic Commissions (in addition, of course, to the Shanghai government) before the State Council approved it.

The highest political leaders seemed to have played little active role in shaping the project. Unlike BJC, the Shanghai company had no serious crisis, and therefore felt less need to appeal to top leaders for aid. Zhao Ziyang's presence at the contract-signing ceremony, however, indicated his support.

Political changes later in the life of the venture may have portended benefit for SVW. In 1989, the city's Communist Party secretary, Jiang Zemin, was elevated to become the national party secretary. SVW sources note he was not particularly helpful to the car factory during his several years of political power in Shanghai; still, Jiang's new authority would most likely speed the city's overall economic development, and allow for incidental benefits to the joint venture.

In 1991, former mayor Zhu Rongji became a national vice premier. As already noted, Zhu had taken several steps to aid SVW while in Shanghai; his background had shown him to be generally sympathetic to foreign automotive projects. Furthermore, SVW officials felt his contacts developed during his previous tenure in Beijing had been quite valuable to the venture, and that he could at times lobby for some preferential treatment. His removal from Shanghai undoubtedly diluted his ability to help the company solve specific problems; his return to the capital, however, gave SVW a powerful voice at high central levels, and, overall, may have been a positive development for the auto factory.

The State Planning Commission played a major role in determining allocations of kit imports, a factor critical to SVW's development and localization success. As noted, the Chinese government rescued the country's automotive joint ventures in the depths of 1989's austerity by purchasing stockpiled vehicles. The State Council and the SPC, which played the major roles in this policy change, further granted SVW 2,000 additional CKD import licenses for 1990; as mentioned above, production nearly doubled in 1991. This sympathetic regulation implies the top central planners hoped to see SVW succeed.

At lower central government levels, SVW found a mixed bag of allies and adversaries. The Bank of China (BOC), subordinate to the ministry-level People's Bank of China, had, as a venture shareholder in the company, a natural inclination to support the project. It could help SVW by granting quick guarantee approval to foreign loan requests. As a bank, however, the BOC had relatively little influence over other central policy-making processes.

The CNAIC must have felt some schizophrenia over the SVW venture. As a partner in the company, it stood to reap financial benefits from the project, and therefore had an incentive to see it prosper. On the other hand, the CNAIC leader, Chen Zutao, harbored the same skepticism about foreign auto investors that became manifest during the BJC crisis. One SVW source sensed Chen had a predilection for "other manufacturers" (most likely a reference to General Motors, which Chen greatly admired). Furthermore, Chen's hostility toward the 1986 BJC settlement seemed to carry over to his 1988 attacks on SVW's local content rate; perhaps he took on the Germans out of a personal sense of spite over his previous bargaining loss. With Chen's retirement at the end of 1988, however, the attitude of the new CNAIC leadership toward SVW was unclear.

As noted above, the Machine-Building Ministry (FMMB) was the first to send representatives to Germany to propose a Shanghai joint venture. FMMB vice minister (later minister and CNAIC chief) Rao Bin was apparently a major proponent of the project. In the subsequent contract negotiations, however, the ministry deferred to the Shanghai government and to VW's future joint venture partners. Major negotiating points, however, were nearly always referred to Beijing, where the FMMB apparently could sway the direction of the talks. Thereafter, the ministry seemed to take little direct interest in SVW, though it could of course shape the venture through its subordinate, the CNAIC.

Like the other joint ventures studied here, then, SVW depended on the central government for production approval, loan guarantees, some raw materials supplies, and sales allocation. To win favor in Beijing, the Germans often relied on local politicians to help influence central leaders. The city government itself, however, was also crucial in solving many of the company's smaller problems.

The Shanghai Municipal Role

For influencing central government policy, SVW had, as mentioned, two natural allies in its partners, the Bank of China and the CNAIC. Shanghai Mayor Zhu Rongji, however, also used his influence, based on his previous posting in Beijing, to aid SVW. On occasion, for example, the central government's allocation of steel to the venture was insufficient. According to SVW sources, Zhu was key to increasing the company's steel quota to satisfy its needs. Such action obviated the need to turn to black market sources, virtually the only recourse when central supplies were too low.

As SVW moved to absorb the remaining space of the Shanghai Car Plant, final permission for the acquisition depended on State Council and CNAIC approval. Chinese sources asserted, however, that Mayor Zhu's opinion could at the time overrule that of the CNAIC, and that it would also hold great weight in the State Council. Zhu apparently expressed support for the merger as he left his mayor's post in April 1991, and the consolidation began in June of that year.

Of course, most local political action related to SVW was directed at solving problems on a smaller scale. The Municipal Automotive Small Group took the lead in coordinating the city's vehicle production policy. Ceremonially led by Zhu, the group in late 1990 included Vice Mayor Huang Ju, who succeeded Zhu as mayor in 1991. Huang, therefore, had some expertise and interest in the industry, and was then likely to extend this concern to his tenure as mayor.

The rest of the small group in 1990 consisted of representatives from the municipal planning, economic, international trade, and construction commissions, and the SAIC leader, Lu Ji'an. Each of the municipal bodies played a role in SVW's development: the international trade commission helped regulate the company's foreign exchange, and the economic and planning commissions charted the long-term localization process.

Second only to Zhu Rongji in securing city governmental support for SVW was SAIC head Lu Ji'an, who also had held the post of SVW board chairman from 1987. Lu had been a deputy economic commission chief in Shanghai since the early 1980s, and had simultaneously held the top SAIC position. With national moves to separate government and industry, Lu relinquished his commission post in 1989. Chinese sources, however, note that his power to influence municipal planning officials remained strong. Lu could, for example, help ensure a reliable municipal supply of electricity and water for the automotive plant by using his connections in the Shanghai government. He maintained his leading role at SVW into 1993.

Under the various commissions came two bodies specifically designed to aid the SVW project. The Shanghai Localization Office was to consult with venture managers on ways to speed the localization process. A "Shanghai Santana Commonwealth" included local research institutes and universities, and was designed to coordinate city-wide efforts to improve production of the German-designed vehicle. Of all the ventures examined in this study, SVW was the only one receiving advice from such an institutionalized forum.

In general, Shanghai seemed to take great pride in the progress of the German auto company. Local political appeals to the central government, combined with concrete steps to solve problems, helped the company reach significant production levels and high profits by the early 1990s. The funding of the Shanghai Volkswagen taxi company, noted above, was one of several important steps the city took to guarantee the venture would succeed. As Shanghai itself moved to reclaim its stake as China's most developed and cosmopolitan city, then, SVW appeared as an important building block in reaching this goal.

Misperception

Probably the best method of avoiding misperception is to emphasize exchange of accurate information and truthful intentions. The German representatives stressed such communication, leaving few surprises to stall SVW's progress. The joint venture contract was quite detailed, and anticipated many of the problems the company would face. As noted above, SVW avoided most of the complications that plagued BJC.

The only indication of Chinese wishful thinking lay in their apparent perception of significant flexibility in the contract. Once the Germans had agreed to a price for engines sold to them from the SVW factory, for example, they believed it was a solid commitment. The Chinese, however, insisted in 1990 that the selling price was too low, and apparently wanted to ignore the contract stipulations. It is unclear exactly how this dispute was settled, though with SVW's high profitability, the Germans were probably willing to make some concession beyond the stated contract terms.

The German trial venture in the early 1980s also served to dispel overoptimistic notions of what the venture could accomplish. Both sides had a chance to experience the levels of technology and quality standards that could be applied in Shanghai, and they thereby acquired realistic expectations for the company's first years of operation.

The SVW case, then, shows a clarity of purpose and achievement unmatched by BJC and the other ventures. Mutual understanding played a significant role in avoiding perceptual problems typical between the Chinese and Western foreign investors.

Policy Process Conclusions

The key to coherent policy making for the SVW project lay in thoughtful planning by the German representatives, and in their amenable Chinese counterparts who cooperated in writing the venture's original contract. When problems arose, the document provided guidance (generally in VW's favor) to indicate a rational course of action.

The central government placed great importance on SVW, and, as was the case with BJC, wanted to see it succeed. Chen Zutao's personal predilections made manifest some ambivalence to such foreign projects, however, and the calls for speedier localization were the major form of political pressure from Beijing. The 1989 central bailout of SVW (and other auto manufacturers), though, showed a consensus behind supporting automotive development.

Finally, local decision makers also displayed some hesitancy over SVW in its early years, moving slowly to take some necessary steps to solve problems. Misperception of their obligation may have contributed to their sloth. The new mayor, Zhu Rongji, however, rallied city officials to support the project, placing its prosperity (along with that of other foreign investments in Shanghai) high on his agenda. With Zhu's ability to influence Beijing officials in their policy making, SVW's future looked bright.

In sum, policy making in this case was somewhat fragmented at the central government level. Local unity came under the leadership of an activist municipal leader and, in a city geographically removed from Beijing, was vital to the success and development of the joint venture project.

Policy Implementation: Zhu Rongji's Catalytic Role

Finally, we look at how quickly the Chinese involved with the venture progressed on the bureaucratic learning curve. What forces helped change set operating procedures?

The early negotiations for SVW were characterized by typical delays, as lower-level officials were obliged to report many of their bargaining positions back to central leaders in Beijing. The contract talks subsequently lasted more than five years. As the discussions moved from the late 1970s into the early 1980s, however, German representatives noted the Chinese partners' eagerness for understanding detail, and that they seemed to become faster at comprehending financial and technological points. The willingness of the Chinese to accept CKD imports showed some improved sophistication, and ability to put faith in a foreign business concept (a difficult step in light of the then-recent Maoist policies of xenophobic self-reliance).

Once the venture was created, early problems of an indifferent municipal bureaucracy began to plague the corporation. Zhu Rongji, however, was able to break the standard political attitude of hesitancy and stultifying inaction. How could he disturb such a pattern?

Zhu seemed to possess a natural leadership quality, one linked to his early childhood hardships and college career. The ability to attract respect, then, played a significant role in his drive to transform Shanghai's political attitude toward automotive development.

Perhaps more important, however, was Zhu's lack of participation in the radical Maoist political stages of Chinese politics, stretching from 1957 to 1978. Zhu had thereby avoided much of the experience of operating in a highly politicized bureaucratic setting; on his reemergence in 1978, he could present a fresh outlook on Chinese policy making, one perhaps based on ideas cultivated over some two decades of political banishment. In sum, Zhu had little patience with the bureaucratic roadblocks he found in Shanghai, and sought to quickly clear them to allow the city to prosper.

Projections for SVW

For Shanghai Volkswagen, local political support, in particular that of Zhu Rongji, and SVW's precise contract helped make the venture a profitable and growing enterprise. With Zhu's return to Beijing, however, what were the company's prospects in the early 1990s?

Zhu's replacement as mayor, Huang Ju, seemed to share the former mayor's interest in the vehicle sector, as he played a leading role in the city's automotive small group. The continued prominence of SVW and SAIC chief Lu Ji'an also hinted of local support into the future.

Perhaps even more promising for the venture, however, was the emphasis the central government began to place in the early 1990s on making Shanghai once again a city of great prominence, one to compete with Hong Kong in economic success. In April 1990, the State Council allowed Shanghai to give tax exemptions to enterprises doing business with foreign investors, to give tax holidays to other foreign-invested projects, and to set up a bonded zone for duty-free imports of raw materials.[50] Foreign investment subsequently soared, adding $2 billion in 1992 to the total of $3.3 billion invested throughout the 1980s; new investment in 1993 alone reportedly topped $6 billion.[51]

Such progress would help guarantee the future success of SVW. The company could look forward to a larger pool of capable parts suppliers, able to deliver goods on a more modern transportation system. A higher standard of living in Shanghai would create a bigger potential sales market for the venture's vehicles. Finally, a more prosperous city government would probably be quicker to respond in an emergency with required aid, should the corporation need municipal assistance. As Shanghai developed, so would SVW. In the mid-1990s, the company's future looked promising.

6

Guangzhou Peugeot: An Island in Guangdong Province

Guangzhou Peugeot's location in wealthy Guangdong Province gave it some great potential for rapid development and freedom from central government scrutiny. "Heaven is high, and the emperor is far away," says a well-known Chinese proverb. Still, the venture did have to rely on Beijing for vital financial favors. With Guangzhou's status as a *jihua danlie* (independent planning unit), moreover, the governor of Guangdong also became a kind of distant emperor to the city; this relationship further shaped the political landscape surrounding the southern joint venture.

As the most recently founded and, generally, least publicized of the passenger car joint ventures operating in the early 1990s, the Guangzhou Peugeot Automobile Corporation (GPAC) presents less empirical and analytical evidence than do the other case studies. Interviews and some limited press coverage, however, paint a picture of a company in which both foreigners and Chinese overcame their geographical isolation and initial industrial deficiencies by using skillful political and organizational tactics. This chapter begins with a brief history of GPAC, then discusses the political maneuvers.

The Birth of Guangzhou Peugeot

With the exception of the Panda Motor Company's home in Huizhou, Guangzhou had the least developed infrastructure for an automotive factory among the present case studies. Lying at the mouth of the Pearl River delta, the fertile Guangzhou area had a tradition of agricultural production, growing rice, fruit, vegetables, and tea in abundance. The surrounding region was also known for its fish supplies. Guangdong Province, however, had few deposits of coal ore, and this deficiency discouraged the development of widespread heavy industry. Inadequate transportation to the region prohibited utilization of northern Chinese coal.[1]

Guangzhou's automotive industry therefore had little on which to build. The city itself began earnest road construction only in the 1920s, and fewer than 900 cars plied municipal streets in 1933.[2] The Canton Bus Company, however, had engaged in some vehicle manufacture, and in importing British and American cars and buses, though on a very small scale.[3] In 1943, a forerunner of the larger Guangzhou Automotive Manufacturing factory appeared as a general machinery plant.[4]

The 1949 Communist revolution brought some hopes to Cantonese desirous of greater industrial capabilities, though the southern Chinese obtained little immediate satisfaction. In 1956, Guangzhou's food-processing industry still constituted 42 percent of local industrial production; textiles took 12 percent, and only 11 percent came from machinery and metals processing.[5] The great costs of converting the light industry hindered rapid industrial development. Rail and road construction in the first years after 1949, however, had facilitated transport to and from the region.

The Great Leap Forward era of the 1950s ushered in efforts to change Guangzhou from a "consumption city" to an industrial base for South China,[6] and automotive production came to play an important role. The year 1962 saw the founding of the Guangzhou-Panyu Red Bridge Bus Assembly Factory. Construction of Peugeot's future partner, the Guangzhou Automotive Manufacturing plant (GAM) began in the adjacent Huangpu zone of the city in 1966, and was completed two years later. GAM built 3.5-ton Red Guard freight trucks and, later, East Wind buses.

The reform era of the 1980s accelerated the movement of heavy industry to the Guangzhou area. Between 1978 and 1985, agricultural output increased by 51 percent, but heavy industrial output more than doubled, from RMB 2.9 billion to RMB 5.9 billion.[7] Plans in Guangdong Province called for establishing automotive parts factories and more assembly plants. As investment dollars poured in from neighboring Hong Kong, the southeastern province was ripe for rapid industrial growth.

Such reforms were only beginning to emerge, however, in the early 1980s, when Guangzhou officials approached France's Peugeot SA to discuss an automotive joint venture.[8] Initial contact came at a French auto fair in Guangzhou in the spring of 1981, and, despite Peugeot's inclination to find a Chinese partner in the more industrialized northeast, concerted talks with Guangzhou municipal officials on a joint venture soon began. The French found the southern Chinese eager to expand automotive industry in their region.

Even in the early 1980s, Guangzhou presented a promising site for the French investors. Successful agricultural reforms were already making Guangdong farmers wealthier, enabling many of them to purchase light trucks imported from Japan.[9] A joint venture had the potential to service this new market.

The French were not alone in looking to Guangzhou; American and Japanese automotive companies were also interested in the developing southern city.[10] Chinese officials note, however, that U.S. economic ties with China were still progressing relatively slowly in the early 1980s. Furthermore, Guangzhou automotive leaders found the Japanese more interested in selling their cars to nascent taxi fleets than in delivering the technology needed to develop a healthy joint venture.

The Chinese side in the following four years of negotiations with Peugeot consisted mainly of officials from the future joint venture partner, GAM. Members of the municipal machinery and electronics bureau (*jidianju*) represented the city government, but the central authorities in Beijing played little role in the talks. The chief of the CNAIC in the early 1980s, Rao Bin, however, reportedly supported the GPAC proposal.

In 1983, Peugeot delivered sample vehicles of the type it hoped to produce in China; the first sent was a 504 model one-ton truck. The Chinese tested the truck for its quality and suitability to domestic road conditions. The model's low compression engine (and that of the model 505 station wagon, later added to the company's production plan) was capable of burning the lower octane gasoline commonly found in China.[11] Unlike Shanghai Volkswagen's development program, however, there was no experimental assembly of vehicles in Guangzhou.

By this time, Beijing Jeep's talks had already ended, with the announcement that the Americans would help develop a completely new vehicle for the Chinese market. According to officials in Guangzhou, however, the event had little impact on the GPAC discussions. Unlike negotiators in both Beijing and Shanghai, the southern Chinese never suggested that the joint venture should or could fashion a new model. Both sides agreed it would be too expensive, and neither wanted to embark on such a project.

The early stages of the venture talks focused on the company's product and technology, with several sessions lasting up to six weeks at a time. The final phases of negotiation turned to salary levels and finances; one Peugeot official implied these discussions were somewhat hurried.

Final agreement came in early 1985, and the contract, calling for twenty years of cooperation, was signed in March of that year. GPAC's initial capital was $52 million, making it France's biggest joint venture in China. Peugeot took a 22 percent share of the company, with GAM holding the largest investment of 42 percent. Other foreign partners included the National Bank of Paris, with 4 percent, and the World Bank's International Finance Corporation (which supplied a $29 million loan) at 8 percent. The rest of GPAC was owned by the Guangzhou branch of the Industrial and Commercial Bank of China, with 4 percent, and the China International Trust and Investment Corporation (CITIC), a central government entity, holding the remaining 20 percent. The Chinese therefore held 66 percent of the venture, and took six of eleven seats on the board of directors.

Although Peugeot held nearly a quarter of the company, it made no capital investment, instead contributing manufacturing equipment, plant design, and manufacturing licenses. The main Chinese partner, GAM, supplied the plant's land and building, together with $4.3 million. GPAC thereby inherited about two-thirds of the GAM factory space.[12] By early 1985, then, GPAC had all the rudiments for a viable automotive venture. How did it fare?

GPAC's Development, 1985–1991

Following GPAC's contract signing in March 1985, the company's board held its first meeting in September. The venture's development plan had three stages: first, it would reach a target annual production capacity of 15,000 504 model trucks; the second stage would raise production to a total of 30,000 vehicles, adding the 505 model station wagon. Finally, the third stage envisaged annual production of 50,000 trucks, station wagons, and a model 505 four-door sedan. The company was further contractually obliged to export one-third of its output; the rest could be sold to domestic Chinese buyers.

GPAC's contract also included an ambitious localization program. Over the first five years of production, the venture was to reach 90 percent local parts content for exported vehicles, and 98 percent localization for domestically sold automobiles.

At the birth of GPAC, China's GAM employed more than 3,000 workers, still producing the plant's East Wind buses and Red Guard trucks.[13] Peugeot's early plan was to spend two years modernizing the plant and adding new equipment. The foreigners further implemented training programs for Chinese, sending more than 100 of them to France to learn techniques of management, engineering, electronics, parts supply, and new technology.[14]

Like Volkswagen's Shanghai venture, GPAC's first troubles were rooted in poor conditions at the old GAM facility. Equipment was outdated and workers' training levels fell far below what the French had expected.[15] Peugeot had to compensate by dispatching more of its expensive foreign managers to Guangzhou, and by training many more Chinese in Europe than initially planned.[16]

At the production level, further problems arose. Chinese resentful of the expatriate managers' high salaries and benefits were slow to take orders. GPAC reportedly fought battles with GAM over factory space (GAM continued to produce buses in its remaining one-third of the plant). Furthermore, the Chinese were ever eager to increase the size of GPAC's labor force beyond what the French wanted.[17] The French, on the other hand, wanted to spur production and pay their employees more than the average auto worker earned at a state-owned factory; but the Chinese at GPAC feared resentment from the GAM employees (who earned standard wages) working nearby.[18]

Faced with such early and unexpected troubles, the additional problem of parts localization came as a further unwelcome burden. Initially, GPAC could find no sources of tires, glass, or other relatively simple items that reached its quality standards; even local paint failed to meet Peugeot's requirements.[19]

The reliance on imported vehicle kits quickly sparked problems similar to those encountered by BJC. In late 1986, production stopped for more than two months, as Peugeot and its Chinese partners disagreed over the price GPAC should pay for the CKDs.[20]

Unlike BJC, Guangzhou Peugeot suffered no shortage of foreign exchange. The company's problems were found in the growing strength of the French franc. GPAC's contract called for the Guangzhou Light Automotive Sales Company (GLASC), a corporation primarily concerned with marketing Peugeot's products, to purchase kits at a fixed franc price. From mid-1985 to early 1987, however, the franc appreciated some 110 percent against the renminbi, making it more difficult for GLASC to sell the more expensive assembled vehicles in China.[21]

In July 1986, GLASC asked Peugeot to lower its CKD price, but the French balked. The disagreement resulted in nearly six months of negotiations. GPAC's contract stipulated the 1985 purchase price to be 47,000 francs, and the 1986 price to rise to 53,580 francs. With the franc's appreciation, however, the price rose from about $5,060 in 1985 to $8,500 by the end of 1986. Eventually, the two sides agreed on a price of 48,000 francs, and orders resumed in early 1987.[22]

Throughout the disagreement, the venture apparently never lacked hard currency. The municipal government had pledged its own foreign exchange reserves to GLASC for kit purchases, and encouraged Guangzhou banks to sell hard currency to the auto marketer at official exchange rates.[23] Furthermore, GPAC could rely on its World Bank partner, the International Finance Corporation, to supply needed hard currency loans (though the central government's Bank of China had to guarantee such transactions).

As with the Volkswagen venture, the municipal government also took the responsibility for investing in parts supplies development to foster the localization process, which began in earnest in 1988. By 1990, the parts for about 19 percent of GPAC's light truck (model 504) and 16 percent of its station wagon (model 505) came from domestic suppliers (see figure 6.1). From 1988 to 1990, the city invested some RMB 200 million to develop localization industry, allowing GPAC to source car seats, headlights, dashboards, carpets, and other items within China. Guangzhou municipal industry had much to gain by the joint venture's success, because, by 1991, the venture's own factory made 30 percent of the Chinese-manufactured parts, Guangzhou-area suppliers contributed 20 percent, while the remaining 50 percent came from other domestic sources, mainly outside of Guangdong.[24]

Despite GPAC's ability to address its localization troubles, the joint venture faced early problems with its contractual commitment to ex-

Figure 6.1. **Localization at Guangzhou Peugeot, 1987-93**

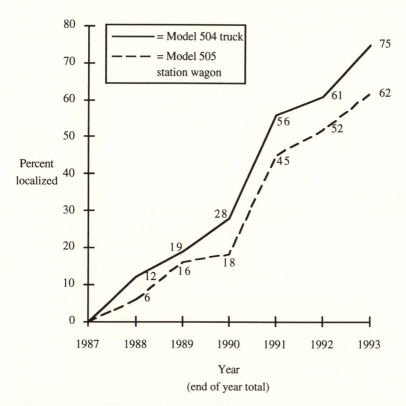

Year
(end of year total)

Sources: For 1988, Thurwachter, "Development of the Chinese Auto Industry," p. 17. For 1989, 1990 interviews in Guangzhou. For 1990, *China Daily*, February 4, 1991, p. 2. For 1991-93, 1994 telephone interview with Guangzhou Peugeot.

port vehicles. As the percentage of local content rose, the French became reluctant to send cars out of China that might have contained substandard Chinese-made parts; they feared the effect such sales would have on the Peugeot brand reputation (Shanghai Volkswagen had shared such a concern). By mid-1990, then, virtually no GPAC automobiles had been sent beyond China's borders.[25] Exports were further inhibited by the high price of the venture's product, which was buoyed by the shipping costs associated with the kit assembly process.

The company thereby failed to meet its contractual pledge to export one-third of its product, and gave little promise of achieving such an ability in the foreseeable future.

Guangzhou Peugeot faced renewed problems in 1989, as China's national economic austerity program discouraged domestic automotive sales by prohibiting factories and firms from buying vehicles without a permit. On November 4 of that year, GPAC stopped production after fulfilling its quota of 4,700 units. Although it had hoped for additional kit import licenses, the central government failed to allow more CKDs into Guangzhou.[26] "Originally, they granted us too few import licenses," complained one Peugeot employee. GPAC managers had believed they could persuade the central government to allow more CKD permits, but the Chinese refused. "They are controlling the economy very tightly," said the venture's source.[27]

The company was further disturbed in 1989 by the hesitancy of CITIC, one of its Chinese partners, to raise its equity investment. When GPAC moved toward the second stage of its development plan in September 1989, GPAC called for a further investment of 250 million French francs (or about $39 million); CITIC was to contribute 20 percent. But China's large trading company had financial problems of its own. "CITIC is in deep trouble—they cannot do anything for us and cannot make further contributions to the equity," said GPAC's French general manager, Bruno Grundeler, in late 1989.[28] (By June of 1990, however, CITIC had contributed its "phase two" equity. In mid-1991, CITIC also helped arrange a loan that further financed GPAC's second stage.)[29]

Financial problems also arose as the central government imposed localization taxes (similar to those faced by SVW). In October 1988, the tax added RMB 25,000 (about $6,700) to the price of each car; with an additional consumption tax of RMB 20,000 ($5,360), a model 505 station wagon cost RMB 200,000 ($53,600) in early 1989. GPAC's Grundeler complained, to no effect. "We told them they would kill the industry, but they ignored us," he said at the time.[30] GPAC, which had held fifth place in 1988 in the ranking of China's top ten joint ventures, disappeared from the list in 1989,[31] perhaps indicating some doubt among central government planners about the company's viability.

These developments contributed to a general feeling of gloom at the venture. One foreign manager commented in late 1989 that "if we had to make the decision to come to China over again, knowing what we know, we wouldn't come."[32]

By January of 1990, however, GPAC had gained some respite from the central government. The Chinese granted permission to construct 5,000 vehicles in 1990, enough, according to a GPAC manager, to allow the corporation a profit. The Bank of China loaned the venture needed capital, and the central government allowed more state enterprises to purchase vehicles. "We have no financial problems at the moment and will be getting additional export credits from France in the near future," said Grundeler, who, at the time, was "very optimistic about the future. It certainly can't be any worse than 1989."[33] In October 1990, GPAC's partner, the National Bank of Paris, showed its confidence by lending the company $15 million.

As figure 6.1 shows, by the end of 1990 localization rates had reached 28 percent for the model 504 truck and 18 percent for the 505 station wagon.[34] The central government, perhaps partly as a reward for such progress, nearly doubled GPAC's production limit for 1990, raising their kit import limit from 4,700 to 8,000. In early 1991, the venture bought more equipment from France to expand production of the model 505 sedan.[35] The company failed, however, to make China's top ten joint venture list in 1991 for a third consecutive year,[36] and, following foreign exchange shortfalls, actual production in 1990 only reached about 6,000 cars, about 75 percent of the limit.[37] In 1991, total production topped 15,000 vehicles, but output stabilized at about 20,000 cars and trucks in 1992 and 1993; the stage two production goal of 30,000 units remained elusive. Local content rates, though, had made progress by 1993 (see figure 6.1), though they fell short of the contract's initial targets.

Although GPAC faced significant economic problems in its early years—ones nearly as severe as those confronting Beijing Jeep—it managed to survive (though perhaps not thrive) with a combination of central government aid, local lobbying efforts (discussed in more detail later), and foreign cash infusions.

Stimuli

Foreign Forces

Peugeot representatives originally sought an automotive partner in the industrialized northeast of China. There, close institutionalized links between the established factories and the central government would have forced the French to take an active interest in courting Beijing officials. In the relative isolation of Guangzhou, however, the foreigners soon grasped the importance of solidifying local political friendships. As an area new to heavy industry, the southern automotive managers were less beholden to central authorities, so the French coalition of partners was able to exploit local needs for managerial guidance and financial support in ways more meaningful than those AMC or (to a lesser extent) VW could have applied.

Peugeot's choice of foreign partners was resourceful and rational. The Paris Bank and IFC were logical choices to provide monetary aid when needed.[38] On the Chinese side, GAM was the natural automotive partner in Guangzhou. It is not clear how CITIC and the Guangzhou Industrial Bank came to be GPAC partners, but their choice seems to have been a poor one: CITIC had chronic troubles in the late 1980s, and the bank's functions may have been superfluous with the French financial forces in reserve. Given the various troubles GPAC faced in its first years, a partner with closer ties to the central government might have been more useful.

The foreigners, however, were able to utilize municipal contacts very effectively to sway Beijing's policy in their favor. In the early 1990s, as southern China's economic and political power began to show signs of a schism with Beijing, such local allies appeared to have been a very valuable investment for the future of the French foreign firm.

Domestic Economic Forces

By the mid-1980s, China had already signed joint venture projects with AMC and VW; the rash of vehicle imports during these years, however, left the Chinese amenable to further cooperative production. A retrospective examination of foreign automotive ventures, though, indicates that Peugeot may have arrived at a disadvantageous period in the economic demand cycle.

Following GPAC's 1985 contract, China signed no more major passenger car joint venture agreements for nearly six years,[39] indicating a weakened market for automobiles. Considering the glut in the passenger car market during the retrenchment year of 1989, the French might have found a more receptive market had they begun production somewhat later.

The impetus for the project, of course, lay more in the economic conditions of southern China than in those of the nation as a whole. As mentioned above, Guangdong's rapidly developing economy cried out for foreign investment, and proved irresistible to the Peugeot team seeking a partner.

The relative lack of heavy industrial infrastructure in the Guangzhou area proved one of the most serious handicaps to the GPAC corporation. The venture encountered outdated factory equipment, and a dearth of suitable suppliers in the immediate Guangzhou area. In some sense, GPAC was meant to fill a vacuum, though the necessary development work was substantial.

The wild card in the domestic economic environment was Hong Kong, and the Pearl River delta area southeast of Guangzhou. After Hong Kong returns to Chinese control in 1997, the former colony stands to be a ready market for Peugeot's nearby manufacturing plant. GPAC expected an edge over Volkswagen manufacturers, as transport costs from northern China would add to the price of selling in Hong Kong and its rapidly developing environs. If Hong Kong is smoothly integrated into the Chinese economy, therefore, the French venture could receive a big boost.

Government Decision Making

Political Bargaining

Beijing's Role

By early 1985, the Chinese central leadership, facing staggering vehicle import bills, seemed to have acquiesced to the notion of foreign-invested automotive projects. Unlike some of the early hostility Beijing Jeep encountered, GPAC sources reported general goodwill among top officials. Zou Jiahua, for example, appeared to have been somewhat of an ally to the venture, helping in May 1990 to get central approval for GPAC to move into the second phase of its production.[40]

GPAC officials felt some threat from the incipient Panda Motor Company forming in the eastern part of the province (see chapter 7). Leaders who opposed or had some reservations about Panda's production plans (including Zou and, to some degree, Li Peng) expressed implied support for an exclusive GPAC right to sell its product in the southern Chinese market.

Significant expressions of central support came in 1989, at the height of the venture's despair. As noted, the central officials approved the purchase of backlogged Peugeot cars and trucks siting in Guangzhou storage lots. Perhaps more important, however, was the permission the company received to import an additional 3,300 kits in 1990; this number stood in contrast to the mere 2,000 extra kits allotted SVW, and some 1,000 to 2,000 kits for BJC.[41] In general, however, top officials showed little interest in the Peugeot project; one GPAC employee asserted that central leaders did not comprehend the problems the company faced, and seldom came to tour the factory.

Day-to day central concern for the joint venture, then, appeared to focus on the ministerial level. CITIC, one of the company's partners, had ministerial ranking at its formation. According to GPAC sources, however, CITIC was more of a burden to the company than a benefit.

CITIC was reluctant in the late 1980s to fulfill its obligation to raise its equity in the corporation. The unwillingness to contribute the required capital came at a critical juncture for GPAC, and may have pushed the joint venture to the brink of collapse. Perhaps more significant, however, was CITIC's general uselessness in influencing central policy to remedy GPAC problems. Foreign and Chinese employees at the Guangzhou company said CITIC actually had little power to sway Beijing officials on policy issues such as the granting of import licenses. In light of this, GPAC very seldom called on CITIC to help solve problems.

The foreign trade ministry, MOFERT, played a decisively greater role in determining GPAC's development, though not necessarily in a positive way. In the spring of 1990, the venture moved toward implementation of the second phase of its development plan. According to GPAC sources, MOFERT claimed the right to unilaterally approve the recapitalization of the corporation; the ministry felt the State Council and SPC need not act on the matter. As the intragovernmental conflict continued, GPAC suffered from the delay in receiving higher production permission. Finally, MOFERT acknowledged that it alone could not approve the expansion plan, and, with higher certification, the venture moved to its second manufacturing phase.[42] A GPAC official put MOFERT's action in the context of a larger conflict, one between northern central government leaders on one side and southern enterprises and politicians on the other, with both seeking the maximum degree of independent policy-making ability.

While MOFERT used the GPAC controversy as a tool to assert its authority over joint venture development, the CNAIC seemed detached from shaping its progress. Both the CNAIC and GPAC officials interviewed placed little importance on the central automotive corporation's involvement in the Guangzhou factory. As Guangzhou was forming its Municipal Automotive Small Group in late 1990, there were no plans to include a CNAIC representative. A GPAC official indicated, however, that the CNAIC would be welcome in the group, as the venture sought a channel of influencing the corporation's decisions.

A CNAIC official noted that the distance from Beijing was a decisive factor in reducing his organization's influence in Guangzhou. Southern aloofness also may have been a factor. Still, a GPAC representative pointed out that, should the CNAIC want to affect the venture's course, it could appeal to the State Planning Commission; the alliance of Zou Jiahua and CNAIC Chief Cai Shiqing in the early 1990s made such a control process more viable.

Before summarizing the powers of the central authorities, we turn to the provincial and municipal levels of government, ones which, as mentioned above, were critical to success in an area far from Beijing's close observation.

Local Politics

The attitudes of the Guangdong provincial and local Guangzhou governments toward GPAC displayed distinct differences. Most sources interviewed indicated Guangdong authorities were generally opposed to the GPAC project. The root of this attitude lay in Guangzhou's designation as a *jihua danlie* (independent planning unit). As such an entity, Guangzhou reported its economic plan directly to Beijing, leaving provincial authorities with little control over the city's development. Guangzhou, then, had a natural incentive to ignore surrounding provincial areas, leaving Guangdong ambivalent about its capital city's progress.

In the case of GPAC, Guangdong leaders originally opposed the venture's founding, according to Chinese sources, fearing the automotive company would siphon off central funds intended for the province. Prominent among those later indifferent to the venture was Ye Xuanping, governor from 1985 to 1991.[43] Over his term in office, the province sought to develop the Sanxing automotive group in the southern Guangdong city of Zhanjiang over GPAC, to avoid a Guangzhou monopoly in the vital industry.[44]

The province's other major planned automotive corporation was Panda Motors. Panda was located in Huizhou, a city that was not a *jihua danlie*; that project, then, was far more attractive to provincial authorities. As chapter 7 notes, Guangdong leaders took several steps to further Panda's development, including the establishment of a special government office to coordinate measures to aid Panda. GPAC, by contrast, enjoyed little of the provincial attention lavished on Panda. There was no special office in Ye Xuanping's organization to help GPAC solve problems.[45] Several sources further indicated that Guangzhou's planning status lent a natural inclination for the municipality to rely on itself to solve problems, and left little dependence on Guangdong's help. One provincial official noted GPAC was "Guangzhou's project," and further implied that Panda was much more of a Guangdong concern.[46] (One GPAC source noted, with some dismay, that his venture was not consulted in the province's process of approving Panda.)

Guangzhou municipal officials, then, were key to GPAC's survival and prosperity. The city had arranged its personnel ranks with the automotive sector in mind: Vice Mayor Xie Shihua had been GPAC's first board chairman, from 1985 to 1987; and the venture's chairman in 1990, Xie Gancheng, was simultaneously the deputy chief of Guangzhou's Machinery and Electronics Bureau.

GPAC officials uniformly praised local officials, in particular for their actions that influenced both provincial and central government policy. In early 1990, for example, Guangdong's provincial price bureau was slow to approve the price of the venture's model 504 pickup truck. Vice Mayor Xie lobbied the bureau to speed its decision process; this allowed GPAC to sell the truck at the certified rate.

Xie Shihua was also key to obtaining concessions from the central government. In 1990, for example, Xie made a special trip to Beijing to lobby for increased kit import permission. He was responsible in part for the extra 3,300 licenses subsequently allowed GPAC.

The municipal government also took many local actions to aid the venture. As noted above, the city was willing to contribute its own hard currency reserves to GPAC when needed. Furthermore, though Guangdong lacked a provincial unit to aid GPAC, Guangzhou created a special city office to coordinate the joint venture's development. In 1991, this office organized localization supply efforts and city investment in parts manufacture. These tasks were of greater benefit to the joint venture than the work of GPAC board chairman Xie Gancheng's municipal Machinery and Electronics Bureau, which formulated industrial regulations and tallied and reported statistics. (Xie's knowledge of the bureau's work, however, undoubtedly was of value to the company.)

To spur automobile sales, the municipal government reportedly decided in 1993 to allow 5 percent of local families to own a car by the year 2005; this would add a potential 50,000 families to the private car market.[47] In 1994, the city took a further step to aid sales, as it moved to cut the number of bicycles on Guangzhou streets from 3 million to 1 million by the year 2010.[48]

GPAC highlights the ironic phenomenon of a provincial capital city operating its industry at odds with its surrounding province. Although municipal officials seemed able to supply the needed support for the automotive venture, the lack of cooperation with Guangdong most likely portended some inconsistent development of the economy in the southern Chinese province.

Misperception

Southern Chinese officials seemed to have avoided the kind of wishful thinking found among negotiators of the Beijing Jeep venture. They realized, as did Shanghai officials negotiating for the SVW company, that an automotive venture would require imported car kits and a localization process. The timetable for achieving high rates of local content, however, was overly ambitious, though not entirely unrealistic.

The generally rational approach Guangzhou leaders took to development of GPAC may be based on previous experience with foreign investors. By 1984, Guangdong Province claimed 492 joint ventures and 1,735 cooperative ventures.[49] Guangzhou had 27 joint ventures, including a large American investment by Beatrice Companies to process food, and 219 cooperative ventures.[50] (For rough comparison, all of China had some 931 joint ventures by the end of 1984.)[51] The experienced southern municipal officials were therefore better able to forecast problems, such as those of hard currency balancing and localization funding.

In the GPAC case, more misperception may in fact be attributed to the foreign investors. Peugeot seemed to think that relatively higher standards of living in southern China would guarantee rapid equipment modernization; they were subsequently frustrated with the slow process of improving GAM's outdated factory and educating poorly trained workers. Peugeot officials also initially believed raw materials were available on free markets, and were surprised that the company was dependent on centrally planned allocations.[52]

In general, then, GPAC's problems were based more in unexpected structural economic problems, such as the fluctuating currency exchange rate and China's austerity measures in the late 1980s, rather than in irrational decision making clouded by Chinese misperception. As noted, however, the foreigners' impression of a rapidly developing southern economy may have raised expectations of technical competence to unrealistic levels.

Policy Process Conclusions

The case of Guangzhou Peugeot points out the significant degree of policy independence achievable in a rapidly developing city far from Beijing. Still, GPAC could not act completely without central approval. China's top central leaders paid little attention to the southern auto venture. Unlike Beijing Jeep, the company was not a national showcase; unlike Shanghai Volkswagen, GPAC was not in a city with close industrial ties to the capital. Furthermore, GPAC's French banking connections made it less dependent on China's centrally controlled foreign cash reserves.

The venture, then, only caught central concern at major development stages; the conflict between MOFERT and the SPC over GPAC expansion approval illustrates this point. The central leaders, of course, also wanted to maintain as much control as possible over the distant factory, and required municipal officials to pay a kind of homage in lobbying for a greater number of import licenses.

Local officials were key to GPAC's success. The French did well to develop friendships in the city government; and the municipal officials had their own interests in seeing GPAC prosper. Once the foreign investors overcame early misconceptions about the possibilities of manufacturing in southern China, the venture partners developed a good cooperative relationship.

The most surprising element in GPAC's political support was the indifference and, at times, opposition displayed by Guangdong provincial officials. In granting Guangzhou planning independence, the reform process encouraged competition, but also divisiveness, in the southern economic development drive. Coordinated policy making became more difficult, and GPAC may have suffered from the province's devoting its expertise and resources to helping Panda Motors and the Sanxing group.

Policy Implementation: GPAC's Course

The most impressive, and at the same time effective, standard operating procedure in the political decision making for the GPAC case was the use of local officials as conduits to higher levels. Municipal leaders had a vested interest in seeing the venture succeed, and the French exploited their willingness to influence Beijing to win aid during China's economic retrenchment period, a higher number of import licenses, and other concessions. Guangzhou typically relied on a vice mayor (Xie Shihua) to solve problems with both the central and provincial governments.

This type of policy process stands in contrast to that of the Beijing Jeep case, in which problems were solved by leaping over local levels to reach central leaders. Here, Guangzhou's industrial history and distance from the capital determined the style of policy making necessary for success.

With generally rational methods of shaping government policy toward GPAC ingrained early on, the local officials apparently found little need, or even possibility, to modify their behavior. Southern officials greeted with the first foreign investments in the late 1970s most likely were unfamiliar with the customs and requirements of capitalist entrepreneurs, and undoubtedly had to adjust their policy making to accommodate the foreign business style. By the time GPAC had established itself, however, officials in Guangzhou seemed to have learned useful procedures for solving policy problems particular to such projects. Structural difficulties remained, of course: it was difficult to quickly modernize equipment or to instill notions of quality in local managers and workers. In general, however, most of the policy "learning" process had taken place before GPAC operation began, leaving the venture with a supportive local bureaucracy capable of accomplishing required tasks.

Summary and Projections

The most limiting factor for the Guangzhou Peugeot venture was the company's distance from areas with developed heavy industry. This factor led directly to foreigner frustrations in the early production stages. As time passed, however, the local and foreign investment in regional localization projects helped ameliorate this problem.

Guangzhou's distance from Beijing was also an obstacle at times. The venture depended on the central government for key elements of its development (import licenses, purchases by government units, etc.), and was hampered by the difficulty of cultivating political ties in the remote capital.

In GPAC's weakness, however, lies great potential future strength. The integration of Hong Kong into China's southern economy promises greatly expanded technical capability and market sales in the early years of the next century. The wealth of local Chinese private businesspeople also has been rising quickly in southern China, and, with uninterrupted progression, will leave many of them prosperous enough to purchase a private vehicle by the end of the decade.

If China's decentralization and economic reform processes continue, Guangzhou's isolation from Beijing could offer GPAC another advantage: as central restrictions and powers decline, local resourcefulness and ability to solve problems could allow the company to function more smoothly than other ventures more dependent on central aid and guidance. Thus, while a company like Beijing Jeep might flounder without central support, GPAC could still prosper in distant Guangzhou, far from Beijing.

7

Panda Motors

In late December of 1988, Dr. Charles Kim, president of Panda Motors Corporation, arrived in Huizhou, Guangdong Province. He soon found that he had reached the end of a long search for a home for his fledgling automobile company. Less than two years later, Panda, the largest wholly foreign-owned enterprise in China, had made giant leaps over bureaucratic hurdles, while at the same time emerging as a potentially powerful wild card in China's automotive development plans. By 1992, however, Panda was essentially dead, killed by its own, rather than Chinese, failures.

This chapter traces the history of Panda from its initial approaches to the Chinese government, through its clever development of ties to the Chinese, and its initial ability to solve serious problems quickly and effectively. As in previous chapters, analysis focuses on the foreign and domestic stimuli acting on the political decision makers, the actions of the politicians, and the resulting development of the automotive project, beginning, however, with a historical narrative of the Panda company.

Panda's Development

The seeds of the Panda project were planted in preliminary discussion among South Korean and Korean-American investors (many of whom remain anonymous) in 1986. The actual company did not manifest itself, however, until September of 1988, when Panda was incorporated in Delaware under an umbrella organization called the Virginia Business Enterprise Group.[1] With headquarters in Vienna, Virginia, the automobile company was a coalition of several companies worldwide, including HWH Holding Group of West Germany, which manufactured automobile parts; the Tong Il Company, a South Korean transmission maker; and an automotive design firm based in the United States.

Although many companies participated in forming the Panda organization, the force behind the project was actually the South Korean–based Unification Church. The church's leader, Reverend Sun Myung Moon, publicly stated his desire to "create an automobile production city in Southern China in order to enhance the People's Republic of China's export opportunities."[2] Panda was also "meant to create a constructive relationship with the top leadership in Beijing so that we might become partners in a new Asian-Pacific era."[3] Moon, furthermore, denied the suggestion that Panda was merely out for profit:

> The purpose of this investment is not so that I can establish a foothold in China as a way of making a fortune for myself. It is my principle that not so much as a penny of the profits from the China project will be taken out of China. These profits will be reinvested in China to construct the International Highway of Peace and to bring China up to international standards in other areas of high technology.[4]

This "International Highway" is based on a 1981 Moon proposal to construct a roadway from Tokyo to London, a route including a tunnel from Japan to South Korea. The road would traverse North Korea, then pass Dandong in Northeast China on its way to Beijing, Moscow, and eventually on to Western Europe. Whether or not this scheme was actually practical, the Unification Church seemed intent on pursuing it, perhaps with the goal of leaving a lasting memorial to the achievements of Moon's church. In 1988, in fact, representatives of the Unification Church approached China's Transportation Ministry with a proposal to build a stretch of highway from Dandong (on North Korea's border with China) to Beijing. These plans actually received tentative approval from then-CCP leader Zhao Ziyang, Premier Li Peng, and State Planning Commission Chairman Zou Jiahua, before being sent to the Transportation Ministry for further consideration.[5]

Panda Motors commenced a drive to raise funds for its automotive project, and soon had reportedly raised at least $200 million to $300 million, much of it in loans from South Korean and Japanese banks. At its 1988 incorporation in the United States, the company had registered capital of $100 million.

Panda apparently chose the United States, rather than South Korea, as its home because China and South Korea at the time lacked diplomatic relations and economic treaties to guarantee the safety of the investment. In assembling the company's top management, the Unification Church recruited Douglas MacArthur II, a former U.S. ambassador to Japan and nephew of the famous World War II general (who, ironically, had fought the Communist Chinese), to be the company's board chairman. Real management power seemed to rest, however, in the hands of former South Korean general Bo Hi Pak, treasurer and vice chairman of Panda and a chief aide to the Reverend Moon. The president of Panda was Dr. Charles Kim, a Korean-American with several years of experience in automotive parts exports. Dr. Kim was also reportedly the brother-in-law of the prominent South Korean politician (and future president) Kim Young Sam.[6]

After Panda had assembled its management team and raised funds, it composed a project feasibility study for the Chinese. Panda presented its project as a wholly foreign-owned enterprise (WFOE), rather than as a joint venture. WFOE's were allowed in China as of 1986, following the National People's Congress adopting a twenty-four-article law outlining the rights and obligations of such entities.[7] Among other points, the advantages of such an arrangement included greater protection of trade secrets that might otherwise need to be revealed to a joint venture partner; enhanced management control; more flexibility to meet changing market demands; and greater control of the corporation's finances.[8] Panda took this route in part to avoid lengthy negotiations with a Chinese partner; furthermore, it recognized that under China's austerity program introduced in mid-1988, there were in any case few funds for a prospective joint venture company to contribute.

Once Panda had chosen to manifest itself as a WFOE, it was bound by conditions of the 1986 Chinese law. This regulation specified that Panda was to "export all or most of their products."[9] Panda therefore promised in its feasibility study to export 100 percent of the cars it was to manufacture in China. Reports vary on the company's projected market, but future sales sites reportedly included Southeast Asia, Eastern Europe, and perhaps India.[10] In any case, Panda promised to make a small, low-priced vehicle, in the $5,000 price area, so it would therefore probably not be competitive in the industrial world's marketplace, already dominated by Japanese and South Korean manufacturers producing slightly more expensive but higher-quality products.

In its presentation to the Chinese, Panda further pledged to invest up to $1 billion over ten to fifteen years to build several factories at the chosen production site. Panda representatives also promised to develop a new car model, but were unclear as to the exact type of vehicle they would manufacture. (In fact, as late as October of 1990, Chinese officials in Huizhou were still ignorant of the type of car that would roll off the assembly line.)

The company had ambitious production goals. For its first assembly plant, Panda forecast manufacture of 50,000 cars by the end of 1990, 200,000 by the end of 1991, and a capacity of 300,000 vehicles reached in 1992. The venture would function initially as an assembly plant, importing much of its needed parts and raw materials. It reportedly promised, however, to localize up to 10 percent of its vehicles composition each year. To this end, the company hinted it might be willing to invest in local parts-supplying factories, to help suppliers reach necessary quality standards.

Panda's feasibility study also outlined requirements for its factory site. First, because the company's cars were to be exported, the production area would have to be near a fairly well developed port, one deep enough to accommodate large ships. Ideally, it would also be close to roads and railways, to allow shipment of incoming parts. Panda promised to construct its own factory, along with housing and other needed structures, but it expected the Chinese to help with roadways and public transportation facilities.

One element omitted from Panda's proposal was reference to the Unification Church. Perhaps the project backers felt Chinese knowledge of the church connection would hamper the venture's chances for acceptance. The official Chinese reaction to the affiliation with the religious group was that the government did not discriminate against investors based on their religion. "There is no link between a person's religious belief and his investment in China," said one government leader in a later reference to the project.[11] As of mid-1991, there was little evidence Panda sought converts to the church's faith in China, though one foreign writer did claim the venture had such a goal.[12] Panda officials denied such conjecture.[13]

By the end of 1988, then, Panda had all it required to approach a prospective Chinese production site: money, a production plan, and a list of the plant site's requirements. Company representatives, led by Dr. Kim, turned first to some of China's more industrially developed cities, including Changchun, Shiyan, Beijing, Dalian, Qingdao, and, as a first choice, Shanghai.[14] These cities held promise of future parts-supplies capability, a necessary feature should Panda seek to accomplish its localization goals.

It is unclear why these cities rejected Panda's proposal. Shanghai Mayor Zhu Rongji reportedly felt the project was unnecessary, and would only be a waste of his city's resources and efforts.[15] Zhu and others apparently also took note of the auto company's short history, and their doubts about Panda's viability grew. In Panda's opinion, however, the sites that rejected Kim were in any case suboptimal for the project. Shanghai, for example, lacked the necessary land for the new factory. Shiyan's proposal to ship vehicles on barges down the Yangtze did not appeal to the company.[16]

When Dr. Kim arrived in Guangdong Province's Huizhou in December, he received a much warmer reception than he had in previous site visits. Why was Huizhou eager to impress Panda? Although Huizhou, a city of some 2.2 million people, lies in the booming Pearl River delta of Guangdong, it had been slow to implement economic reforms, and felt a desire to catch up with its prosperous neighbor, Shenzhen (figure 7.1). Huizhou authorities had been strong supporters of Mao Zedong's policies, and city leaders were loyal to the radical military leader Lin Biao until his fall in the early 1970s. The city delayed implementing reforms until 1984, by which time it was obvious that surrounding areas were leaving Huizhou behind. A new leadership saw the need for foreign investment to compete, and such investment from 1988 to 1990 averaged $294 million each year, four times that of each of the four years from 1984 to 1987.[17]

The city was also attractive to Panda officials, for several reasons. First, Huizhou is close to Hong Kong; by sea, the port of Autou is only forty-seven nautical miles from the British colony. The Shenzhen special economic zone is also quite near. Second, because the land near the factory site is hilly, there was little agricultural activity, so the development of industry would not be accompanied by the difficulties arising from displaced peasantry. Furthermore, Autou represents a natural port site, and the regional government saw much potential for developing shipping import and export.

Dr. Kim's first meetings were with a Huizhou delegation led by Vice Mayor Lin Xushen and Municipal Party Secretary Deng Huaxuan. Kim presented the officials his company's feasibility study, to-

138

Figure 7.1. Map of Huizhou Region

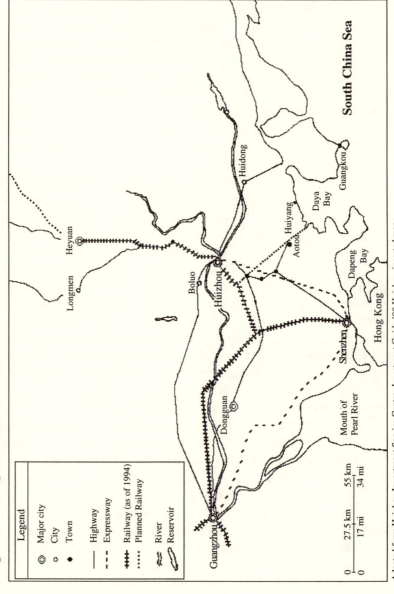

Adapted from Huizhou Investment Service Centre, *Investment Guide '90 Huizhou*, inserted map.

gether with some detailed financial information. Local municipal technicians also examined the plans, and apparently gave a favorable report. Huizhou officials knew Panda was a new company, but were impressed by the presence of Douglas MacArthur II as board chairman. One high-ranking Huizhou official commented in an interview that he believed MacArthur would not work for a bad company.[18]

The Huizhou government may also have felt there was little substantial risk involved in the Panda project. Panda officials have pointed out that, were the project to fold after a year or two, the region would still benefit from infrastructural improvements brought by construction investment. Construction workers would receive salaries, and, if the project did successfully begin production, plant workers would gain valuable skills. Furthermore, if Panda managed to turn a profit, it would pay taxes.[19] By February of 1989, then, Huizhou's enthusiastic officials had approved the project.[20]

In the early months of 1989, the central government's State Council sent a small group of specialists (*zhuanjia xiaozu*) to Huizhou to investigate Panda's plans. According to article six of the 1986 WFOE law mentioned above, the State Council or its agents had to approve the project before it could proceed. After ascertaining that Panda's finances were in order, and that raw materials would be imported from outside China, and automobiles would be exported, the group approved the new venture.[21] Still, Beijing leaders needed some further prodding, and only after sustained lobbying by Huizhou Mayor Li Jinwei and Vice Mayor Li Hongzhong would the State Council actually allow the project to go ahead.[22] One of the project's key supporters at this time reportedly was Communist Party Secretary Zhao Ziyang.

Dr. Kim returned to Huizhou in March 1989, as the project sailed through Guangdong's provincial bureaucracy. On March 7, the province gave its approval in principle, pending further research. Ten days later, the provincial government approved Panda's feasibility study and company organization; on March 20, the Guangdong foreign economic relations and trade commission (COFERT) signed on. Finally, on March 23, Panda got its operating license (*zhunshengzheng*) from the province.[23] Only three months after its initial presentation in Huizhou, Panda was then officially established. (This approval time stood in sharp contrast with that noted in the previous case studies; the other ventures took five years or more to get Beijing's certification. The rapidity of Panda's licensing is analyzed in later sections.)

Progress and Problems

Once the project had been approved, Huizhou authorities began to promote spending designed to aid the new auto company. The city government allocated RMB 200 million (about $53 million) to build two thermal power plants capable of producing 60 megawatts of power. The authorities also promised the required port, one capable of serving ships weighing 35,000 dead-weight tons.[24]

Panda moved forward with its plans throughout the turbulent events during Beijing's 1989 spring student demonstrations. The June 4 killings, however, brought pause to the company officials working in China. On June 5, Panda administrators appeared for the first time at the commercial section of the U.S. consulate in Guangzhou, obviously shaken and hoping for advice. The fall of their supporter Zhao Ziyang may have contributed to their anxiety.

The crisis time soon abated for the Panda people, however, and the company carried on with its plans. On June 27, 1989, Panda held its ground-breaking ceremony in Huizhou; present at the event were Mac-Arthur, Dr. Kim, Bo Hi Pak, and Guangdong Vice Governor Kuang Jie, who led the Chinese delegation.[25] Panda's inauguration, held fewer than four weeks after the Tiananmen Square incident, was to provide Chinese propaganda organs with a grand example of new foreign investment in the face of contract cancellations and world economic isolation. In a series of articles, the official press emphasized the huge scale of the "American" investment.[26] One publication later claimed that "Panda had rendered a great service in breaking [foreign] economic sanctions."[27] No Chinese public media, however, reported the company's ties to the Unification Church, though Chinese leaders knew of the connection by early 1989.[28]

Panda's investment, though of great propaganda value, was actually not revealed until the middle of September 1989. One possible reason for this delay may have been Panda's fear of publicity before it had established itself; the company may also have wanted to avoid criticism for beginning a project so soon after the Tiananmen events.

A further reason for delaying the announcement, however, may have been central government hesitation over the project's viability. On July 9, 1989, Vice Governor Kuang Jie went to Beijing to report to Premier Li Peng. Li was apparently annoyed that Panda had avoided steps to coordinate its project with the national automotive agencies and the State Planning Commission. On July 19, then, Li Peng personally organized a second central government delegation to visit Huizhou, this one led by Chen Zutao, who was by then retired from his duties as chief of the CNAIC. The group stayed for ten days, studying the site and examining documents on Panda's background. At the end of the investigation, Chen recommended approval of the venture, citing his admiration of MacArthur's participation and Panda's pledge to export 100 percent of its product.[29] One source quoted Dr. Kim as saying at these meetings that "if we lacked the ability to export, we would not have invested hundreds of millions of dollars to build a factory."[30] Li Peng is said to have later emphasized this promise, proclaiming that "not one" Panda car would be sold within China.[31]

The company's first goal was to prepare the Huizhou site's land for construction. Panda had leased six square kilometers, rented for fifty years at RMB 10 (about $2.70) per square meter per year.[32] The chosen land was hilly, though, so construction teams were hired to flatten and pack the earth for the factory's foundation. This work was finished on some 400,000 square meters by the spring of 1990, and Panda began the construction of its assembly and stamping buildings later that year.

Panda had also rented the whole twenty-fifth floor of Hong Kong's new Bank of China building, apparently as its Asia headquarters. By early 1990, the company had only some ten employees working there, though, in addition to about fifteen in the United States, seven to ten in China, and others in various international offices. The Huizhou staff was led by Senior Vice President Xu Liyun, a Chinese citizen with permanent U.S. resident status.

Panda's next mission was to acquire machinery for its China factories. In late 1989, it bought stamping equipment from a closed General Motors factory in Hamilton, Ohio, and also purchased GM's four-cylinder engine tooling.[33] Up to the end of 1990, Panda refused to reveal the type of vehicle it would produce with this equipment, though it apparently planned to keep to the small model vehicle envisaged in its initial proposal.

The venture made steady progress in completing the factory's outer steel frame, but had discovered by early 1990 that the port facilities at Autou would not be ready to receive the large ships needed to carry the plant's equipment. On January 12, 1990, Dr. Kim met in the morning with Wang Renzhong, deputy director of the central National People's

Congress (or NPC, China's nominal parliament) standing committee, apparently to discuss the venture's troubles. Later that day, Kim and Vice President Xu met with Guangdong Governor Ye Xuanping and Vice Governor Kuang Jie; Chen Zutao was also present, sent by Beijing to advise Guangdong on Panda's affairs.

At this meeting, Kim expressed concern over the pace of construction of the needed Autou port. During the coming year, Panda planned to import some 1,200 forty-foot containers, and in 1991 wanted to bring in stamping presses, parts of which weighed up to 175 tons. The Autou port had only a single 3,000-ton class wharf, and no equipment to handle containers. Kim asked for immediate dredging of the harbor, so ships could at least arrive at the shore. The only alternative to this would be for Panda to ship its equipment to Hong Kong or Guangzhou, then transship the machinery to Autou in smaller vessels. This would be much more expensive.

Governor Ye listened to Panda's problems, and asked about other troubles. The Panda representatives expressed concern over their ability to recruit workers for the factory, noting they would need some 100,000 employees. Ye commented that the training period would take a minimum of one year.

The Guangdong governor went on to suggest a "shadow cabinet," headed by Chen Zutao, that would work closely with Panda to try to solve the type of problems mentioned at the meeting. He said the government would attempt to hurry construction of the needed port facilities, perhaps in conjunction with the Transport Ministry. Finally, according to a transcript of the meeting,

> the governor again praised Dr. Kim's determination to succeed, and promised the province's full support. The project was so critical to the province that failure was absolutely unthinkable. Yet, the governor advised Dr. Kim to be more realistic with his timetable, appreciating that China was not the U.S.[34]

Before the meeting closed, Panda officials thanked Ye for contributing his calligraphy for Panda's logo.

Early the next month, a delegation of nearly a dozen former U.S. congressmen, led by Democrat Richard Ichord of Missouri and Republican Robert Wilson of California, journeyed to China. Wilson and Ichord were reportedly paid lobbyists for Panda,[35] and their meetings with Premier Li Peng and Party Secretary Jiang Zemin received much media attention in China, in the wake of the post-Tiananmen U.S. travel ban on high-ranking American officials going to China. It is unclear whether Wilson and Ichord won any concessions for Panda, but the former congressmen made a visit to Huizhou after leaving Beijing. In any event, both Li and Jiang benefited by the positive feelings generated in being seen meeting important Americans.

Soon after the congressmen left China, Premier Li Peng toured the Panda facilities as part of a February inspection tour of Guangdong. Li was greeted by a small model of future factory buildings at the Huizhou site. The series of visits was a success for Panda, as Li later promised RMB 30 million (about $6.4 million) of state money to help develop the Autou port.

A trip for Guangdong and Huizhou officials in the spring of 1990, to visit Panda facilities in the United States, may also have generated good will. Travelers on this voyage reportedly included Huizhou Mayor Li Jinwei, Guangdong Vice Governor Kuang Jie, and Panda adviser Chen Zutao.

The auto company plodded along until June, when Shell Oil announced plans to form a joint venture petrochemical plant off the coast of Huizhou. Panda representatives complained that fumes from the factory might affect the paint applied to the company's cars. The new petrochemical joint venture, however, projected to cost $2.4 billion, was also a high-priority investment in the area, and Panda's objections apparently had little influence on the progress of the large project's negotiations. Guangdong did show its continuing concern for the venture, though, by creating the provincial Panda Automotive Small Group Office in Guangzhou in September 1990.[36]

Panda's most serious problem rose to the fore gradually as 1990 drew to a close. Where would the company sell its vehicles? In a mid-October interview, Huizhou municipal officials expressed anxiety over their belief that Panda had no certain market for the cars it would produce. They indicated that even Dr. Kim was unsure where his company would be selling. Panda treasurer Bo Hi Pak journeyed to Beijing in the autumn to meet CCP Secretary Jiang Zemin.[37] On this trip, he asked for permission to sell 30 percent of the company's output within China.

While such a proposal was permissible under WFOE laws, Panda's previous promises to export all of its cars may have made a policy switch politically difficult. It is unclear what reply the Beijing leadership gave Pak, though one source reported the Chinese government might have allowed Panda to sell some of its vehicles domestically if the company were in serious trouble.[38]

The company was also plagued by tardiness in finalizing its vehicle design. As mentioned above, Panda's project plan omitted reference to the exact model the company would be manufacturing, and when Panda officials were questioned about their production plans, they declined comment.[39]

Panda's future was further threatened in 1991 by the weak world auto market brought on in part by global recession. In March, Panda temporarily halted its plant construction because of the weak international market. By then, the company had spent some $106 million to finish the factory building's steel frame.[40] Some of Panda's investors reportedly were reluctant to further finance the transport and installation of equipment for the venture's factory, fearing the inability of the company to market its cars, and doubtful that Panda even had the ability to decide on a practical design.[41]

Panda also reorganized its personnel in a bid to keep its prospects alive. In February 1991, Dr. Kim was replaced as company president by Sung Kyun Moon, a relative of the Reverend Moon.[42] Bo Hi Pak became chairman of the board, apparently replacing MacArthur, whose role in the project had remained somewhat nebulous from the start. By April, though, Panda was seeking an outside investor to acquire the company's land lease (perhaps its most enticing remaining asset) and its license to produce vehicles; it put the presses and engine line purchased from General Motors up for sale; and the offices in Hong Kong were nearly all closed.[43]

The company did not completely disappear, however. In July 1992, Panda hosted a photography reception in Washington, D.C., for an exhibition organized by Yang Shaoming, a son of China's president, Yang Shangkun. Bo Hi Pak himself introduced Yang. Even at such a moribund stage of its development, the Panda officials strove to win favor with important Chinese officials.

Stimuli

Foreign Forces

Panda's initial approach to several Chinese cities met a lukewarm response. These cities realized that the company was an unknown player, one that was proposing a complex project based on little apparent experience or background. Panda's feasibility study was extremely weak, as, for example, it could not say exactly what type of vehicle the company would manufacture. Furthermore, Panda's reluctance to publicize its connections to the Unification Church may have added to the suspicion of potential local sites.

As a wholly foreign-owned enterprise, Panda may also have carried undesirable features. Local politicians might have preferred a joint venture, because that kind of investment brings more control to the municipal officials. Furthermore, in some of the cities Panda approached, including Shanghai, Shiyan, and Changchun, joint ventures were already operating or under discussion, and the local governments may have feared competition with the established factories.

On the other hand, however, status as a WFOE also stood to benefit a local city. The venture could probably be approved and begin operation somewhat faster than could a joint venture, as lengthy negotiations, such as those faced by the other automotive joint ventures, would be avoided.

Panda's greatest asset in its approach to the Chinese, though, was its promise of lucrative monetary investment. At a time of economic austerity, little central government money was available to begin new local projects. Panda's promise of $1 billion, paid in hard currency, was a tempting prize for the cities approached.

Besides its financial resources, Panda's most useful tool was its skillful approach to the Chinese political system. The company realized it could make much faster progress as a WFOE than as a joint venture. This was key to deflecting SPC opposition, as procedures for approval of WFOEs were considerably less stringent.

When Panda encountered trouble from central government officials, the company made effective use of its celebrity lobbyists, Wilson and Ichord, to gain sympathy and concessions from Beijing. The ability to win the confidence of such an important player as Chen Zutao also reflects well on Panda's persuasive skills. In sum, once the new auto company had overcome problems in finding a suitable site, it used its monetary and political skill effectively to make rapid progress in gaining approval and support.

Domestic Economic Forces

At the time Panda approached China about building a new factory, the country was just beginning an economic retrenchment that significantly restricted the spending power of the central government. There was, therefore, an impending investment vacuum, and Panda's pledge promised to help alleviate the shortfall.

The large amount of spending could have an impact in several ways. First, workers needed for constructing the factory would find immediate employment. If the plant began producing cars, employees of the company would gain useful technical and managerial skills. Of course, the salaries earned by the factory workers would help stimulate the local economy. Further benefits might be gained from multiplier effects of such a large manufacturing concern. Parts suppliers in the factory area would be needed, and such companies would provide additional employment. The infrastructural improvements at the Panda plant site could also have beneficial effects for the local economy.

The Panda project did potentially carry some economically harmful attributes. Because the company lacked a joint venture partner, Panda would probably have to draw skilled workers away from the established auto joint ventures, and the domestic state-owned factories, to engage employees in the manufacturing process. Employees interviewed in 1990 from both Beijing Jeep and Shanghai Volkswagen expressed interest in working for Panda; they sought the higher salaries and more freedom they envisaged in working for a WFOE.[44] Such a migration could have damaging effects on the auto manufacturers outside of Huizhou.[45]

If Panda failed completely, the Chinese economy as a whole might also be adversely effected. As the Beijing Jeep case demonstrated, the international reputation of China's investment climate was still quite vulnerable. When projects with such great investment as Panda faltered, other foreign investors could not help but reconsider their own plans. Of course, the Panda project was somewhat unorthodox from the beginning, so the effect a Panda collapse would have on the whole of China's investment climate was not clear.

This analysis assumes Panda would keep to its pledge to export all the vehicles it produced. If, however, one supposed Panda could sell its cars on the Chinese internal market, as the company actually desired in late 1990, other domestic factors appear for brief consideration. First, the joint ventures and domestic producers would probably suffer from competition with the wholly foreign-owned enterprise. The Chinese domestic producers would lose some of their market share.

On the other hand, Panda cars sold within China might bring some substantive benefits to the economy. Assuming Panda could produce on the scale it predicted (a possibility based on the company's ability to avoid initial demands to localize, and on the utilization of modern factory equipment), Panda's cars could theoretically represent viable import substitution for the thousands of Japanese cars needed to replace aging taxis in the early 1990s. Panda cars would be assembled with Chinese labor, and transportation costs would probably be lower than for imported vehicles. Furthermore, the new venture's cars would be smaller than the Santana model (with a 1.3-liter engine versus Volkswagen's 1.8-liter Santana), and such models might be somewhat more appropriate for China's narrow and crowded streets.

In comparison with the earlier joint venture auto projects, the stimuli represented by the Panda representatives and the domestic forces acting on the central government at the time were probably somewhat less imperative. By the late 1980s, China had already made substantial progress in absorbing advanced passenger car technology, and joint venture production was showing gradual progress toward satisfying the nation's needs. These two vital domestic factors were therefore less salient at the time Panda officials approached the Chinese authorities.

The foreign representatives of Panda, however, were able to stimulate the Chinese political system in ways different from those adopted by the joint ventures. In bypassing negotiations for a Chinese partner, the WFOE would have far greater latitude in interacting directly with the pertinent Chinese authorities. Panda people were free to move quickly, pinpointing the officials who could make the important concessions needed by the foreign venture; and, once found, these leaders were subjected to the pressures Panda felt would bring the desired response. Panda's identity as wholly foreign-owned, combined with a certain political acumen on the part of its representatives, made the company a formidable force in shaping the actions of the relevant members of the automotive decision-making officials. The next section focuses on the actual political process that pushed the Panda project forward at a rapid clip.

Government Decision Making

Political Bargaining

Beijing's Role

At the top, the State Council seemed to present little initial opposition to the Panda project. Zhao Ziyang, as party secretary, was reportedly a supporter of the plan, though he was busy with events surrounding political demonstrations soon after the venture was proposed and approved.

Premier Li Peng seems to have felt early ambivalence toward the company. Under his stewardship, the State Council reportedly did investigate the proposal in early 1989, when the first small expert group toured Huizhou and recommended State Council approval. Perhaps Li had not paid proper attention to this investigation, for by mid-July Li's attitude was that "it is not that I oppose [the project], but if it is done, it should be done well,"[46] and he dispatched a second group to Huizhou for further information.

Li appears to have been greatly influenced by the report of this second group, which included his trusted friend, Chen Zutao. The premier's attitude seems to have shifted from suspicion to muted support, as shown by Chen's later posting to Guangdong as a special adviser, and by Li's visit to Huizhou and promise of financial assistance. (Still, the top leader's approval was conditional on Panda's pledge to export its product.)

Li's opinion was influenced by more than just the July report. The Panda-engineered visit by former U.S. congressmen to Beijing was of some vital propaganda use to the premier, and to new Party Secretary Jiang Zemin, and the ploy probably further influenced the government leaders. But a more important factor may have been the encouragement of then-CNAIC Vice President Bo Xiyong, who, reportedly feeling it had great practical potential, took an instant liking to the auto proposal. Bo proceeded to champion the merits of the company directly to Li; and the premier, a personal friend of this son of elder leader Bo Yibo, took his advice to heart.

While the top government leaders seemed to stand behind Panda, SPC Chairman Zou Jiahua led the opposition. His stance was most likely based on a report the SPC had commissioned to a private foreign research organization, assigned to investigate the Panda project and the company's background.[47] The report, citing Panda's suspect background and poorly outlined production plan, gave a negative opinion of Panda, and from that time on Zou seems to have fought the project.

The SPC also had political motivation for fighting the venture. As a WFOE, Panda could, and did, argue that it would operate completely outside of the national economic plan. Because of this, the SPC theoretically lacked jurisdiction over the auto venture, and thereby lost its right to veto the proposal. Panda therefore represented an inherent threat to the planning body that could set a very dangerous precedent for future wholly foreign-owned enterprises in China. Zou's attitude, then, was most likely based on protecting the prerogatives of his bureaucratic entity.

One should note that Zou was the brother-in-law of Guangdong Governor Ye Xuanping, one of Panda's biggest supporters. Although scholars often assign such familial bonds great importance in analyzing political actions, in this case the ties seem to have made little difference in either administrator's stance.

Although Zou's administrative portfolio included only the SPC chairmanship, he retained great influence at his former Ministry of Machine-Building and Electronics Industry, and at the MMEI's subordinate organization, the CNAIC. Once Chen Zutao had retired from the leadership of the CNAIC, Zou's ally Cai Shiqing was apparently willing to comply with SPC wishes. By late 1989, then, the CNAIC had issued instructions to its staff to refrain from aiding the Panda organization. Furthermore, the auto bureaucracy also apparently attempted to prevent its employees and workers at the state-owned auto factories in Changchun and Wuhan from leaving their posts to work for the new venture.[48]

Although the new CNAIC leadership took part in a drive against Panda, there is evidence that the organization lacked unanimity in its efforts. First, CNAIC Vice President Bo was an early supporter of Panda, and his position did not change, though by late 1990 he had moved to the more sympathetic Ministry of Aeronautics and Aerospace (or MAAS). Other sources report a kind of "underground" within the CNAIC, consisting of lower-ranking officials supporting Panda, perhaps in the hope of obtaining a future position in the company.[49] Such a force may have been further influenced by the former chief of the CNAIC, Chen Zutao, who had by then become an adviser assigned to aid Panda. Chen reportedly harbored a great dislike of SPC Chairman Zou, and may have relished the opportunity to help foster a project he knew was opposed by the SPC. In fact, there were some signs that by late 1990, CNAIC opposition to Panda had faded somewhat, as one Panda official reported that a CNAIC-subordinate company had bid to supply the venture with spare parts.[50]

While the SPC and the CNAIC represented the main opposition to Panda, other ministries supported the company. The aeronautics ministry, MAAS, was an early fan of the auto venture, as its civilian production units stood to earn money from selling parts. The MAAS minister, Lin Zongtang, saw such sales as a way to counteract cuts in China's military spending that hurt the expansion of his ministry's production.

MAAS took several concrete steps to demonstrate its interest in sales to Panda. In late 1989 or early 1990, the ministry arranged for flights around China in special government planes to show Panda representatives the facilities that could supply parts to the venture. Later, in 1990, the ministry appointed Bo Xiyong, reportedly a personal friend of Minister Lin, as vice president of its Civilian Production Development Company. Finally, the ministry put in a bid, competing with the CNAIC, to become the exclusive parts supplier to Panda.

The Transport Ministry may have played a peripheral role in the development of the auto company. As noted above, the Unification Church had approached the ministry in 1988, proposing the construction of some portions of its "International Highway" in China, and the ministry apparently favored the proposal. When Panda later had trouble in speeding the construction of the vital Autou port, Guangdong Governor Ye suggested the Transport Ministry might somehow aid the port's progress. One Chinese automotive official suggested that a kind of *quid pro quo* might have emerged to link these issues, with Panda potentially receiving Transport Ministry help in exchange for progress on the highway project which, as of late 1990, was still on the Chinese planning agenda.[51]

Local Politics

For Guangdong Province officials, Panda represented a chance to develop a region near the rapidly developing Shenzhen special economic zone (SEZ), one that would be under closer provincial control than Shenzhen. After achieving SEZ status, Shenzhen (like Guangzhou) was declared a *jihua danlie* (independent planning unit), and could then make its economic plans with far less provincial influence. Huizhou, however, was not a *jihua danlie*, so more credit for and control over its growth would rest with Guangdong authorities.

In addition to the desire to see Huizhou develop for these reasons, Panda represented a kind of provincial challenge to the growing Peugeot venture in Guangzhou. This rivalry seemed particularly ironic, considering that Guangzhou is the capital city of Guangdong. Still, the competition gave provincial officials further incentive to help the Panda cause.

Support for the new company seemed to be unanimous within the Guangdong government, though Governor Ye and Vice Governor Kuang were the main Panda boosters. The quick approval granted the venture was the earliest manifestation of the province's goodwill, and Kuang's July 1989 visit to Beijing demonstrated further support for the project. Ye's meeting in early 1990 with Panda officials, detailed above, shows how deep the governor's concern ran.

Perhaps the most telling sign of Guangdong's support for the project was the founding in September 1990 of the above-mentioned provincial automotive work group assigned to help Panda. This organization was to coordinate the development of the new venture with potential resources in the rest of the province. It was specially created by the governor's office to help with problems that Huizhou could not solve alone.

One example of provincial intervention came in late 1990. Panda wanted permission to operate a 700-horsepower boat in the waters around Autou, as a prelude to establishing a ferry service to Hong Kong; the Guangdong regulations limited boats to 60 horsepower. Once the special work group was informed of the problem, however, it moved quickly to grant the auto company an exemption.[52]

Huizhou city had many reasons to support Panda, and few to oppose the company. Like any municipality during the austerity policy of the late 1980s, Huizhou welcomed the cash infusion and the benefits that would accompany such a large construction and production project. The city was therefore willing to make the previously cited pledges of investment in power and port facilities.

Perhaps Huizhou's more important contribution, however, was the effort local leaders mounted to lobby the national government in Beijing. Mayor Li Jinwei's journey to the capital seemed key to Panda's gaining initial central government support, as did Vice Mayor Li Hongzhong's moves to convince those with technical expertise of the project's viability. This local support probably was instrumental in persuading the State Council to grant the new enterprise the required approval.

In one instance, the interests of the city actually ran counter to those of the national government. By late 1990, the Autou port was deep enough to allow 3,000-ton ships to enter the harbor. Beijing had approved dredging the harbor to a depth of eight meters, to allow in 10,000-ton ships. But the city had plans to deepen the harbor to eleven meters, to permit 35,000-ton ships passage. One source hinted that Huizhou might go ahead with the unauthorized dredging, later presenting the central government with a *fait accompli* that might not fit into the central government's plans for regional port development.[53] (It is unclear as of this writing, however, whether Huizhou actually proceeded with this plan.)

The Huizhou leaders were probably taking the biggest political risk of any officials in backing Panda. Were the project to fail, national repercussions would not be very great, as little central government money had been diverted to help the project, and the effect on the investment climate in China would probably be minimal. Local officials, however, would be embarrassed by their miscalculation of Panda's potential. Furthermore, the municipality would be forced to spend time and money to convert the infrastructure left by Panda to other uses. Huizhou would also be left with the many unemployed workers from a failed venture.

Misperception

Considering the negotiating experiences Chinese leaders had with the three extant auto joint ventures, the enthusiastic welcome extended by many of them to Panda is somewhat surprising. Would not Panda, with no actual car company or experience behind it, prove to be a far greater strain on rational auto development than had been the relatively slowly progressing Shanghai Volkswagen project, not to mention the initially ill-conceived Beijing Jeep company? If the Chinese believed that to be the case, were there mitigating factors that blurred the perception of the new venture in the eyes of the Panda supporters?

One element seems to supplement the list of reasons, noted above, for the Panda boosters' stance: namely, the prevalence of a kind of unnatural obsession to attract money. The affliction may have been accentuated by the prevailing austerity policy, yet it probably also played some role in the approval of the earlier automotive joint ventures (and, potentially, in any other type of foreign investment involving large monetary infusions).

In the Panda case, the Chinese supporters seem to have been somewhat blinded by the promise of a huge investment. Because of this, many officials appear to have formed a kind of mental block to some of the shortcomings of the company itself, and to its plans in China. One foreign source familiar with the project reported that many Guangdong Province officials affiliated with developing the venture believed that Panda was a large American auto manufacturer; Panda, for its part, was probably loath to shatter such an illusion. Huizhou officials did not worry about the enormous cost the company would of necessity have to endure to create a new model vehicle, asserting that, though two years after arriving in China the company had yet to name the type of car it would produce, there would be no problem on the issue. Some of Panda's support, therefore, was at least partly based on the irrational belief that large amounts of money guaranteed success.[54]

One surprising perception twist appears in Chen Zutao's stance. Although Chen had been a bane to the Beijing Jeep and Shanghai Volkswagen ventures, he appeared as one of Panda's staunchest supporters. His attitude may have been based partly on his apparent faith in the virtues of exporting automobiles, and his opposition to allowing foreigners a share of the domestic market. In criticizing Beijing Jeep and SVW, Chen's referent was quite clear, as both ventures were obviously initiating domestic sales on a scale unforeseen in the companies' planning stages. Panda, however, promised to export all of its product, and its status as a WFOE seemed to lend the credence of Chinese law to this pledge. If Chen's past experience influenced his stance on Panda, his support, even in light of the inherent weakness of the company and its plans, is not surprising, though it may be somewhat irrational.

Policy Process Conclusions

The Panda case vividly displays many of the political processes associated with bureaucratic politics and irrational influences within the decision-making process. At the central government level, we see the emergence at the top of a small group, led by Li Peng, Bo Xiyong, and Chen Zutao, supporting the Panda project for various personal reasons. The main central government opposition had a more bureaucratic-political tinge, as Zou Jiahua hoped to defend his ministry's prerogatives against the upstart wholly foreign-owned enterprise. The CNAIC was torn between the commands issued from above, initially emanating from the powerful Zou, and its own inclination to help Panda—and itself—by selling parts. Peripheral players included the MAAS and the Transport Ministry, both of which had incentives to support Panda in order to help advance their ministerial goals.

From such a setting emerges a picture of fragmentation, and of top leaders subject to manipulation by the foreign investors. The State Planning Commission seems to have been the only body reacting to rational, apparently objective input in the form of the foreign firm's feasibility study it had commissioned. The SPC, however, was also subject to bureaucratic pressures that may have made its stance somewhat less than completely objective. The main Panda supporters apparently had rather narrow goals in mind in advancing the project, and their clever manipulation by the Panda officials testifies to great political acumen on the part of the foreign forces. The troubles Panda encountered in 1991 tend to highlight the lack of rational judgment in the top leaders' decision process.

Local officials in Guangdong and Huizhou were dependent on the Beijing politicians for both project affirmation and material support. The united front of provincial and municipal leaders lobbying the pertinent members of the central government seems to have been of invaluable aid to Panda. At the times when it appeared central government help would be slow in coming, the local officials even dared to push forward, though cautiously, on their own.

Finally, the positive political response to Panda was nourished by a general aura of enthusiasm for the company, based partly on the Chinese fascination with Panda's monetary pledge. Although other factors worked in the foreign project's favor, the respect generated by Panda's seemingly unlimited fiscal resources added to the company's political support.

Policy Implementation: Panda's Path

In contrast to the previously discussed cases of automotive joint ventures, Panda, as a WFOE, was far less at the mercy of the Chinese political system. The relatively quick implementation of government policies reflects the luxury of Panda's greater independence.

Without a joint venture partner, Panda was relieved of the obligation to consult with lower-ranking automotive officials who lacked decision-making powers, and, more importantly, had spent decades entrenched in a slow-moving political process. The new foreign investors were also fortunate that Huizhou politicians, unaccustomed to large, heavy-industry projects in their region, were also apparently generally free of the bureaucratic shackles that contributed to delay in development of such ventures.

At the local level, then, the relative absence of standard operating procedures (SOPs) left from the prereform era, combined with the lack of a joint venture partner, seems to have been a factor in allowing officials to move Panda along the bureaucratic conveyor belt more quickly. The venture's quick approval and its progress in developing its factory facilities testify to this assertion.

The central government's actions may also have depended on Panda's independent status. As noted, the company representatives could directly approach the pertinent top leaders for the help required. Furthermore, Panda was able to avoid such large institutions as the SPC and the CNAIC, as neither had to approve the company's plans, and, at least in the early stages, their help was unnecessary. Implementation at this level effectively excluded those offices that would tend to rely on slow and perhaps inappropriate SOP responses. For comparison, one should note that the above-mentioned Shell refinery, a joint venture project, was still under negotiation in early 1991 after more than three years of discussions.[55]

Although the Panda case is noteworthy for its minimal amount of political intervention, is there any evidence that the bureaucracies involved actually displayed the type of "learning" that represents behavior different from and more rational than that of the past? Probably the biggest sign of rational advance by any governmental body is seen in the SPC's actions toward Panda. The planning commission's study, done by an outside source, displayed the shortcomings of Panda's plans. Although bureaucratic goals may also have played a role in the planning commission's opposition to the project, the SPC showed competence in accepting the negative opinion of a neutral source, even though rejection of the venture could have cost the nation millions of dollars in hard currency investment. It is not clear whether such outside studies preceded the other Chinese automotive projects; in any case, though, the process of rejecting a venture based on such projections of problems similar to those previously encountered (such as obvious planning problems by the foreign investor) is novel, and a sign of advancement, in the automotive policy sector.

Except for the SPC, however, the rest of the pertinent political branches seem to have made little progress. Both central government leaders and local officials fell into a pattern similar to that which characterized the Beijing Jeep case in particular, and the other auto ventures to a lesser extent: a foreign firm arrives in China with grand plans and promises of large investment. Then, when difficult times arrive, often because of poor planning, the Chinese government feels obligated to come to the rescue.

Although Panda seemed at first to fall outside of the usual pattern, enough elements were visible that the bureaucracy should have seen impending problems. The continued susceptibility to a kind of "monetary" misperception, however, and SOPs that were probably designed more for absorbing any money offered than for rationally choosing ventures show that little progress was made from the approach the Chinese took to the AMC bid in the early 1980s, to the actions taken toward Panda at the end of the decade.

Summary and Projections

Probably the most striking feature of the Panda case is the speed with which the venture was able to move through, or often past, the Chinese bureaucracy. Actually, the Panda story has few elements that are necessarily peculiar to that company alone. It is likely, then, that unless China's investment rules change, other wholly foreign-owned enterprises might be able to follow Panda's path, to achieve rapid progress in establishing themselves and solving problems. Such companies, however, would need to develop the kind of political acumen that seemed innate to the Panda representatives.

As of this writing, Panda faltered for precisely the reasons the SPC felt suspicion toward the company: the company had failed to formulate a practical plan for construction of a vehicle model that still had not been designed; furthermore, there was little market for the venture's product even if it were to roll off the Huizhou assembly line. Therefore, any company that wished to emulate Panda's success with the Chinese bureaucracy, and remain a viable and profitable entity, would need to make its plans much more carefully and rationally than did Panda.

8

Measuring Chinese Economic and Policy Progress

The four case studies presented here chronologically parallel the development of China's "open policy" to foreign investment from the end of the 1970s to the early 1990s. In looking at the record of the foreign-invested passenger car industry, then, this study has measured the progress of the relevant industrial bureaucratic sectors over the first fifteen years of reform.

This final chapter begins with a review of the economic and political progress made in the automotive sector in the post-Mao era. In doing so, it summarizes the impact central and local government forces have had on China's vehicle manufacturing sector, and tells how foreign businesspeople adapted to changing policies. Following this analysis, we look toward the future of China's automotive industry in light of the economic imperatives of the 1990s.

Chinese Automotive Achievements

The original impetus for inviting foreign automotive investment in China was based in the desire to stem a rising tide of imported passenger cars, and to develop an export capable industrial sector. How far did the country go in meeting these goals?

Table 8.1 charts the increase in production at the ventures noted in this volume (Panda, we saw, produced no cars). Even considering the drop in output during the 1988–91 economic retrenchment, production at each facility grew rather steadily. Table 8.2 shows that local content also rose in every case, with Shanghai Volkswagen achieving its aim

Table 8.1. Major Chinese Foreign-Invested Passenger Car Production, 1985-93

	1985	1986	1987	1988	1989	1990	1991	1992	1993
Beijing Jeep (Cherokees)	300	1,500	3,500	5,000	6,600	7,100	15,797	20,808	10,400
Shanghai Volkswagen (Santanas)	3,356	8,031	10,470	15,549	15,700	18,500	35,000	65,000	100,000
Guangzhou Peugeot[a]	---	169	2,715	5,354	4,700	6,000	15,500	22,500	ca. 20,000
Tianjin Daihatsu (Charades)	---	---	100	2,873	1,275	2,920	11,261	29,950	47,850
Volkswagen Changchun	---	---	---	---	---	---	---	12,100	20,000
Total Passenger Car Production[b]	5,207	12,297	20,865	36,798	28,820	42,409	81,055	162,725	250,000

Sources: For Beijing Jeep, figures from 1994 correspondence with Chrysler Corporation. For Guangzhou Peugeot (1986-88), see Thurwachter, "Development of the Chinese Auto Industry," pp. 13 and 17 (respectively). For Guangzhou Peugeot in 1991 and 1992, see *Guangzhou tongji nianjian* (Guangzhou Statistical Yearbook), 1993, p. 83. Guangzhou Peugeot figure for 1993 is from a 1994 phone interview with a company representative. For Tianjin Daihatsu, 1987 and 1988 figures from *Tianjin jingji nianjian* (Tianjin Economic Yearbook), 1989, p. 357; 1989 and 1990 figures from *Tianjin jingji nianjian*, 1991, p. 375; 1991 figure from *Tianjin jingji nianjian*, 1992, p. 342; 1992 figure from *Statistical Yearbook of Tianjin*, 1993, p. 145; 1993 figure from *China Auto 4*, no. 1 (January-February 1994): 17. For Volkswagen Changchun, figures from 1994 correspondence with Volkswagen, Germany. For total production figures, see sources in figure 2.6. For other figures, see references in the text.

---: Indicates pre-production year.

[a] These figures are totals of model 504 and 505 vehicles.

[b] Totals do not add in all cases, as national production figures include some vehicles produced at non-Sino-foreign venture facilities; futhermore, variation of sources for venture output induces some distortion.

Table 8.2. Growth in Local Content at Joint Venture Manufacturers (years needed to reach various local content levels)

	Local content (percent of Chinese-made parts)			
	20 percent	40 percent	60 percent	80 percent
Beijing Jeep	3 years	6 years	7 years	---
Shanghai Volkswagen	4 years	5 years	5 years	7 years
Guangzhou Peugeot	3 years	4 years	6 years	---

Sources: See references in figures 4.1, 5.1, and 6.1.

of 80 percent local content in only seven years. The result, then, was a fairly effective import substitution program, with, however, little opportunity for meaningful export in sight. (Figures 2.7 and 2.10 summarized the country's import and export achievements.)

The Chinese, then, seem to have made good progress in meeting many of the goals set in the early 1980s. How does this progress compare with automotive advances in other developing countries? Table 8.3 shows India's achievements in passenger car production over several decades. (Most of the 1980s' increase in production, however, was the result of a new joint venture with Japan's Suzuki which began manufacturing cars in 1983.) Though the pace of production growth was slower, India was able to export some 114,000 cars and Jeeps over the one-year period from mid-1986 to mid-1987;[1] figure 2.10 showed that by the mid-1990s, China's exports were still negligible. (The vast majority of the Indian vehicles, however, were sent to developing countries in Asia and Africa.)[2] Meanwhile, as noted in chapter 2, South Korea kept production high, at nearly 1.2 million cars in 1991. The Koreans were able to export some 379,000 cars and trucks, and sold about 80 percent of these vehicles to the United States, Canada, and Europe.[3] In sum, the Chinese had made much faster progress than India, but still lagged behind the Koreans in both production and export capability.

By most measures, however, the decision to invite foreign automo-

Table 8.3. **Indian Car Production (selected years),** **1948-89**

Year	Number of cars produced
1948-50	3,089 (annual average)
1951-55	4,611 (annual average)
1956-60	12,949 (annual average)
1961-65	21,743 (annual average)
1966-70	33,725 (annual average)
1971	38,304
1975	23,075
1981	42,106
1985	102,456
1989	177,190

Source: *Automotive Industry of India, Facts and Figures, 1989-1990*, p. 7.

tive investment to China was a good one. The case studies show that the country could incorporate foreign technology and managerial expertise quickly and rather effectively. The general strength of Chinese production capability and the ability of the domestic market to absorb its output, with the exception of the retrenchment period of 1988–91, remained firm over the first decade of cooperative vehicle manufacture.

Evolution of Central Politics

The initial decisions to reorganize the automotive bureaucracy with the passing of the Maoist creed came from the very top leaders. The early 1980s, then, saw the reappearance of the CNAIC, and opening to foreign automotive companies. Both developments reflected policies first pursued in the early 1960s. Had China not veered off the path set before the Cultural Revolution, then, the country might have developed a viable vehicle industry ten to fifteen years earlier than it actually did. In fact, the radical Maoist years suppressed leaders who might have introduced market-oriented reforms similar to those adopted with success in the late 1970s.

Who were the leaders responsible for reforming China's automobile industry? Deng Xiaoping was well known for his advocacy of technology import from capitalist nations, and for greater reliance on expert knowledge. Based on the profiles in chapter 3, however, the top leaders concerned with heavy industry were also likely associated with the early post-Mao moves. Thus, Bo Yibo, one of the elder leaders throughout the 1980s and into the early 1990s, was a key proponent of both the CNAIC and automotive modernization in general. Very few of the top leaders, in fact, seemed to object to the reorganization of the industry or to greater technological contacts with the West. As Margaret Pearson notes, there was little organized opposition in general to the opening to foreign investment.[4]

Still, the early experiences of Beijing Jeep and, to some extent, those at Shanghai Volkswagen showed some lingering central doubts about the national emphasis on joint ventures. In BJC's case, for example, the government was reluctant to bail the company out of its foreign exchange balancing problems. SVW had to suffer under threats over its slow localization pace. Some leaders, though perhaps not at the pinnacle of power, resisted the trend to increasing foreign economic participation.

On closer examination of these automotive problems, one finds it was often the quasi-ministerial levels, rather than the top leaders, that most handicapped the foreign ventures. In the cases of both BJC and SVW, it was Chen Zutao, as CNAIC chief, who led the auto bureaucracy against the companies; he opposed import concessions for AMC and campaigned for faster local content in Shanghai. MOFERT, furthermore, failed to rescue Beijing Jeep; as regulator of foreign exchange, it could have moved with more alacrity to ameliorate the venture's predicament.

BJC's problems were solved when Zhao Ziyang and Zhu Rongji intervened, effectively overruling the CNAIC chief and the MOFERT leadership; SVW could breathe easier in 1989, after Chen Zutao took forced retirement, likely at the insistence of his former boss and one of China's rising stars, Zou Jiahua. Leaders at the commission level and above, then, acted effectively to remove obstacles to foreign investment that originated at the ministerial level and below. Although the bureaucrats were able to set up effective roadblocks to reform, a strong central hand could, if necessary, still sweep them away.

By the late 1980s, the central government was generally united in its acceptance of foreign automotive corporations. The CNAIC played a less antagonistic (though greatly reduced) role in regulating the ventures; Guangzhou Peugeot, far from the capital, seemed barely to notice the national corporation. The central commissions took steps that stifled automotive sales in 1989; this move, however, was part of a general economic austerity program, and should not be viewed as a targeted attack on the auto industry.[5] Other foreign-invested industries similarly effected also made no claim that the problems represented an end to the reform era.

The Panda case illustrates one more recent attempt of middle-level bureaucrats (including Chen Zutao and Bo Xiyong) to create a split in central policy making. Although the commission-level authorities (led by Zou Jiahua) expressed grave reservations about the project, Chen Zutao was able to mobilize top-level support (from Premier Li Peng) to gain central approval. The events also document an instance of central leaders, in approving the project, disregarding the opinion of technical experts. Although China has emphasized the importance of scientific and technological education for its new generation of officials, it is not clear that the opinions of the resultant experts will be honored in the face of concerted, politically motivated opposition.

The failure of the Panda project is unfortunate from our analytical viewpoint, as its continued existence and progress would have provided useful data on an instance of sharp disagreement among top central and commission-level leaders. In the end, however, the middle-level officials, along with their local allies, lacked the strength to sustain central support for the flawed foreign proposal. Even in the more liberal days of decentralizing reform, then, central leaders were still capable of effectively exerting their influence when they focused their attention on a single issue.

David Bachman has suggested that there were various industrial "coalitions" within the Chinese government that existed mainly in the 1950s. He described an environment in which "organizational interests profoundly colored leadership behavior in China."[6] He found bureaucratic goals centered on the Ministry of Finance (which opposed unbalanced budgets) and the Machine-Building Ministry (which lobbied against aid for the rural sectors) during the period leading to the pre-1960 Great Leap Forward.[7] The bureaucracies studied here did sometimes act as such coalitions: as noted, the alliance of Chen Zutao (with some CNAIC support), Bo Xiyong (of the Aeronautics Ministry), and, for a time, Premier Li Peng was able to push through policies favoring the Panda project. It is difficult, however, to pinpoint instances in this study of this kind of coalition leading to a long-term alliance.

In sum, the central government decision process often resembled Graham Allison's Model III (see chapter 1), as bureaucrats struggled to protect their institutional prerogatives. Although the top central leaders were eventually able to impose their wills, bureaucratic resistance was sometimes surprisingly strong (even in cases where Bachman-type coalitions were absent).

Evolution of Local Politics

Local politicians in the larger Chinese cities seem to have caught the centrally inspired reform spirit by the early 1980s. The automotive cases point out the rather rapid evolution of local political economic autonomy, and the willingness of regional governments to cooperate with foreign investors to enhance productive abilities. In each city considered in this study, except Beijing, local leaders came to identify with and support the joint ventures to a degree even the foreign businesspeople may have found surprising.

In Shanghai, municipal officials were initially, in the mid-1980s, disorganized in addressing SVW problems. The city leadership's attitude was transformed by two significant events. First, Mayor Zhu Rongji galvanized Shanghai to seize the chance to develop a lucrative, high-technology heavy industry; and, second, central government targeting of Shanghai as a site for rapid modernization and foreign investment made city leaders more respectful of the role SVW played in building the local economy.

The future of Shanghai's economic development therefore seemed bright. With SVW functioning smoothly, heavy industry would have a secure foundation for development. The legacy of Zhu Rongji (and his potential continued support with his new roles in Beijing) further enhanced the city's prospects. Emphasis in the early 1990s on development of the Pudong development zone in the eastern section of the city (along with other measures noted in chapter 5) demonstrated continued interest in Shanghai's prosperity.[8]

Unlike the Shanghai city leaders, the Guangzhou municipal officials had already experienced several years of foreign contracts and were accustomed to many of the problems of incorporating new ventures in the area, and of wresting concessions from Beijing. Peugeot found a welcome local political climate even as it began its talks in Guang-zhou. Changes in local policy toward the automotive sector over the company's first six years were therefore not significant. This stability was reassuring to the company, and in fact stood as an attractive fea-ture to many foreign investors. Guangdong Province as a whole, for example, had attracted about 36 percent of Hong Kong's industry by 1992, and had absorbed a total of some $8 billion from the capitalist British colony.[9] Southern China's regional investment environment, then, in terms of political stability, was perhaps the strongest in the nation.

This analysis also extends to the case of Panda Motors. The company's representatives arrived in Huizhou as the area was joining boom times in the Pearl River delta. Municipal officials acted boldly in helping the company win central approval, and in accommodating the auto company's needs at the factory site. The actual involvement of Huizhou leaders with Panda lasted only about two years, however, so it is difficult to document the evolution of local policy there.

Again, distance from Beijing, along with the amenable policies in-stituted by the provincial leadership, made Guangdong a prime target for foreign economic participation. Even though Panda failed, Hui-zhou's success in attracting other projects, such as the Shell refinery, show the importance of liberal policy for foreign businesspeople.

Finally, the Beijing Jeep case illustrates a retreat of local policy participation in a foreign-invested venture. The city and BJC's partner, Beijing Auto Works, both took responsibility for the company's initial plan to produce Cherokees from CKD kits; after the crisis of 1985 showed the city unable to meet its obligations, and the Americans turned to the central government for aid, the local Beijing leaders were relegated to a more minor role in fostering BJC's development. At least until Don St. Pierre left the company in 1989, Beijing Jeep looked first to central government leaders (Zhu Rongji and others) for needed assistance.

Other ventures in Beijing most likely felt similar pressure from the hand of the central government. Of course, this type of political inter-vention could have important advantages, as national leaders naturally had more resources at their disposal. Companies in the Chinese capital that were targeted by central leaders, however, lacked the ability to focus on the smaller subset of local leaders key to prosperity; they were forced to face the often fractionalized politics of the national government. With appropriate sponsors, however, such as Zhu Rongji in the case of BJC, a foreign venture could still make gains even in close proximity to the country's top officials.

One must note here that, though regions far from Beijing often acted *independently* from central influence, they did not necessarily act in *opposition* to national leaders. In each case discussed, even that of Panda, the local action was meant to improve the economic picture in an important region of the country. Such progress did in fact generally conform to central ideals of the reform process.

The immediate future for local political-economic policy development would probably show a stronger role for municipal governments, such as those in Shanghai and Guangzhou. As cities capitalized on foreign investment and rapid economic development, their financial (though not necessarily political) independence from Beijing would potentially grow ever greater. Hong Kong's return to China promises more benefit to the southern cities, including Huizhou (where a possibly resuscitated Panda stands to prosper). Only the Beijing local government would find difficulty asserting its own objectives, as it lies under the watchful eyes of central leaders.

Lessons for Foreign Investors

The automobile industry cases show how various strategies employed by foreign entrepreneurs produced different financial results. There was, first, a strong temptation to deceive the Chinese, who may have been seen initially as inexperienced in negotiating with foreign businesspeople. Representatives from American Motors, for example, apparently tried to tempt the Chinese with overstated promises to develop a new vehicle model; meanwhile, virtually all of Panda's presentation was bluff. Of course, these were the two companies that had the most problems with their investments; companies that were more straightforward, such as VW and Peugeot, ran more smoothly.

The lesson here is that, though the Chinese may appear gullible, they are capable of holding the foreign company to its word, and may not easily back down merely to spur progress in the foreign investment process. BJC did win a temporary reprieve, following its 1986 crisis, though in fact the Americans, in the mid-1990s, are taking steps to fulfill their pledge to design a new vehicle model for China. Panda's plans, however, faced virtually complete failure. Foreign investors in other fields might do better by following the German and French examples, where honesty brought respect and generally good results.

Relations between the foreign corporations and the various levels of Chinese government were also highlighted in the automotive case studies. The above sections have outlined the strategies the corporations used to win favor at both the central and local levels. Again, however, those companies with the most rational, best-formed production plans, and the most appropriately chosen Chinese venture partners had the greatest chance for good political ties, with the resultant aid given when needed. Although a company like Panda could use somewhat devious means to strengthen relations with key political figures, its lack of a feasible development scheme doomed it. Potential future foreign investors should be careful to recognize that good political ties alone do not guarantee success.

The cases discussed here also contain lessons for manufacturers that depend on good quality in locally supplied products. In their drive for import substitution, the Chinese have been slow to recognize the importance of meeting world standards in parts supply; this factor is relevant not only for domestic sales, but also for potential future exports. The insistence that companies meet rather arbitrary local content goals very quickly meant, for the automobile manufacturers, the inability to export their product. China's possible entry into the General Agreement on Tariffs and Trade (GATT) regime (discussed later) could also put the substandard vehicles at a competitive disadvantage against a renewed resurgence of imported cars. The investors of the late 1990s will have to be careful in agreeing to a localization scheme they might find too quick to ensure acceptable quality levels. (Of course, Chinese incentives to increase local content, such as offering corresponding reductions of import taxes or abatements of import license requirements, would be tempting inducements to the foreign corporations.)

One further question remained about the established joint venture projects: what would happen at the expiration of a corporation's contract? In the vehicle sector, BJC's agreement is due to end in the year 2003, SVW's in 2009, and GPAC's in 2005. (As a wholly foreign-owned enterprise, Panda's project had no time limit.) Again, however, economics indicate the contracts might be extended. China will still be a developing country even in the early years of the twenty-first century, and will therefore still rely on advanced Western technologies. Although it stands to approach the technical levels of capitalist nations after several decades of modernization efforts, it will probably be forced to rely on the joint venture partners' continued technology infusions (in both the automotive and other high-technology sectors) for at least a few years beyond the time limits of the joint venture agreements. By then, if profit levels of the early 1990s are any indication, the foreign companies will have earned handsome returns on their investments. The Chinese, moreover, will continue their advance toward world-standard production and quality levels.

Finally, in a broader analysis, we ask whether there is any correlation between foreign nationality and success in the automobile sector. From such a small sample, it is impossible to generalize about the differences in American, French, German, and South Korean approaches. An earlier study by Victor A.T. Koh in 1986, however, noted that Chinese managers surveyed found West German investors honest and dependable; the French were seen as hard-working but rather inflexible and offering equipment at prices too high; and Americans received good marks for honesty and willingness to share knowledge (the study omitted South Korea).[10] Although Koh's findings do not strictly correspond to the data in this volume, the case study results show some correlation. Of course, with multinational corporations often consisting of representatives of various nationalities, any such conclusions are tenuous. The finance manager of Peugeot's GPAC in the late 1980s, for example, was British; BJC's president, Don St. Pierre, was Canadian-American. And Panda representatives were South Korean, American, and even overseas Chinese.

Over the fifteen years after VW and AMC made their first bids for automotive cooperation in 1978, foreign investors in general became more sophisticated and better able to wrest favorable treatment from central leaders. Although the early years were most difficult, by the time Panda lobbyists appeared, a combination of Chinese economic maturation and a blossoming refinement of foreign lobbying brought favorable results for the outside investors. Future foreign automotive investors would be wise to take heed of some of the tactics employed by the ventures chronicled in this study.

The Politics of Foreign Investment into the Next Century

By the end of the 1990s, China's revolutionary elder leaders will most likely have all died (or be in very fragile health in their middle or late nineties). These elder leaders interested in the development of heavy industry and the success of joint ventures include Deng Xiaoping, Bo Yibo, and Gu Mu, all of whom are likely soon to pass from the scene. What lies in their wake?

The leadership level under the elders, as of mid-1994, includes Premier Li Peng, CCP Secretary Jiang Zemin, and Vice Premiers Zhu Rongji and Zou Jiahua. Li and Jiang are typically labeled "conservative" by many China political scholars, Zou is called a "moderate," and Zhu is dubbed a "liberal." All of these leaders at one time or another expressed varying degrees of support for development of the automotive sector (though Zou was at times somewhat hesitant). The minimum goal of acquiring an import substitution capability was, in fact, seldom in question over the 1980s.

In the event of a peaceful transition of power within Communist ideological parameters, then, the foreign ventures have little to fear from the demise of Deng Xiaoping's generation. The support of the elder officials was key to earlier advances in the late 1970s and 1980s, but those leaders apparently effectively transferred their beliefs on development to the potential succeeding leadership group.

Should a smooth transfer of power to either conservative or liberal Communists not materialize, what might be the consequences? Certain key elements of a new regime would probably be critical in determining the fate of the foreign corporations; namely, how politically and territorially cohesive would the nation be under a noncommunist government?

Political instability is a natural bane to any business operation. The foreign-invested companies in China would likely lose their carefully nursed personal political connections instantly, and face leaders unfamiliar with their particular problems. New national import regulations, tax codes, quality standards, or other rules stand seriously to disturb steady growth. Modifications in stringent Communist regulations on workers' rights to strike, or to change jobs, would also work against the investments.

If China were to disintegrate geographically in a manner similar to that seen in the Soviet Union in the 1990s, the ventures would experience further difficulties. Each company studied here, for example, depends on parts shipped from outside the plant and, in some cases, from manufacturers in distant provinces. A schism between northern and southern provinces, for example, would have the greatest impact in the

vehicle sector on GPAC (or perhaps Panda), which took parts from
central provinces. (Of course, any of the companies could probably
rely on necessary parts sent from the home company in a time of crisis,
implementing a "delocalization" process.) The ventures would be further affected by disruption in long-distance sales networks, new
"quasi-national" regulations, and myriad other problems.

Still, the macroeconomic trend in China generally favors continued
industrial growth under even difficult circumstances. Such conditions
suggest that even a new regime would find a place for the automotive
corporations.

Economic Challenges to the Future
of the Automobile Industry

Where will economic forces lead the central policy makers in the
future? For the vehicle sector, chapter 2 cited projections of increased
needs for passenger cars and light trucks in China. Consideration of
such requirements most likely inspired two new joint venture passenger car projects, to join those already discussed in this volume. In early
1991, China signed contracts with France's Citroën in Hubei, and with
Volkswagen in Changchun. Citroën took part of a $800 million venture
designed for production of up to 300,000 ZX model cars by the end of
the century; VW's plant, owned 40 percent by the Germans and also
costing some $800 million over five years, was to produce 150,000
Jetta model cars each year by 1996.[11]

A problem with these plans lies in China's ability to absorb all of
the vehicles envisaged by these projects. GPAC's capacity was some
100,000 light trucks and sedans, SVW's was 300,000 Santanas, and
Tianjin's Daihatsu factory projected manufacture of up to 80,000 cars.
State Planning Commission projections for national car requirements
forecast 480,000 vehicles sold per year by the year 2000.[12] Unless the
country could reach export quality standards by this time, and, perhaps
more importantly, find a market for its product, the nation faced either
a glut of automobiles within its borders, or several factories operating
below capacity. China would have solved its import substitution problems, but would have wasted money in constructing unnecessary production facilities.[13]

The examples here show a reluctance of Chinese leaders to reject a
large-scale foreign investment proposal, even in the light of possible

disruption to the national economy. In approving a joint venture bid, the Chinese are naturally in a position to absorb foreign capital, managerial expertise, and other beneficial elements of such projects. Blindly accepting such investment, however, may in the long run prove detrimental to the national economy; the two new car ventures, for example, if unneeded, could come to be a waste of the country's capital, energy, and time.

Still, the Volkswagen plant in Changchun got off to a rather quick start. By 1993, as table 8.1 indicates, the factory was already making 20,000 Jettas, with local content up to 20 percent.[14] (Other ventures had taken five to six years to reach such levels.) The company further claimed to be monitoring quality using a Japanese-style "lean production" system; a company brochure speaks of quality circles and *kaizen* (Japanese for "continuous improvement") to imply the company is aiming at world-class production standards.[15] Should the company actually attain such quality, some Jettas (models more advanced than the Santanas) might in fact be competitive on export markets.

A final new company worth brief mention because of its troubles even in the investment environment of the early 1990s is General Motors' $100 million joint venture with Shenyang's Jinbei (Gold Cup) Automotive Company. GM took a 30 percent share in agreeing to the cooperative venture in early 1992; the company was to make GM's S-10 pickup truck.[16] By early 1994, however, company sales had stopped, as a new national austerity drive at the time limited automobile purchases by state-owned agencies.[17]

Such new potential and actual problems bring us back to a challenge policy makers had never quite met throughout the decades of China's automotive development: that of formulating a cohesive national policy to guide the industrial sector's progress. (Foreign investment policy in general, in fact, was made on an ad-hoc basis, as Pearson's work has implied.)

This policy shortcoming was accentuated in 1993, with China's proposed entry into the GATT trade regime. Participation in GATT would require a more open market for imported goods. Given the choice between the joint venture products, now loaded with sometimes inferior Chinese parts and carrying price tags bloated with various taxes, and the efficient, less expensive imports from Japan, Europe, and the United States, many potential Chinese automobile customers would naturally opt for Toyotas, Nissans, and perhaps Fords and Fiats.

An auto import binge, the likes of which have not been seen since the mid-1980s (and betokened in figure 2.7), looms on the horizon; one source reported the motor vehicle import bill for 1992 totaled some $2.4 billion.[18] China's pre-GATT move in early 1994 to lower import tariffs from 150 percent to 110 percent for small cars and from 220 percent to 180 percent for large cars would most likely accelerate this trend.[19]

In addition to the fiscal impact GATT entry would have on the trade balance in the automotive sector, joint ventures and domestic vehicle and parts manufacturers also stand to suffer. Competition could force some producers into virtual bankruptcy, and even the joint ventures are threatened with reduced production volumes. (SVW's managing director, Fang Hong, noted in late 1992 that "[a]t the moment, we are not competitive. If they were to open the market, we could not compete.")[20]

The revived CNAIC took some tentative steps to prepare for GATT's impact on the industry. In November 1992, CNAIC leaders asked the Chinese central bank to establish a special development fund to finance vehicle modernization projects. The automotive bureaucrats also called for an acceleration in foreign investment in their sector,[21] perhaps hoping a capital infusion would bolster the industry against import competition.

The problems accompanying entry to GATT, of course, will also touch other foreign-invested sectors. Those elements of China's economy cooperating with overseas investors, however, stood to be more resistant to the new competition from imported goods than the purely state-owned enterprises, as their quality levels were, in general, higher than those of comparable producers working without foreign capital and managerial guidance.[22]

The resurgence of the CNAIC in trying to plan a strategy to cope with GATT entry indicates at least one organization within the bureaucracy was in fact capable of understanding an economic challenge, and of attempting to use policy tools to ameliorate the situation. Other industrial sectors that would face similar problems might also seek recourse from their administrative sponsors.

Chapter 2 and the case studies showed the shortcomings in central attempts to rationally develop the country's vehicle production facilities. Following an irrational proliferation of assembly and parts production plants in the 1960s and 1970s, the reintroduction of sophisticated government planning personnel (in the guise of the CNAIC), and new cooperative schemes with foreign corporations, were meant to add order to the nation's manufacturing system. As decentralization of foreign investment practices increased in the late 1980s and early 1990s, irrational approval of some projects began to pose a potential future problem in the automotive sector. Perhaps market forces, leavened by the increasing influence of technically educated bureaucratic experts, and of foreign-run joint venture managers, could bring order to the vehicle industry, and to other important areas of the national economy. Efforts by the CNAIC in the face of the GATT challenge show some evidence that a rational political policy may in fact, of necessity, be emerging. If it is not, China stands to see further bumps on its road to a modern, efficient, and rationally ordered automobile industry.

Notes

Chapter 1

1. Harry Harding, *China's Second Revolution*, pp. 136–39.
2. Barry Naughton, "Central Control over Investment," pp. 51–80.
3. Ezra Vogel, "Politicized Bureaucracy: Communist China," p. 564.
4. A. Doak Barnett, *Cadres, Bureaucracy, and Political Power in Communist China*, p. 84.
5. Ibid., p. 430.
6. Ibid., pp. 431, 441.
7. U.S. Department of Commerce, *Survey of Current Business*, p. 28. Figure is in 1987 constant dollars.
8. Yamaichi Research Institute, *Japanese Industries Today (1993)*, p. 124.
9. Ibid., p. 124.
10. Nihon Keizai Shimbun, *Japan Economic Almanac, 1992*, p. 107.
11. *Country Report: South Korea and North Korea*, p. 26.
12. Michael Yahuda, "China's Foreign Relations and the Modernization Programme," pp. 37–54.
13. James H.T. Tsao, *China's Development Strategies and Foreign Trade.*
14. Nicholas Lardy, *China's Entry into the World Economy.*
15. A. Doak Barnett, *The Making of Foreign Policy in China.*
16. Rosalie Tung, *China's Industrial Society after Mao.*
17. Ryosei Kokubun, "The Politics of Foreign Economic Policy-Making in China: The Case of Plant Cancellations with Japan."
18. Michel Oksenberg, "Economic Policy-Making in China: Summer, 1981."
19. Lin Jianhai, *Foreign Investment in China.*
20. Victor A.T. Koh, *Cultural Expectations for International Marketing and Business in the People's Republic of China.*
21. Philip Wik, *How to Do Business with the People's Republic of China.*
22. Randall Stross, *Bulls in the China Shop.*
23. Graham T. Allison, *Essence of Decision.*
24. Allison's work was later the topic of criticism: international relations theorists claimed Model I's parsimony was more valuable than the added description obtained in the other two models (see, for example, Kenneth Waltz, *Theory of*

173

International Politics). Others claimed bureaucratic models gave excuses to leaders for their shortcomings and errors (see Stephen Krasner, "Are Bureaucracies Important?").

25. John Steinbruner, *The Cybernetic Theory of Decision.*

26. Ibid., p. 79.

27. Robert Jervis, *Perception and Misperception in International Politics.*

28. Kenneth Lieberthal and Michel Oksenberg, *Policy Making in China: Leaders, Structures, and Processes.*

29. Ibid., p. 14.

30. Ibid., p. 16.

31. Ibid., p. 22.

32. Ibid., p. 3.

33. Ibid., p. 31.

34. Ibid., pp. 248–49.

35. Margaret Pearson, *Joint Ventures in the People's Republic of China.*

Chapter 2

1. Tom O. Jones, *Motor Vehicles in Japan, China, and Hawaii*, p. 44.

2. William Irvine, *Automotive Markets in China, British Malaya, and Chosen*, p. 3.

3. Ibid., p. 4.

4. Ibid., p. 6.

5. Hollington K. Tong, ed., *China Handbook, 1937–1945*, p. 217.

6. U.S. Department of Transportation, *Highway Statistics, Summary to 1965*, p. 119.

7. Jones, *Motor Vehicles*, p. 43.

8. Irvine, *Automotive Markets*, p. 53.

9. Ibid., p. 10.

10. H.G.W. Woodhead, ed., *The China Year Book, 1936*, p. 293.

11. Irvine, *Automotive Markets*, p. 41.

12. *Zhongguo qiche gongye nianjian* (Chinese Automotive Industry Yearbook), 1984 ed., p. 131.

13. Much of the following historical information is from China Automotive Technology Research Center, *Zhongguo de qiche gongye* (The Motor Industry of China), 1986 ed., pp. 14–23.

14. The ZIS 150 itself was based on American World War II–vintage Ford trucks. See Maria and Bohdan Szuprowicz, *Doing Business with the People's Republic of China*, p. 319.

15. Barry M. Richman, *Industrial Society in Communist China*, p. 566.

16. *Far Eastern Economic Review*, May 6, 1954, p. 567 (cited in Jim Mann, *Beijing Jeep*, p. 31).

17. Charles Lynch, *China: One Fourth of the World*, p. 92.

18. Jack Baranson, "The Automotive Industry," p. 173.

19. Maurice Meisner, *Mao's China and After*, p. 224.

20. Baranson, "The Automotive Industry," p. 173.

21. Ibid., p. 186.

22. China Automotive Technology and Research Center, *Zhongguo de qiche gongye* (The Motor Industry of China), 1986 ed., p. 16.

23. Szuprowicz and Szuprowicz, *Doing Business*, p. 319.

24. *Zhongguo qiche gongye nianjian (*China Automotive Industry Yearbook), 1991 ed., p. 124.

25. Szuprowicz and Szuprowicz, *Doing Business*, p. 318.

26. Motor Vehicle Manufacturers Association of America, *World Motor Vehicle Data*, pp. 10, 14.

27. By then, the Shanghai plant was also capable of producing the "Sea Swallow" car, a very small vehicle with a 0.3-liter engine.

28. *Zhongguo qiche gongye nianjian* (China Automotive Industry Yearbook), 1991 ed., p. 124.

29. Ibid., p. 119.

30. Szuprowicz and Szuprowicz, *Doing Business*, p. 318.

31. Charles E. Edwards, *Dynamics of the United States Automobile Industry*, pp. 155, 161. One should also note that in the year 1916, Buick was already able to produce 73,827 units of one popular model in its product line. See Jerry Heasley, *The Production Figure Book for U.S. Cars*, p. 89.

32. Baranson, "The Automotive Industry," p. 172.

33. Ibid., p. 172.

34. Ibid., p. 174.

35. *Zhongguo qiche gongye nianjian* (China Automotive Industry Yearbook), 1991 ed., p. 536.

36. Szuprowicz and Szuprowicz, *Doing Business*, p. 323.

37. Baranson, "The Automotive Industry," p. 184.

38. Ibid., p. 184.

39. Ibid., p. 184.

40. Ibid., p. 186.

41. Szuprowicz and Szuprowicz, *Doing Business*, p. 324.

42. Ibid., p. 322.

43. Zhao Hong and Xiong Zhaoxiang, "Dui tiaozheng woguo qiche gongye de kanfa" (Opinions on adjusting our automotive industry), pp. 26–30.

44. *China Daily* (North American ed.), March 7, 1994, Business Weekly p. 1.

45. Sun Xi, "Dui woguo qiche gongye chanpin gaizao wenti de fenxi" (An analysis of the problems of transforming our automotive industrial products), p. 26.

46. Luo Maoxuan and Liao Guojun, "Woguo qiche gongye chanxiao qingkuang diaocha" (An investigation of our automotive industry's production and marketing), p. 27.

47. China Automotive Technology and Research Center, *Zhongguo de qiche gongye* (Automotive Industry of China), 1989 ed., p. 4. The exchange rates used in this text for U.S. dollars to renminbi for the years 1979 to 1994 are shown in the chart at the top of page 176.

48. China Automotive Technology and Research Center, *Zhongguo de qiche gongye* (Automotive Industry of China), 1989 ed., p. 5.

49. Ibid., p. 29.

50. *Zhongguo qiche gongye nianjian* (China Automotive Industry Yearbook), 1991 ed., p. 124

51. Ibid., p. 124.

Year	Average annual exchange rate (RMB/$)
1979	1.55
1980	1.50
1981	1.71
1982	1.89
1983	1.98
1984	2.33
1985	2.94
1986	3.45
1987	3.72
1988	3.72
1989	3.77
1990	4.78
1991	5.32
1992	5.51
1993	5.77
1994	8.70

Sources: For 1979–90: Lardy, *Foreign Trade and Economic Reform*, pp. 148–49. For 1991–92: International Monetary Fund, *International Financial Statistics Yearbook*, p. 279. For 1993–94: author's estimates from various published figures.

52. Todd Thurwachter, "Development of the Chinese Auto Industry: Foreign Participation and Opportunities," p. 4.

53. *Zhongguo qiche gongye nianjian* (China Automotive Industry Yearbook), 1991 ed., p. 536.

54. Ibid., p. 529.

55. Thurwachter, "Development of the Chinese Auto Industry," p. 4; according to this report, China spent more money on Hainan car imports than on the island's eight major projects.

56. Ibid., p. 5.

57. *Zhongguo qiche gongye nianjian* (China Automotive Industry Yearbook), 1991 ed., p. 536.

58. Both these organizations are described in greater detail in chapter 3.

59. Thurwachter, "Development of the Chinese Auto Industry," p. 5.

60. See chapter 3 for further discussion of Chen's policies.

61. Chen Zutao, "Woguo qiche gongye da fazhan de ji xiang juece" (Policies of the general development of our automotive industry), p. 14.

62. Ibid., p. 14.

63. Ji Zhuoru, "Fenfa tuqiang zhenxing woguo qiche gongye" (Go all out to make the country work, and promote our automotive industry), p. 6.

64. Ji Jie, "Yinjin xianjin jishu jiakuai woguo qiche gongye de fazhan" (Introduce advanced technology, speed our automotive industry's development), p. 7.

65. Lei Liulong and Li Huidong, "Guanyu zhongguo qiche gongye fazhan zhanlüe wenti" (On questions of China's automotive industrial development strategy), p. 7; and Zhao Ying, "Shilun woguo qiche gongye baohu zhengce" (Policies

on protecting our automotive industry), p. 41.

66. For more information on the Argentinean case, see Jack Baranson, *Automotive Industries in Developing Countries*, pp. 43–49. Baranson also briefly examines the cases of Brazil and Mexico on pages 35–42. A good detailed discussion of Mexico's automobile industry is found in Douglas Bennett and Kenneth Sharpe, *Transnational Corporations versus the State*.

67. United Nations Center on Transnational Corporations, *Transnational Corporations in the International Auto Industry*, p. 131.

68. Ibid., p. 133.

69. Baranson, *Automotive Industries*, p. 33.

70. Bennett and Sharpe, *Transnational Corporations*, p. 134.

71. Ibid., p. 132.

72. Ibid., p. 135.

73. Ibid., p. 136.

74. See, for example, Yang Lincun, "Dui fazhan woguo jiaoche gongye de ji dian kanfa" (A few opinions on developing our passenger car industry), p. 26; and Hu Zixiang et al., "Jiasu fazhan woguo xiao jiaoche gongye de tantao" (An inquiry into speeding our small passenger car industry's development), pp. 20–23.

75. Jiang Xianfen, "Fazhan jiaoche, shi zai bi xing" (It is imperative to develop passenger cars), pp. 15–16. Stross, however, found some sentiment in late 1970s China that a *lack* of automobiles, along with the resulting traffic and air pollution, instilled some sense of superiority in Chinese officials who had heard of such problems in more advanced nations (see his *Bulls in the China Shop*, p. 36).

76. *Asiaweek*, March 23, 1994, p. 7.

77. Yang Lincun, "Dui fazhan woguo jiaoche gongye de ji dian kanfa" (A few opinions on developing our passenger car industry), p. 27.

78. This figure is for 1986 production in the United States. See Sean P. McAlindon, "The Importance of Motor Vehicle Manufacturing in the U.S. Economy," appendix 1.2A, table 5.

79. Su Lian, "Lun qiche gongye de diwei he zuoyong" (On the automotive industry's status and effect), p. 15 (my translation).

80. *Far Eastern Economic Review*, March 13, 1986, p. 9. This study later recommended, among other steps, production of passenger cars at FAW and SAW, and tighter restrictions on imports of cars and auto parts. See also *Jingji cankao* (Economic Reference), August 3, 1987, p. 4.

81. Wu Facheng, "Qiche gongye wu nian lai de xin fazhan ji qi jin hou de fazhan zhanlüe" (The automotive industry's progress over the past five years and future development strategy), pp. 30–31.

82. Thurwachter, "Development of the Chinese Auto Industry," p. 9.

83. Wu Facheng, "Qiche gongye wu nian lai de xin fazhan ji qi jin hou de fazhan zhanlüe" (The automotive industry's progress over the past five years and future development strategy), p. 31.

84. See, for example, He Ling, "Ruce xiaqu jianbucheng zhongguo de 'Detelu'" (If things go on like this, there will never be a Chinese "Detroit"), p. 14 (on Shanghai Volkswagen); Li Hongqi, "Cong shan shenchu qiche cheng" (An automotive city in the depths of the mountains), p. 44 (on SAW); and "'Auto Town' is underway" (no author cited), *China Daily*, September 20, 1989 (on Panda Motors).

85. *China Daily* (North American ed.), March 7, 1994, Business Weekly, p.1.

86. *Zhongguo qiche bao* (China Automotive News), January 4, 1990, p. 3.

87. Zhou Jiayi, "China's Passenger Car Industry," pp. 22–24.

88. China Automotive Technology and Research Center, *Zhongguo de qiche gongye* (Automotive Industry of China), 1989 ed., p. 28. (For comparison, the United States had about 3.9 million miles of surfaced road in 1990; see U.S. Department of Transportation, *Highway Statistics*, 1990 ed., p. 122.)

89. Cited in *China Daily* (North American ed.), June 29, 1991, p. 4.

90. One Chinese estimate in 1989 forecast that in the year 2000, there would be a minimum of 3 million (and a maximum of 14 million) passenger cars on China's roads. The same source suggested that in 1989, some 400,000 to 600,000 families in China already had sufficient income and the desire to purchase a passenger car (Zhou Jiayi, "China's Passenger Car Industry," pp. 6, 12). The 1993 figure is from *China Daily* (North American ed.), February 1, 1993, Business Weekly, p. 2.

91. Thurwachter, "Development of the Chinese Auto Industry," p. 4.

92. China's Ministry of Foreign Economic Relations and Trade (MOFERT) statistics indicate passenger car imports from Japan fell from 17,454 in 1985 to 844 in 1986, and to only 145 in 1989. These figures, somewhat incompatible with those from the *China Automotive Industry Yearbook* cited above, are most likely too low. See *Almanac of China's Foreign Economic Relations and Trade*, 1987 to 1990 editions.

93. *China Daily* (North American ed.), June 28, 1993, Business Weekly, p.2.

94. Isuzu, however, has had a successful joint venture producing light trucks in Beijing. See Thurwachter, "Development of the Chinese Auto Industry," p. 11. In early 1993, the company signed a new $30 million agreement with a Jiangxi factory to make trucks. See *China Daily* (North American ed.), February 6, 1993, p. 2.

95. *Beijing Review*, August 19–28, 1991, p. 18.

96. *International Herald Tribune*, November 30, 1993, p. 17.

97. Based on several discussions in China, 1989–90.

98. Thurwachter, "Development of the Chinese Auto Industry," p. 11.

99. *Far Eastern Economic Review*, May 23, 1985, p. 75.

100. *Financial World*, December 8, 1992, p. 50.

101. One observer notes, however, that 1986 rules on equity joint ventures served to attract increased Japanese investment attention. See Allen Whiting, *China Eyes Japan*, p. 106.

102. Ibid., p. 116.

103. Ibid., p. 117.

104. *International Herald Tribune*, November 30, 1993, p. 17.

105. Ibid., p. 1.

106. *Financial World*, December 8, 1992, p. 51.

Chapter 3

1. See, for example, Lieberthal and Oksenberg, *Policy Making in China*, pp. 35–41.

2. The following three biographical sketches are based primarily on information found in *Zhongguo dang zheng jun renwu zhi* (Annals of China's

Party, Governmental, and Military Personalities), and in *Who's Who in China*.

3. Bo Yibo, "Guowu weiyuan Bo Yibo tongzhi zai zhongguo qiche gonye gongsi dongshihui di yici huiyi shang de jiang hua" (State Council Member Bo Yibo's speech at the first China National Automotive Industrial Corporation [CNAIC] board meeting [summarized]), pp. 3–7.

4. Bo Yibo, "Bo Yibo tongzhi zai zhongguo qiche gongye gongsi shou jie wuci ji er jie yici dongshihui shang de jiang hua" (Comrade Bo Yibo's speech at the first session-fifth meeting and second session-first meeting of the CNAIC board [summarized]), pp. 9–10.

5. The CNAIC and Bo Xiyong are discussed in more detail in this chapter and in the following case studies.

6. For more detail on Gu, see David Lampton, *Paths to Power: Elite Mobility in Contemporary China*, ch. 4 (on the career of Gu Mu).

7. Ibid., pp. 119, 145.

8. Ibid., p. 142.

9. Based on July 1990 interview in Beijing.

10. Based on 1990 interview with a foreign source in Beijing.

11. Ma Hong, "Tantao juyou zhongguo tese de qiche gongye fazhan zhanlüe" (A discourse on a development strategy for China's distinct automotive industry), pp. 12–15.

12. *Reuters* news service dispatch, March 24, 1992, from cnd-editor@ bronze.ucs.indiana.edu, *China News Digest* (News Global) March 26, 1992, item no. 2.

13. This figure is valid as of 1989; most of the ventures noted in this study were approved before that year.

14. Lieberthal and Oksenberg, *Policy Making in China*, p. 72.

15. *Zhongguo qiche gongye nianjian* (Chinese Automotive Industry Yearbook), 1988 ed., p. 6.

16. Based on July 1990 interview in Beijing.

17. Much of the information in these two sections is based on the following sources: China Automotive Technology and Research Center, *Zhongguo de qiche gongye* (The Motor Industry of China), 1986 ed., pp. 14–23; China Automotive Technology and Research Center, *Zhongguo de qiche gongye* (Automotive Industry of China), 1989 ed., pp. 25–27; and *Dangdai zhongguo de jixie gongye* (China's Current Machinery Industry), part 1.

18. Chu-Yuan Cheng, *The Machine Building Industry in Communist China*, pp. 8–9.

19. The Second Ministry of Machine Building specialized in defense-related production.

20. Cheng, *The Machine Building Industry in Communist China*, p. 11; by the 1960s, however, the Fourth Ministry had taken over the electronics industry (see ibid., p. 120).

21. The Ministry of Commerce also lost some rights in this field.

22. China Automotive Technology and Research Center, *Zhongguo de qiche gongye* (The Motor Industry of China), 1986 ed., p 17.

23. The MBI Commission thereby disbanded.

24. *1987 China Directory*, p. 28. By 1990, as noted above, Zhou was head of the State Council's Machinery and Electronics Import Inspection Office.

25 Two new vice ministers, however, arrived in December 1985, to aid leading MBI Vice Minister He Guangyuan.

26. *China Aktuell* (Topical China), December 1986, p. 763.

27. The CNAIC thereby took over the functions of the Sixth Bureau, which was then abolished.

28. *Dangdai zhongguo de jixie gongye* (China's Current Machinery Industry), p. 46.

29. Ibid., p. 432.

30. Rao Bin, "Rao Bin tongzhi zai zhongguo qiche gongye gongsi shou jie wuci ji er jie yici dongshihui shang de jiang hua" (Comrade Rao Bin's speech at the first session-fifth meeting and second session-first meeting of the CNAIC board [summarized]), pp. 13–15.

31. Rao Bin, "Rao Bin tongzhi zai zhongguo qiche gongye fazhan zhanlüe taolunhui shang de jianghua" (Comrade Rao Bin's speech at the Chinese Automotive Industry Development Strategy Conference), pp. 16–20.

32. Based on 1991 interview in Beijing.

33. See "Zhongguo qiche gongye gongsi zhangcheng" ("The CNAIC constitution"), pp. 55–57.

34. For more detail on some of these factories, see Martin Weil, "Overhauling the Automotive Industry," pp. 28–33.

35. Ibid., p. 32.

36. Ibid., p. 32.

37. *The China Business Review*, March-April 1984, p. 9.

38. Based on 1990 interview in Beijing.

39. Kenneth Lieberthal et al., *U.S.–China Automotive Industry Cooperation Project*, vol. 1, section 3, p. 34.

40. Based on 1991 interview in Beijing.

41. Rao subsequently died in August 1987.

42. The company retained, however, its English acronym "CNAIC."

43. Based on 1991 interview.

44. From 1991 interview.

45. In March 1993, MOFERT was renamed the "Ministry of Foreign Trade and Economic Cooperation," and assumed the acronym "MOFTEC."

46. As noted above, the descriptions in the following section are pertinent mainly to the large cities capable of supporting joint venture vehicle manufacturers. The information, therefore, is not necessarily applicable to smaller municipalities that also had automotive output.

47. Of course, each municipality under study here also had a local Communist Party hierarchy; information gathered during interviews, however, indicated that day-to-day management and planning in the automotive arena generally was reserved for the political and bureaucratic structures. In the case of Shanghai, the mayor (Zhu Rongji) was simultaneously party secretary.

48. Huang Ju, however, had been a member of the city's automotive leading small group, discussed below.

49. One must note, however, that joint ventures had a considerably greater degree of financial and political independence, based on special joint venture laws, than did state-owned companies, in their relations with the automotive industrial groups.

50. The discussions below are based in part on biographies found in several sources, including: *Zhongguo dang zheng jun renwu zhi* (Annals of China's Party, Governmental, and Military Personalities); *Zhonggongdangshi Renwu Lu* (Records of CCP Era Personnel); Wolfgang Bartke, *Who's Who in the People's Republic of China*; and *Who's Who in China*. For Zhu Rongji, see also *Tansuo* magazine (also titled *The Quest*), August 1991, pp. 77–79; on Zou Jiahua, see *Tansuo*, December 1989, pp. 69–70. Most of the information on Chen Zutao is based on interviews.

51. The identity of Chen Zutao's mother is unclear. Harrison Salisbury reported Chen Changhao was married to former textile vice minister Zhang Qinqiu (1904–1968) in the mid-1930s; she died, however, during the Cultural Revolution, and sources interviewed in 1990 indicated Chen Zutao's biological mother was still alive. She was most likely, then, an earlier wife of Chen Changhao. (For Salisbury's account, see *The Long March*, p. 151.)

52. As Chen Changhao's apparent second wife, Zhang Qinqiu, took part in the Long March, Chen Zutao's mother may have been left in central China to raise the young boy.

53. One source reports that Chen, like Li Peng, was personally raised by Zhou Enlai and his wife Deng Yingchao (see Mann, *Beijing Jeep*, p. 284). Chen's later problems during the Cultural Revolution, however, cast some doubt on the assertion of such close ties to Zhou.

54. This was the same place future CCP General Secretary Jiang Zemin received instruction in 1955.

55. GM did sign an agreement in 1988 with a Beijing engine plant to produce two-liter gasoline engines.

56. The commission, led by State Councilor Song Jian, may have gained added importance in late 1991 when Deng Nan, one of Deng Xiaoping's daughters, joined it as a vice minister.

57. See Zhu Rongji, ed., *Guanli xiandaihua* (Management Modernization); one section of the text analyzes General Motors, pointing out features of its large corporate management structure (see pp. 61–68).

58. "I can't speak the Shanghai dialect, but I can understand what Shanghai people are saying," he told the local press on assuming the office. See the *Wall Street Journal*, November 22, 1988, p. A10.

59. Ibid., p. A10.

60. *New York Times*, November 5, 1989, p. 21.

61. Zhu shunned the term, commenting that "if I were the Gorbachev of China I'd be in a lot of trouble now." See *Asiaweek*, April 26, 1991, p. 36.

62. *Ming Bao* (Hong Kong), October 31, 1992, p. 6, cited in Foreign Broadcast Information Service (FBIS), November 2, 1992, p. 19.

63. *South China Morning Post*, November 5, 1991, Business p. 3.

64. Premier Li Peng, one year older than Zhu, spent seven years in the USSR, as did Vice Premier Zou Jiahua; Jiang Zemin studied one year as a trainee in Moscow, and Politburo member Li Tieying spent six years in Czechoslovakia in the 1950s.

65. *New York Times*, November 5, 1989, p. 21.

66. *Time*, November 30, 1992, p. 21.

67. Zou's younger brother, Zou Jingmeng, later became a director of China's

Meteorological Bureau, and an alternate CCP Central Committee member. Nothing is known of Zou's (probably younger) sister.

68. See Howard Boorman, ed., *Biographical Dictionary of Republican China*, pp. 319–21 for further detail on Zou Taofen.

69. Chen Zutao also studied at the Bauman Institute, and most likely knew Zou at this time.

70. Li Peng's father, Li Suoxin, was killed by the Chinese Nationalists in 1931; Zhou Enlai adopted Li Peng and helped raise him at the Yan'an base camp.

71. *Asiaweek*, April 26, 1991, p. 34.

72. Based on 1990 interviews in China.

73. *Journal of Commerce and Commercial*, August 30, 1991, p. 2A.

Chapter 4

1. For more detail on the early history of the venture, see the comprehensive study *Beijing Jeep*, by Jim Mann. Mann, a reporter for the *Los Angeles Times*, based his book primarily on lengthy discussions with the Americans involved in the Beijing Jeep venture (primarily the company's former president, Don St. Pierre, and other American Motors executives). The book is thorough in chronicling the history of the Jeep venture, and I use some of his empirical work to supplement my own interview and documentary findings. Though his research is sound, Mann's narrative is interspersed with comparisons to other foreign investment projects in China, some of which (such as the nuclear power industry) are quite peripheral to the automotive case. Other anecdotes about expatriate life in China are often distracting. Mann's conclusion is apparently influenced greatly by the 1989 Tiananmen massacre, which occurred just before the book was published. Perhaps this made him more pessimistic about Beijing Jeep's long-term prospects than the company's success over the past three years (noted later in this chapter) would warrant. In general, Mann saw a "short, unhappy romance" of American business in China. My findings in this and following chapters, however, indicate that, though the "romance" of foreigners looking for an unlimited market among the vast Chinese population may have been over, opportunities for foreign venture success in China remained.

2. *Beijing Review*, November 4, 1985, p. 21.

3. *Zhongguo qiche gongye nianjian* (China Automotive Industry Yearbook), Beijing, 1986 ed., p. 507.

4. Mann, *Beijing Jeep*, pp. 47–48.

5. Ibid., p. 61. The talks apparently foundered on Japanese unwillingness to part with the technology the Chinese desired. (See chapter 2 of this volume for more discussion of Japanese investment attitudes.)

6. *Beijing Review*, November 4, 1985, p. 22.

7. *Christian Science Monitor*, June 14, 1983, p. 10.

8. *Beijing Review*, November 4, 1985, p. 22.

9. Ibid., p. 22.

10. Ibid., p. 21.

11. Ibid., p. 22.

12. *Christian Science Monitor*, June 14, 1983, p. 10.

13. Ibid., p. 10.

14. Ibid.

15. *Beijing Review*, November 4, 1985, p. 21.

16. Ibid., p. 23.

17. *New York Times*, April 11, 1986, p. D4.

18. Ibid.

19. Erik J. de Bruijn and Xianfeng Jia, "Managing Sino-Western Joint Ventures: Product Selection Strategy," p. 355.

20. *Beijing Review*, November 4, 1985, p. 24.

21. *New York Times*, April 11, 1986, p. D4.

22. Ibid.

23. Information from Don St. Pierre is based on an interview conducted in Hong Kong in January 1989.

24. Mei Bo and Zhang Cailin, "O! Beijing Jipu . . . " (Oh! Beijing Jeep . . .), p. 32.

25. Mann, *Beijing Jeep*, p. 177

26. Mei and Zhang, "O! Beijing Jipu . . . " (Oh! Beijing Jeep . . .), p. 32.

27. The Chinese report that St. Pierre wrote the letter on March 12, 1986. See ibid., p. 33.

28. *Business Week*, April 7, 1986, p. 50.

29. *Wall Street Journal*, April 30, 1986, p. 23.

30. Ibid., p. 23.

31. Ibid.

32. This information is based on an interview held in Beijing in January 1989.

33. Mei and Zhang, "O! Beijing Jipu . . . " (Oh! Beijing Jeep . . .), p. 34.

34. The Chinese suspect the Americans picked these days to coincide with a May 10 visit by Treasury Secretary James Baker to Beijing, and Yao Yilin's May 16 visit to Washington. Baker did in fact discuss the problem with Premier Zhao. See ibid., p. 34.

35. Based on my interview with St. Pierre, 1989.

36. Mei and Zhang, "O! Beijing Jipu . . . " (Oh! Beijing Jeep . . .), p. 35.

37. *Asian Wall Street Journal Weekly*, August 25, 1986, p. 4.

38. Ibid.

39. Based on January 1989 interview with St. Pierre.

40. Mann, *Beijing Jeep*, p. 273.

41. Based on January 1989 interview with St. Pierre.

42. There is no evidence, however, that the Chinese (or even Americans) actually used the "Daqing" terminology to refer to the BJC project. Mann makes a somewhat inappropriate comparison to the rural village of Dazhai, a model commune during the 1960s. See *Beijing Jeep*, pp. 222–35.

43. See chapter 3 for more information on the function of the BAIC.

44. Mann, *Beijing Jeep*, p. 225.

45. Ibid., p. 262.

46. Ibid., pp. 225, 281.

47. Ibid., p. 228.

48. *China Daily*, November 20, 1990, p. 2; Wu Yi became minister of the renamed foreign trade ministry, MOFTEC, in March 1993.

49. From May 1990 interview at BJC.

50. *Wall Street Journal* (western ed.), January 11, 1994, p. B4.

51. *China Daily*, October 17, 1988, p. 2.
52. Mann, *Beijing Jeep*, p. 297.
53. *China Daily*, March 12, 1990, p. 2.
54. *China Daily*, July 31, 1990, p. 2.
55. *China Daily*, August 27, 1990, p. 2.
56. From 1994 correspondence with Chrysler Corporation. The company's target for 1994 was 20,000 Cherokees.
57. *China Daily* (North American ed.), February 19, 1993, p. 2.
58. *Journal of Commerce and Commercial*, December 16, 1992, p. 4A.
59. *China Daily*, October 23, 1990, p. 1.
60. *China Daily*, December 8, 1990, p. 2.
61. *Wall Street Journal* (eastern ed.), February 27, 1992, p. B2.
62. Based on August 1990 interview.
63. De Bruijn and Jia, "Managing Sino-Western Joint Ventures," p. 354.
64. Mann, *Beijing Jeep*, p. 215.
65. Xiao Ming, "Zhao Ziyang zong shuji shicha Beijing Jipu Gongsi" (Secretary General Zhao Ziyang inspects the Beijing Jeep company), p. 6.
66. Ibid., p. 9.
67. Mann, *Beijing Jeep*, p. 283.
68. Ibid., p. 163.
69. Ibid., p. 283.
70. Ibid.
71. Ibid., p. 217.
72. Based on 1989 interview with Don St. Pierre.
73. Based on 1990 interview in Beijing.
74. From 1990 interview in Beijing.
75. Mann, *Beijing Jeep*, p. 177.
76. Beijing mayor Chen Xitong, burdened with the additional duties as a state councilor in the central government, appears to have played no significant role in policy making for the Jeep venture.
77. Mann, *Beijing Jeep*, pp. 262–63.
78. Ibid., p. 138.
79. Ibid., p. 156.
80. Ibid., pp. 160, 162

Chapter 5

1. Marie-Claire Bergere, " 'The Other China': Shanghai from 1919 to 1949," p. 4.
2. Ibid., p. 4.
3. Ibid., p. 10.
4. Ibid., pp. 21–22.
5. For details on these factories, all of which still existed into the 1980s, see *Zhongguo qiche gongye nianjian* (Chinese Automotive Industry Yearbook), 1986 ed., pp. 530–37.
6. Woodhead, *The China Year Book, 1936*, p. 293.
7. Christopher Howe, "Industrialization under Conditions of Long-Run Population Stability: Shanghai's Achievement and Prospect," p. 160.

8. Ibid., pp. 160–61.

9. Ibid., pp. 158, 175.

10. Ibid., p. 161.

11. Ibid., p. 180.

12. Most of the following discussion of Volkswagen negotiations is based on interviews conducted in Shanghai in 1990.

13. VW also considered a venture with the Second Auto Works in Hubei, but rejected it because the site had only a rail transport connection, and no port.

14. The Chinese team was led by four officials: Qiu Ke, manager of the Shanghai Automotive Industrial Corporation (SAIC); Jiang Tao, vice chairman of the Shanghai municipal planning committee; Zhou Mengxiang, vice manager of the Bank of China's Shanghai Trust and Consultancy Corporation; and Zhang Xingyue, a deputy manager of the CNAIC. This team represented all four of VW's future joint venture partners.

15. Although the Chinese eventually accepted the Santana, they found its shock absorbers too weak for domestic roads, and its back seats too small for adults to sit comfortably.

16. Xia Chuanwei, "Shanghai pai jiaoche de shichang fenxi yu xiaoshou yuce" (Analysis of the Shanghai brand sedan's market and sales forecast), pp. 38–41.

17. Wang Changda, "Dui Shanghai jiaoche gongye fazhan zhanlüe wenti de tantao" (Inquiry into problems of the Shanghai brand sedan industrial development strategy), pp. 26–30.

18. This particular plan (in ibid., pp. 29–30) set out a detailed (though, in retrospect, vastly overoptimistic) schedule: by 1985, the factory should have exported up to 1,000 vehicles, mainly to Hong Kong and Macao; by 1990, it would sell up to 30,000 vehicles per year to overseas Chinese in Southeast Asia; by 1995, Africa and Latin America would buy 50,000 vehicles per year; and by the year 2000, up to 100,000 Shanghai cars would be sold all over the world. (In 1990, Shanghai Volkswagen actually produced 18,500 cars, and exported none.)

19. Ibid., p. 27.

20. *China Reconstructs* (North American ed.), November 1985, p. 33.

21. *Far Eastern Economic Review*, May 23, 1985, p. 75.

22. *China Reconstructs* (North American ed.), November 1985, p. 33.

23. He Ling, "If Things Go On Like This, There'll Never be a Chinese Detroit," *The China Business Review* (July–August 1986), p. 35.

24. Ibid.

25. Based on 1990 interview in Shanghai.

26. Zhang Wei et al., "Dui Shanghai jiaoche gongye fazhan de shi dian jianyi" (Ten suggestions for the development of Shanghai's passenger car industry), pp. 46–47.

27. *Shanghai Volkswagen 1989 Annual Report*, p. 8.

28. Ibid.

29. Joint Publications Research Service—China Economic Affairs (JPRS-CEA), October 1, 1986, p. 47.

30. *Zhongguo qiche bao* (China Automotive News), June 30, 1988; and *Shanghai qiche bao* (Shanghai Automotive News), August 2, 1988, p. 1.

31. James P. Womack, et al., *The Machine that Changed the World*, pp. 216–17.

32. Thurwachter, "Development of the Chinese Auto Industry," p. 16.

33. Based on 1990 interview in Shanghai.

34. *China Daily* (North American ed.), February 1, 1993, Business Weekly, p. 2.

35. Ibid.

36. *South China Morning Post*, January 6, 1990, Business page 1.

37. Ibid.

38. *China Daily*, April 25, 1990, p. 2.

39. For 1989 list, see ibid.; for 1990 list, *China Daily* (North American ed.), June 24, 1991, Business Weekly, p. 2; for 1991 list, *China Daily* (North American ed.), June 29, 1992, Business Weekly, p. 3; for 1992 list, *China Daily* (North American ed.), May 12, 1993, p. 2.

40. *China Daily* (North American ed.), February 1, 1993, Business Weekly, p. 2, and 1994 correspondence with Volkswagen.

41. For 1989 figure: *Shanghai Volkswagen Annual Report*, 1989 ed., p. 45; for 1989 figure: *Shanghai Volkswagen Annual Report*, 1992 ed., unpaginated reference.

42. *International Herald Tribune*, September 11, 1991, p. 16.

43. *China Daily* (North American ed.), February 1, 1993, Business Weekly, p. 2.

44. *Automotive News*, October 28, 1991, p. 8.

45. A peripheral problem loomed for outside factories that had previously supplied parts for the Shanghai Brand vehicle, and were then required to transform their production. For a discussion of this transition, see Ying Hailong, "Yi Shanghai pai jiaoche yao bu yao xiama wei shili, tan jingying zhanlüe ju zhen fenxi de yingyong" (A discussion of the use of management strategic matrix analysis, using the Shanghai-Brand sedan as an example of whether production should cease), pp. 49–51.

46. *International Herald Tribune*, December 2, 1993, p. 11.

47. *International Herald Tribune*, December 23, 1993, p. 13.

48. *Wall Street Journal* (western ed.), December 10, 1993, p. R4.

49. In late 1990, France's Citroën announced plans to produce passenger cars at the Hubei complex.

50. *International Herald Tribune*, December 23, 1993, p. 13.

51. Ibid.

Chapter 6

1. Ezra Vogel, *Canton under Communism*, p. 17.

2. Ibid., p. 27.

3. *Far Eastern Economic Review*, May 6, 1954, p. 567; cited in Mann, *Beijing Jeep*, p. 31. This factory apparently was rechristened in October 1949, and continued production as the "Guangzhou Bus Company" into the 1990s.

4. Li Huiqin, "Zenyang geng wei youxiao di liyong waici" (How to use foreign capital more effectively), p. 44.

5. Vogel, *Canton under Communism*, p. 16.

6. Ezra Vogel, *One Step Ahead in China: Guangdong under Reform*, p. 197.

7. Ibid., p. 208.

8. The rest of this section, unless otherwise noted, is based on interviews held in Guangzhou in 1990 and 1991.

9. Thurwachter, "Development of the Chinese Auto Industry," p. 17.

10. One source reports that up to ten foreign companies vied for the Guangzhou venture site. See Li Huiqin, "Zenyang geng wei youxiao di liyong waici" (How to use foreign capital more effectively), p. 44.

11. Thurwachter, "Development of the Chinese Auto Industry," p. 17.

12. Ibid.

13. Ibid.

14. Ibid., p. 18.

15. Ibid., p. 17.

16. Ibid.

17. Ibid.

18. *Asian Wall Street Journal Weekly*, February 2, 1987, p. 15. By 1987, however, GPAC workers had received a 30 percent pay raise, still less than the French proposed.

19. Thurwachter, "Development of the Chinese Auto Industry," p. 17.

20. *Asian Wall Street Journal Weekly*, February 2, 1987, pp. 1, 15.

21. Ibid., p. 1.

22. Ibid., p. 15.

23. Ibid.

24. Gearboxes, for example, came from Hangzhou.

25. Some fifty vehicles were shipped to Vietnam that year, according to a GPAC source. In early 1991, the company exported ten cars to Hong Kong. See *China Daily* (North American ed.), April 8, 1991, Business Weekly, p. 2.

26. *South China Morning Post*, January 6, 1990, Business Section, p. 1.

27. *Newsweek* (Asia ed.), December 4, 1989, p. 49.

28. *South China Morning Post*, October 20, 1989, Business section, p. 4.

29. *China Daily* (North American ed.), March 7, 1991, p. 2.

30. *South China Morning Post,* October 20, 1989, Business section, p. 4.

31. *China Daily*, April 25, 1990, p. 2.

32. From anonymous source, December 1989.

33. *South China Morning Post*, January 6, 1990, Business section, p. 1.

34. *China Daily* (North American ed.), February 4, 1991, p. 2.

35. Ibid.

36. *China Daily* (North American ed.), June 24, 1991, Business Weekly, p. 2 (for 1990 list), and *China Daily* (North American ed.), June 29, 1992, Business Weekly, p. 3 (for 1991 list).

37. *Automotive News*, March 4, 1991, p. 33.

38. Foreign loans, however, still required a guarantee by the central Bank of China.

39. Panda Motors, discussed in the next chapter, was wholly foreign-owned.

40. Based on 1990 interview in Guangzhou.

41. Based on 1990 interview in Guangzhou.

42. Based on 1990 interview in Guangzhou.

43. Ye's action is particularly striking considering that he had been mayor of Guangzhou from 1983 to 1985. Some analysts assert this position would have influenced him to favor the GPAC project had he not been promoted.

44. Sanxing's productivity, however, was much smaller than that of GPAC. In 1990, it made only 1,600 vehicles (mostly light trucks), and 2,000 in 1991. Its goal was 20,000 vehicles in 1995. See *China Daily* (North American ed.), April

22, 1991, Business Weekly, p. 2, and *China Daily* (North American ed.), January 6, 1992, Business Weekly, p. 2

45. The Guangdong Automobile Industry Office, however, was charged with coordinating all of the province's automotive industry.

46. Based on 1991 interview in Guangzhou.

47. *China Daily* (North American ed.), July 24, 1993, p. 3.

48. *Asiaweek*, March 23, 1994, p. 7.

49. *Guangdong tongji nianjian* (Guangdong Province Statistical Yearbook), p. 275.

50. Guangzhou nianjian (Guangzhou Yearbook), p. 299.

51. *Almanac of China's Economy, 1985–1986*, p. 132.

52. *Asian Wall Street Journal Weekly*, February 2, 1987, p. 15.

Chapter 7

1. Much of this information is based on interviews conducted in China in 1990. Some of the discussion appeared in a different form in my essay, "China's Elusive Panda," pp. 44–47.

2. *International Herald Tribune*, December 14, 1989, advertisement.

3. *Unification News*, December 1989, p. 7.

4. *Today's World*, April 1990, p. 19.

5. Based on 1990 interview.

6. See Su Ya and Jia Lusheng, *Shei lai chengbao zhongguo?* (Who Will Contract for China?), p. 358.

7. See "The Law of the PRC on Wholly Foreign-Owned Enterprises," pp. 52–53. Further "implementing regulations" on WFOEs were enunciated in December 1990. These regulations made few substantive changes in the original laws.

8. For more analysis of WFOEs, see *The China Business Review*, January–February 1990, pp. 30–35.

9. See "The Law of the PRC on Wholly Foreign-Owned Enterprises," p. 52 (article 3 of the law).

10. *Cincinnati Enquirer*, October 3, 1989, p. C6, and *Washington Post*, December 4, 1989, p. 1.

11. *San Francisco Examiner*, July 9, 1990, p. A11.

12. See Anson Shupe, "Sun Myung Moon's Mission in Retreat," p. A12.

13. *Far Eastern Economic Review*, November 1, 1990, p. 31.

14. Based on October 1990 interview in China.

15. *Hong Kong Standard*, September 7, 1989.

16. Based on October 1990 interview in China.

17. *China Trade Report*, volume 29, January 1991, p. 8.

18. October 1990 interview in Huizhou.

19. Harwit, "China's Elusive Panda," p. 45.

20. Based on October 1990 interview in Huizhou.

21. *Wen Hui Bao*, Hong Kong, September 15, 1989, p. 2.

22. Thurwachter, "Development of the Chinese Auto Industry," p. 18.

23. Based on October 1990 interview in Huizhou.

24. *China Daily*, September 20, 1989, p. 2.

25. Su and Jia, *Shei lai chengbao zhongguo?* (Who Will Contract for China?), p. 358.

26. See, for example, *Renmin Ribao* (Haiwaiban) (Overseas People's Daily): September 19, 1989, p. 3; November 4, 1989, p. 2, and November 21, 1989, p. 1.

27. Su and Jia, *Shei lai chengbao zhongguo?* (Who Will Contract for China?), p. 360 (my translation).

28. The first foreign accounts of the Unification Church ties came in late September 1989.

29. Su and Jia, *Shei lai chengbao zhongguo?* (Who Will Contract for China?), p. 359.

30. Ibid.

31. Based on interviews held in Beijing, 1990.

32. Based on an October 1990 Huizhou interview.

33. Harwit, "China's Elusive Panda," p. 44.

34. Based on anonymous source in Guangzhou.

35. Based on a February 1991 interview with an American National Security Council advisor in Washington, D.C.

36. Based on January 1991, interview.

37. *Far Eastern Economic Review*, November 1, 1990, p. 24.

38. Based on May 1991 interview.

39. Based on October 1990 interview in Huizhou.

40. *Far Eastern Economic Review*, March 28, 1991, pp. 6–7.

41. From May 1991 interview.

42. *Wall Street Journal* (eastern ed.), September 11, 1991, p. A13.

43. *Automotive News*, April 22, 1991, p. 51.

44. In fact, Huizhou officials confirmed Panda was considering paying some of its Chinese employee payroll in U.S. dollars.

45. Panda officials claimed they could train their own workers, if necessary, to avoid such hostility from other factories. They also said workers trained by foreigners would lack "bad work habits" typical of Chinese laborers. From a February 1990 interview.

46. Su and Jia, *Shei lai chengbao zhongguo?* (Who Will Contract For China?), p. 359 (my translation).

47. Based on 1990 interview.

48. Based on 1990 interview in Beijing.

49. Based on 1990 interview.

50. Based on October 1990 interview with Richard Cummins, chief executive officer of Panda's China office.

51. Based on interviews in Beijing, 1990.

52. Based on January 1991 interview in Guangzhou.

53. Based on 1991 interview.

54. Such support, however, could be a double-edged sword. When Huizhou officials seemed reluctant to move on Panda's complaint about potential fumes from the proposed Shell oil refinery, the politicians may have been reacting to the size of the Shell investment which, at $2.4 billion, would be twice that of Panda's fiscal promise.

55. *China Trade Report*, vol. 29, January 1991, p. 8.

Chapter 8

1. *Automotive Industry of India, Facts and Figures, 1989–90*, p. 71.
2. Ibid., pp. 73–74.
3. *Automotive News, 1992 Market Data Book*, p. 4.
4. Pearson, *Joint Ventures in the People's Republic of China*, pp. 21–25.
5. The policies also hit the steel production, power generation, and agricultural sectors. See *The China Business Review*, January–February 1990, pp. 27–29.
6. David M. Bachman, *Bureaucracy, Economy, and Leadership in China*, p. 44.
7. Ibid., p. 219.
8. For further information on the development of Pudong, see Thomas B. Gold, "Can Pudong Deliver?," and Norman P. Givant, "Putting Pudong in Perspective."
9. *The China Business Review*, May–June 1992, p. 14.
10. Koh, *Cultural Expectations*, pp. 284, 301, 307–8.
11. *China Daily* (North American ed.), April 8, 1991, Business p. 3.
12. *China Daily* (North American ed.), March 12, 1991, p. 2.
13. One source in China's planning sector claimed the Citroën project was approved at the personal insistence of elder leader Li Xiannian, a native of Hubei Province. Since this book did not focus on the two newest auto ventures, it is difficult to substantiate or elaborate on the assertion.
14. From 1994 correspondence with Volkswagen.
15. *FAW-Volkswagen*, p. 23 (?) (unpaginated brochure).
16. The GM team that created the venture was led partly by Ronald Gilchrist, who had worked for AMC in establishing the Beijing Jeep venture in the early 1980s.
17. *International Herald Tribune*, November 12, 1993, p. 1. Other observers noted that the truck lacked seating space preferred by Chinese passengers; it could accommodate only two people, while the Chinese wanted space for five or six. See *Wall Street Journal* (western ed.), January 11, 1994, p. B4. Following personnel cuts of up to 30 percent, General Motors officials reportedly were beginning to hire bodyguards for protection on the streets of Shenyang. See *Far Eastern Economic Review*, February 24, 1994, p. 14.
18. *Country Report: China and Mongolia*, p. 4. As noted in figure 2.7, in fact, 1992 imports included some 90,000 passenger cars, and, in the summer of 1993, China bought about 15,000 cars, trucks, and minivans from General Motors, Chrysler, and Ford. See *China Daily* (North American ed.), October 21, 1993, p. 2. This move, however, may have been meant to quiet American criticism of China's growing trade surplus with the United States as much as to satisfy demand for imported vehicles.
19. *International Herald Tribune*, January 3, 1994, p. 7.
20. *Financial World*, December 8, 1992, p. 50.
21. *Xinhua News Agency*, November 22, 1992, in English, cited in FBIS-CHI–92–226, November 23, 1992, p. 41.
22. For further discussion of China and the impact of entry to the GATT, see Harold K. Jacobson and Michel Oksenberg, *China's Participation in the IMF, the World Bank, and GATT*.

Bibliography

Books and Articles

Allison, Graham T. *Essence of Decision*. Boston: Little, Brown, 1971.
Almanac of China's Economy, 1985–1986. Hong Kong: Modern Cultural Company Limited, 1986.
Almanac of China's Foreign Economic Relations and Trade. Hong Kong: China Resources Trade Consultancy Co., 1987 to 1993 editions.
Automotive Industry of India, Facts and Figures, 1989–90. New Delhi: Automotive Component Manufacturers Association of India, 1990.
Automotive News, 1992 Market Data Book. Detroit: Crain Communications, 1992.
Bachman, David M. *Bureaucracy, Economy, and Leadership in China*. Cambridge: Cambridge University Press, 1991.
Baranson, Jack. *Automotive Industries in Developing Countries*. Baltimore: Johns Hopkins Press, 1969.
———. "The Automotive Industry." In William Whitson (ed.), *Doing Business with China*, pp.170–89. New York: Praeger, 1974.
Barnett, A. Doak. *Cadres, Bureaucracy, and Political Power in Communist China*. New York: Columbia University Press, 1967.
———. *The Making of Foreign Policy in China*. Boulder, CO: Westview Press, 1985.
Bartke, Wolfgang. *Who's Who in the People's Republic of China*, 2d ed. Munich: K.G. Sauer, 1987.
Beijing Jeep Company brochure. 1988.
Bennett, Douglas, and Sharpe, Kenneth. *Transnational Corporations versus the State*. Princeton, NJ: Princeton University Press, 1985.
Bergere, Marie-Claire," "'The Other China': Shanghai from 1919 to 1949." In Christopher Howe (ed.), *Shanghai*, pp.1–34. Cambridge: Cambridge University Press, 1981.
Bo Yibo. "Bo Yibo tongzhi zai zhongguo qiche gongye gongsi shou jie wuci ji er jie yici dongshihui shang de jiang hua" (Comrade Bo Yibo's speech at the first session-fifth meeting and second session-first meeting of the CNAIC board [summarized]). In *Zhongguo qiche gongye nianjian* (Chinese Automotive Industry Yearbook), pp. 9–10. Beijing: Jixie gongye chubanshe, 1986.

————. "Guowu weiyuan Bo Yibo tongzhi zai zhongguo qiche gongye gongsi dongshihui di yici huiyi shang de jiang hua" (State Council member Bo Yibo's speech at the first China National Automotive Industrial Corporation [CNAIC] board meeting [summarized]). In *Zhongguo qiche gongye nianjian* (Chinese Automotive Industry Yearbook), pp. 3–7. Beijing: Jixie gongye chubanshe, 1984.

Boorman, Howard, ed. *Biographical Dictionary of Republican China*. New York: Columbia University Press, 1970.

Chen Zutao, "Woguo qiche gongye da fazhan de ji xiang juece" (Policies of the general development of our automotive industry). *Juece yu xinxi* (Policy and Information), no. 2 (1985): 12–15.

Cheng Chu-Yuan. *The Machine Building Industry in Communist China*. Chicago: Aldine-Atherton, 1971.

China: A General Survey. Beijing: Foreign Languages Press, 1982

China Automotive Technology and Research Center. *Zhongguo de qiche gongye* (The Automotive Industry of China; also translated as "The Motor Industry of China"). Changchun Wenyi Printing House (1986 ed.) and Jilin Science and Technology Press (1989 ed.).

1987 China Directory. Tokyo: Radiopress, 1986.

Country Report: China and Mongolia. London: The Economist Intelligence Unit, first quarter, 1994.

Country Report: South Korea and North Korea. London: The Economist Intelligence Unit, second quarter, 1993.

Dangdai zhongguo de jixie gongye (China's Current Machinery Industry). Beijing: Zhongguo shehui kexue chubanshe, part 1, 1990.

De Bruijn, Erik J., and Jia Xianfeng. "Managing Sino-Western Joint Ventures: Product Selection Strategy." *Management International Review, 33* (1993–1994): 335–60.

Dongxifang bankuai de zhuangji (OK, Beijing Jeep: Widely Exchange [sic] between the East and the West). Xiamen: Lujiang Publishing House, 1988.

Edwards, Charles E. *Dynamics of the United States Automobile Industry*. Columbia: University of South Carolina Press, 1966.

FAW-Volkswagen. FAW-Volkswagen Automotive Company brochure, 1993.

Givant, Norman P. "Putting Pudong in Perspective." *The China Business Review 18*, no. 6 (November-December 1991): 30–32.

Gold, Thomas B. "Can Pudong Deliver?" *The China Business Review 18*, no. 6 (November–December 1991): 22–29.

Gray, Jack, and White, Gordon, eds. *China's New Development Strategy*. London: Academic Press, 1982.

Guangdong tongji nianjian (Guangdong Province Statistical Yearbook). Guangdong sheng tongji jubian, 1985.

Guangzhou nianjian (Guangzhou Yearbook). Guangzhou: Guangzhou nianjian bianzuan weiyuanhui bianji chuban, 1985.

Guangzhou tongji nianjian (Guangzhou Statistical Yearbook). Guangzhou: Zhongguo tongji chubanshe, 1993.

Harding, Harry. *China's Second Revolution*. Washington, DC: Brookings, 1987.

Harwit, Eric. "China's Elusive Panda." *The China Business Review 17*, no. 4 (July–August 1990): 44–47.

He Ling, "If Things Go On Like This, There'll Never be a Chinese Detroit." Trans. in *The China Business Review 13*, no. 4 (July-August 1986), p. 35.

He Ling, "Ruce xiaqu jianbucheng zhongguo de 'Detelu' " (If things go on like this, there will never be a Chinese "Detroit"). *Shijie jingji daobao* (World Economic Herald), March 3, 1986, p.14.

Heasley, Jerry. *The Production Figure Book for U.S. Cars.* Osceola, WI: Motorbooks International, 1977.

Howe, Christopher. "Industrialization under Conditions of Long-Run Population Stability: Shanghai's Achievement and Prospect." In Christopher Howe (ed.), *Shanghai*, pp. 153–87. Cambridge: Cambridge University Press, 1981.

————, ed. *Shanghai.* Cambridge: Cambridge University Press, 1981.

Hu Zixiang et al. "Jiasu fazhan woguo xiao jiaoche gongye de tantao" (An inquiry into speeding our small passenger car industry's development). *Gongye jingji guanli congkan* (Industrial Economic Management Collection), no. 9 (1987): 20–29.

Huizhou Investment Service Centre of Taiwan Compatriots, ed. *Investment Guide '90. Huizhou.* Huizhou, [1990?].

International Monetary Fund. *International Financial Statistics Yearbook.* Washington, DC: IMF, 1993.

Irvine, William. *Automotive Markets in China, British Malaya, and Chosen.* Washington, DC: Bureau of Foreign and Domestic Commerce, 1923.

Jacobson, Harold K., and Oksenberg, Michel. *China's Participation in the IMF, the World Bank, and GATT.* Ann Arbor: University of Michigan Press, 1990.

Jervis, Robert. *Perception and Misperception in International Politics.* Princeton, NJ: Princeton University Press, 1974.

Ji Jie. "Yinjin xianjin jishu jiakuai woguo qiche gongye de fazhan" (Introduce advanced technology, speed our automotive industry's development). *Gongye jingji guanli congkan* (Industrial Economic Management Collection), no. 3 (1985): 2–7.

Ji Zhuoru. "Fenfa tuqiang zhenxing woguo qiche gongye" (Go all out to make the country work, and promote our automotive industry). *Juece yu xinxi* (Policy and Information), no. 3 (1986): 4–6, 24.

Jiang Xianfen. "Fazhan jiaoche, shi zai bi xing" (It is imperative to develop passenger cars). *Qiye yanjiu* (Industrial Research), no. 7 (1987): 15–16.

Jones, Tom O. *Motor Vehicles in Japan, China, and Hawaii.* Washington, DC: U.S. Department of Commerce, 1918.

Koh, Victor A.T. "Cultural Expectations for International Marketing and Business in the People's Republic of China." Ph.D. diss., Ohio State University, 1986.

Kokubun, Ryosei. "The Politics of Foreign Economic Policy-Making in China: The Case of Plant Cancellations with Japan." *China Quarterly*, no. 105 (March 1986): 19–44.

Krasner, Stephen. "Are Bureaucracies Important?" *Foreign Policy*, no. 7 (Summer 1972): 159–79.

Lampton, David. *Paths to Power: Elite Mobility in Contemporary China.* Ann Arbor: University of Michigan, 1986.

————, ed. *Policy Implementation in Post-Mao China.* Berkeley: University of California Press, 1987.

Lardy, Nicholas. *China's Entry into the World Economy.* Lanham, MD: University Press of America, 1987.

————. *Foreign Trade and Economic Reform in China, 1978–1990*. Cambridge: Cambridge University Press, 1992.

"The Law of the PRC on Wholly Foreign Owned Enterprises." Reproduced in *The China Business Review 13*, no. 4 (July–August 1986): 52–53.

Lei Liulong and Li Huidong. "Guanyu zhongguo qiche gongye fazhan zhanlüe wenti" (On questions of China's automotive industrial development strategy). *Qiye yanjiu* (Industrial Research), no. 5 (1986): 4–7.

Li Hongqi. "Cong shan shenchu qiche cheng" (An automotive city in the depths of the mountains). *Ban yue tan* (Semi-Monthly Chatter), no. 23 (1982): 44.

Li Huiqin. "Zenyang geng wei youxiao di liyong waici" (How to use foreign capital more effectively). *Guangzhou yanjiu* (Guangzhou Research), no. 4 (1986): 44–46.

Lieberthal, Kenneth, et al. *U.S.-China Automotive Industry Cooperation Project*, vol. 1. Ann Arbor: University of Michigan, 1989.

Lieberthal, Kenneth, and Oksenberg, Michel. *Policy Making in China: Leaders, Structures, and Processes*. Princeton, NJ: Princeton University Press, 1988.

Lin Jianhai. "Foreign Investment in China." Ph.D. diss., Georgetown University, 1986.

Luo Maoxuan and Liao Guojun. "Woguo qiche gongye chanxiao qingkuang diaocha" (An investigation of our automotive industry's production and marketing). *Guangdong jinrong yanjiu* (Guangdong Finance Research), no. 2 (1982): 25–28.

Lynch, Charles. *China: One Fourth of the World*. Toronto: McClelland and Stewart, 1965.

Ma Hong. "Tantao juyou zhongguo tese de qiche gongye fazhan zhanlüe" (A discourse on a development strategy for China's distinct automotive industry). In *Zhongguo qiche gongye nianjian* (Chinese Automotive Industry Yearbook), pp. 12–15. Beijing: Jixie gongye chubanshe, 1988.

Mann, Jim. *Beijing Jeep*. New York: Simon and Schuster, 1989.

McAlindon, Sean P. "The Importance of Motor Vehicle Manufacturing in the U.S. Economy." In Kenneth Lieberthal et al., *U.S.-China Automotive Industry Cooperation Project*, appendix 1.2A, table 5. Ann Arbor: University of Michigan, 1989.

Mei Bo and Zhang Cailin. "O! Beijing Jipu . . ." (Oh! Beijing Jeep . . .). In *Dongxifang bankuai de zhuangji* (OK, Beijing Jeep: Widely Exchange between the East and the West), pp. 28–54. Xiamen: Lujiang Publishing House, 1988.

Meisner, Maurice. *Mao's China and After*. New York: The Free Press, 1986.

Motor Vehicle Manufacturers Associaton of America. *World Motor Vehicle Data*. Detroit: Public Affairs Division of the Motor Vehicle Manufacturers Association, 1992.

Naughton, Barry. "Central Control over Investment." In David Lampton (ed.), *Policy Implementation in Post-Mao China*, pp. 51–80. Berkeley: University of California Press, 1987.

Nihon Keizai Shimbun. *Japan Economic Almanac, 1992*. Tokyo: NKS, 1992.

Oksenberg, Michel. "Economic Policy-Making in China: Summer, 1981." *China Quarterly*, no. 90 (June 1982): 165–94.

Pearson, Margaret. *Joint Ventures in the People's Republic of China*. Princeton, NJ: Princeton University Press, 1991.

Rao Bin. "Rao Bin tongzhi zai zhongguo qiche gongye fazhan zhanlüe taolunhui shang de jianghua" (Comrade Rao Bin's speech at the Chinese Automotive Industry Development Strategy Conference). In *Zhongguo qiche gongye nianjian* (Chinese Automotive Industry Yearbook), pp. 16–20. Beijing: Jixie gongye chubanshe, 1988.

Rao Bin. "Rao Bin tongzhi zai zhongguo qiche gongye gongsi shou jie wuci ji er jie yici dongshihui shang de jiang hua" (Comrade Rao Bin's Speech at the first session-fifth meeting and second session-first meeting of the CNAIC board [summarized]). In *Zhongguo qiche gongye nianjian* (Chinese Automotive Industry Yearbook), pp. 13–15. Beijing: Jixie gongye chubanshe, 1986.

Richman, Barry M. *Industrial Society in Communist China*. New York: Random House, 1969.

Riggs, Fred W., ed. *Frontiers of Development Administration*. Durham, NC: Duke University Press, 1970.

Salisbury, Harrison. *The Long March*. New York: Harper and Row, 1985.

Shanghai Volkswagen Annual Report. 1989 and 1992.

Shupe, Anson. "Sun Myung Moon's Mission in Retreat." *Wall Street Journal*, November 1, 1989, p. A12.

Statistical Yearbook of Tianjin. Tianjin: Zhongguo tongji chubanshe, 1993.

Steinbruner, John. *The Cybernetic Theory of Decision*. Princeton, NJ: Princeton University Press, 1974.

Stross, Randall. *Bulls in the China Shop*. Honolulu: University of Hawaii Press, 1990.

Su Lian. "Lun qiche gongye de diwei he zuoyong" (On the automotive industry's status and effect). *Gongye jingji guanli congkan* (Industrial Economic Management Collection), no. 9 (1987): 12–19.

Su Ya, and Jia Lusheng. *Shei lai chengbao zhongguo?* (Who Will Contract for China?). Guangzhou: Huacheng chubanshe, 1990.

Sun Xi. "Dui woguo qiche gongye chanpin gaizao wenti de fenxi" (An analysis of the problems of transforming our automotive industrial products). *Jingji lilun yu jingji guanli* (Economic Theory and Economic Practice), no. 1 (1982): 25–29.

Szuprowicz, Maria, and Szuprowicz, Bohdan. *Doing Business with the People's Republic of China*. New York: Wiley, 1978.

Thurwachter, Todd. "Development of the Chinese Auto Industry: Foreign Participation and Opportunities." Guangzhou: U.S. and Foreign Commercial Service document, 1989.

Tianjin jingji nianjian (Tianjin Economic Yearbook). Tianjin: Tianjin renmin chubanshe, 1989, 1991, 1992.

Tong, Hollington K., ed. *China Handbook, 1937–1945*. New York: Chinese Ministry of Information, 1947.

Tsao, James H.T. *China's Development Strategies and Foreign Trade*. Lexington, MA: Lexington Books, 1987.

Tung, Rosalie. *China's Industrial Society after Mao*. Lexington, MA: Lexington Books, 1982.

United Nations Center on Transnational Corporations. *Transnational Corporations in the International Auto Industry*. New York: UNCTC, 1983.

United States Department of Commerce. *Survey of Current Business*. Washington, DC: March 1993.

United States Department of Transportation. *Highway Statistics Summary to 1965.* Washington, DC: 1967.

————. *Highway Statistics, 1990.* Washington, DC: 1991.

Vogel, Ezra. *Canton under Communism.* Cambridge, MA: Harvard University Press, 1969.

————. *One Step Ahead in China: Guangdong under Reform.* Cambridge, MA: Harvard University Press, 1989.

————. "Politicized Bureaucracy: Communist China." In Fred W. Riggs (ed.), *Frontiers of Development Administration*, pp. 556–68. Durham, NC: Duke University Press, 1970.

Waltz, Kenneth N. *Theory of International Politics.* Reading, MA: Addison Wesley, 1979.

Wang Changda. "Dui Shanghai jiaoche gongye fazhan zhanlüe wenti de tantao" (Inquiry into problems of the Shanghai brand Sedan industrial development strategy). *Caijing yanjiu* (Finance Research), no. 2 (1983): 26–30.

Weil, Martin. "Overhauling the Automotive Industry." *The China Business Review* 13, no. 4 (July–August 1986): 28–33.

Whiting, Allen. *China Eyes Japan.* Berkeley: University of California Press, 1989.

Whitson, William., ed. *Doing Business with China.* New York: Praeger, 1974.

Who's Who in China. Beijing: Foreign Language Press, 1989.

Wik, Philip. *How to Do Business with the People's Republic of China.* Reston, VA: Reston Publishing Company, 1984.

Womack, James P. et al. *The Machine that Changed the World.* New York: Macmillan, 1990.

Woodhead, H.G.W., ed. *The China Year Book, 1936.* Shanghai: The North-China Daily News and Herald, 1936.

Wu Facheng. "Qiche gongye wu nian lai de xin fazhan ji qi jin hou de fazhan zhanlüe" (The automotive industry's progress over the past five years and future development strategy). *Jingji yanjiu cankao ziliao* (Economic Research Reference Data), no. 180 (1988): 25–36.

Xia Chuanwei. "Shanghai pai jiaoche de shichang fenxi yu xiaoshou yuce" (Analysis of the Shanghai brand sedan's market and sales forecast). *Yuce* (Forecast), no. 2 (1982): 38–41.

Xiao Ming. "Zhao Ziyang zong shuji shicha Beijing Jipu gongsi" (Secretary General Zhao Ziyan inspects the Beijing Jeep company). In *Dongxifang bankuai de zhuangji* (OK, Beijing Jeep: Widely Exchange between the East and the West), pp. 5–11.

Yahuda, Michael. "China's Foreign Relations and the Modernization Programme." In Jack Gray and Gordon White (eds.), *China's New Development Strategy*, pp. 37–54. London: Academic Press, 1982.

Yamaichi Research Institute. *Japanese Industries Today (1993).* Tokyo: 1992.

Yang Lincun. "Dui fazhan woguo jiaoche gongye de ji dian kanfa" (A few opinions on developing our passenger car industry). *Zhongguo keji jitan* (China Technical Compendium), no. 5 (1987): 25–28.

Ying Hailong. "Yi Shanghai pai jiaoche yao bu yao xiama wei shili, tan jingying zhanlüe ju zhen fenxi de yingyong" (A discussion of the use of management strategic matrix analysis, using the Shanghai Brand sedan as an example of whether production should cease). *Shanghai guanli kexue* (Shanghai Management Science), no. 4 (1986): 49–51.

Zhang Wei et al. "Dui Shanghai jiaoche gongye fazhan de shi dian jianyi" (Ten suggestions for the development of Shanghai's passenger car industry). *Shanghai guanli kexue* (Shanghai Management Science), no. 3 (1986): 46–47.

Zhao Hong, and Xiong Zhaoxiang. "Dui tiaozheng woguo qiche gongye de kanfa" (Opinions on adjusting our automotive industry). *Caizheng yanjiu ziliao* (Finance Research Data), no. 90 (1981): 26–30.

Zhao Ying. "Shilun woguo qiche gongye baohu zhengce" (Policies on protecting our automotive industry). *Jingji yanjiu cankao ziliao* (Economic Research Reference Data), no. 37 (1987): 35–41.

Zhonggongdangshi renwu lu (Records of CCP Era Personnel). Chongqing: Chongqing chubanshe, 1986.

Zhongguo dang zheng jun renwu zhi (Annals of China's Party, Governmental, and Military Personalities). Hong Kong: Wide Angle Press, 1989.

"Zhongguo qiche gongye gongsi zhangcheng" ("The CNAIC constitution"). In *Zhongguo qiche gongye nianjian* (Chinese Automotive Industry Yearbook), pp. 55–57. Beijing: Jixie gongye chubanshe, 1984.

Zhongguo qiche gongye nianjian (Chinese Automotive Industry Yearbook). Beijing: Jixie gongye chubanshe, 1984, 1986, and 1988.

Zhongguo qiche gongye nianjian (Chinese Automotive Industry Yearbook). Changchun: Jilin kexue jishu chubanshe, 1991.

Zhongguo qiche gongye nianjian (Chinese Automotive Industry Yearbook). Zhongguo qiche gongye nianjian bianji bu bianji chuban, 1994.

Zhongguo tongji nianjian (Chinese Statistical Yearbook). Zhongguo tongji chubanshe, various years.

Zhou Jiayi. "China's Passenger Car Industry." Graduate School of the Academia Sinica, May 1989. Photocopy.

Zhu Rongji, ed. *Guanli xiandaihua* (Management Modernization). Beijing: Kexue puji chubanshe, 1983.

Periodicals and Computer Services Cited

Asian Wall Street Journal Weekly.
Asiaweek.
Automotive News.
Beijing Review.
Business Week.
China Aktuell (Topical China).
China Auto.
The China Business Review.
China Daily.
China News Digest (News Global), from cnd-editor@bronze.ucs.indiana.edu.
China Reconstructs (North American ed.).
China Trade Report.
Christian Science Monitor.

Cincinnati Enquirer.
Far Eastern Economic Review.
Financial World.
Foreign Broadcast Information Service (FBIS).
Hong Kong Standard.
International Herald Tribune.
Jingji cankao (Economic Reference).
Joint Publications Research Service—China Economic Affairs.
Journal of Commerce and Commercial.
Newsweek (Asia ed.).
New York Times.
Renmin Ribao (Haiwaiban) (Overseas People's Daily).
San Francisco Examiner.
Shanghai qiche bao (Shanghai Automotive News).
South China Morning Post.
Tansuo Magazine (also titled *The Quest*).
Time.
Today's World.
Unification News.
Wall Street Journal.
Washington Post.
Wen Hui Bao (Hong Kong).
Zhongguo qiche bao (China Automotive News).

Index

A graduate of Cornell University, **Eric Harwit** received a diploma from the University of International Business and Economics in Beijing in 1990 and his Ph.D. in political science from the University of California at Berkeley in 1992. He is currently an assistant professor of Asian studies in the School of Hawaiian, Asian, and Pacific Studies (SHAPS) at the University of Hawaii, Manoa.